The European Diary of
Hsieh Fucheng

The European Diary of Hsieh Fucheng

Envoy Extraordinary of Imperial China

■ ■ ■

Translated by Helen Hsieh Chien

Introduced and annotated by Douglas Howland

St. Martin's Press
New York

First published in the United States of America 1993

Printed in the United States of America

ISBN 0-312-07946-X

Library of Congress Cataloging-in-Publication Data

Hsüeh, Fu-ch'eng, 1838–1894
    The European diary of Hsieh Fucheng : Envoy Extraordinary of
Imperial China / translated by Helen Hsieh Chien ; introduced and
annotated by Douglas Howland.
        p.   cm.
    Includes index.
    ISBN 0-312-07946-X
    1. Hsüeh, Fu-ch'eng, d1838-1894—Diaries. 2. Diplomats—China—Diaries.
I. Chien, Helen Hsieh. II. Howland, Douglas, 1955- .
III. Title.
DS764.23.H75A3 1993
951'.033'092—dc20
                                                                93-18496
                                                                CIP

Contents

Translator's Preface

I first became aware of my famous great-grandfather, Hsieh Fucheng, when I was seven years old, after the funeral of my grandfather in 1934. Several pairs of bright red, wooden placards, which had been brought out from storage to be paraded through the city streets to the burial ground as part of the funeral procession, were left standing behind the benches on the side of the spacious entrance hall of my ancestral home in Wuxi, China. On the surface of each pair, large gilt characters were painted to indicate the title and location of my great-grandfather's official posts. The pair that made the deepest impression in my mind was the last pair by the heavy, black, massive double door. The four characters on the left denoted his title, "Envoy Extraordinary," whereas those on the right displayed the locations he served: England, France, Belgium and Italy. In retrospect, I don't think that my grandfather would have approved of such an ostentatious display of his father's glory at his own home. Otherwise, the placards would not have been in storage for all those years. For my grandfather, by nature, was a true Taoist even though he would never make a public claim of his belief for fear of tarnishing his reputation as a Confucian scholar.

The literary achievement of my great-grandfather was virtually unknown to me at that time. I did recall, however, that I had caught a glimpse of the original edition of his complete works when all the books in his library were taken out in the summer to be aired. The library, filled with all the books that my great-grandfather had collected throughout his lifetime, was a two-storey building located in the garden at the back of my Wuxi home. After my grandfather's death, the library was kept locked all year long.

At the outbreak of the Sino-Japanese War of 1937, our entire family made the house in the International Concession of Shanghai our permanent home. I was ten years old then and had been in school for five years. Since my father did not trust the public school system, my brother and I had begun our schooling in Wuxi by studying the Chinese classics at home, as my father had done. Our tutor, who had also been my father's teacher, had earned a degree of *Xiucai* (Cultivated Talent) during the last period of imperial rule in China. In those five years of schooling,

I made no progress in my studies because the tutor was lazy and callous. The only task he set for me was to recite a stack of several volumes of ancient Chinese classics without stopping or making a mistake. The penalty for a blunder was to receive a "chestnut" on my head (a knock from the crooked index finger of the old tutor). I was very fortunate to have a photographic memory, and after the initial "chestnut," I never received another one. My brother, however, suffered a great deal under such tyranny until my mother intervened.

Although the war brought wrath to the entire Chinese population, it brought happiness and joy to me, because my father then found a noted professor, Wang Chou Cheng, to be our private tutor. Professor Wang, who had distinguished himself in the field of Chinese classics, was also a professor at the two prestigious universities in Shanghai, Fudan and Zhoutung. With his inspiring guidance, I became an avid reader. At that time, the complete collection of personal journals written by all the literary giants from the Tang dynasty (618–907) to the Manchu dynasty, the last dynasty of China (1644–1911), had just been published. Professor Wang, an admirer of my great-grandfather's literary achievement as well as his integrity as a diplomat, made a point of informing me that the personal journal of my great-grandfather was included in that collection. I subsequently purchased the complete set. These journals were written in the style of present-day newspaper articles, filled with stories of palace intrigue, sensational court trials, colorful local anecdotes and memorable family history, all faithfully reported and commented on by each writer during the tour of his various official duties. Among these stories there were also supernatural and ghost tales that inevitably attracted a child's attention. I was particularly delighted with my great-grandfather's ghost stories as they were tinged with the local color of Wuxi, where I spent a major part of my early childhood. I asked my father about my great-grandfather's more serious works, and he had taken the trouble to show me a few volumes, but I was too young then to comprehend such writing. However, I did have the chance to study one of the entries in his European diary (16th of the intercalary Second month, 1890), which had been included among the selections in the standard high-school textbooks at that time under the resounding title "The Paris Art Gallery Tour." Professor Wang believed that I should be made aware of neoclassics (the prose of the Song dynasty [960–1279] to the Manchu dynasty [1644–1911]) as well as the ancient classics. But since the neoclassics were written strictly in a prose style (as compared to the lyrical ancient classics), they were much harder to memorize, and therefore I did not appreciate my great-grandfather's writing as much as I should have.

I don't know whether any of my great-grandfather's essays were chosen for inclusion in the college textbooks of that time because I only majored in Chinese literature at the University of Peking for one term. Unable to cope with the bleakness of student life in the north, with its daily diet of black dumplings and boiled cabbage, I returned home to enter the University of Shanghai, where I majored in English for the rest of my college years. However, Nailene Chou Wiest, a reporter at Reuters, mentioned during a recent exchange of correspondence that she had the opportunity to study my great-grandfather's works during her college years in Taiwan.

In 1948, I left China with my husband to continue our education in the United States. We were each admitted to different universities, I to Mills College in California and he to the University of Minnesota. At that time, however, neither of us was aware of the distance between the two states, and after we reached San Francisco, I made the sacrifice of following my husband to Minnesota. We did not stay long in Minnesota due to a housing shortage there. With the help of one of his former professors, my husband was later admitted to the graduate school at the University of Detroit. We made our home in Michigan for more than twenty years.

My own studies, however, were interrupted, first by pregnancy and then by the eruption of revolution in China. Facing poverty with our financial resources now completely severed, my husband had to work to support our growing family, and I subsequently took over part of his school load by doing book reports for him. It was during that period, as I read through books by distinguished scholars of Chinese history such as Professor John K. Fairbank, that I realized that the acclaimed literary fame of my great-grandfather had reached the West. Unfortunately, my husband's major field was economics, so I spent more time struggling with financial terminology than enjoying reading about my great-grandfather's achievements as a statesman of his era.

Since we made the journey to America by plane, I was unable to bring my books. Therefore, it was not until I reached my late forties that I finally had the opportunity to obtain the complete collection of my great-grandfather's works through a friend of my husband's in Taiwan. This edition, however, was just photocopies of the original books compressed into two large, hardcover volumes.

I assume that one of my cousins must have brought a set to Taiwan, because my grandfather, who was solely responsible for the publication of the complete collection of his father's works, had distributed many sets of the first edition to his relatives and friends. Three years after his father's death in 1894, he went through all his father's notes, which had already been edited by Zhang Mai Jung, his father's secretary in Europe, and diligently copied them into ten volumes. When Zhang came to Wuxi in the spring of 1897 to pay a gravesite visit to my great-grandfather, my grandfather asked him to stay as his house guest and finished editing the materials for the four volumes of the *Overseas Essay Collection*, two volumes of the *Memorials of the Overseas Mission* and ten volumes of the *Official Correspondence of the Overseas Mission.* He then added the six volumes of the earlier published edition of the European diary as well as his father's personal journal, edited by his brother-in-law, Chen Kwan Sung. All of these volumes were published in 1898. My grandfather later collected all of his father's former publications, including four volumes of the *Essay Collection of Yung An,* two volumes of the *Sequel to the Essay Collection,* four volumes of the *Additional Essay Collection,* one volume of the *Analysis of Foreign Policy,* and four volumes of the *Defense of the Eastern Coast of Zhejiang,* and had them reprinted for distribution with the previous publications.

In 1973, my husband and I moved to Toronto, as he was seriously ill with a heart ailment. During his illness, I had to work to supplement our family income, and I did not have the chance to carefully study my great-grandfather's writings.

In 1976, my husband recovered from his illness and accepted a position in Saskatchewan, Canada. While there, I began to find the time to read through the European diary of my great-grandfather and subsequently undertook its translation. Since I did the work on an old typewriter, I managed to finish only the first two years of the diary before I became seriously ill. In 1983, while I was slowly recovering, my husband died suddenly of a heart attack, and consequently, my youngest son Paul brought me to Sacramento, California, where he had been working since his graduation from California State University. For my first five years there I suffered from a deep depression and could not stand to be left alone in the house. I spent all my time visiting the homes of my other five children. Finally, tired of traveling, I made up my mind that I had to finish the translation. It was good therapy and gradually lifted me out of my depression.

As I ventured deeper into my great-grandfather's diary, I was inspired by his keen interest in science and his fascination with the creation of the universe, which raised my own spirit to a higher level of consciousness. As a result, the first draft of my manuscript was filled more with my great-grandfather's private thoughts than with scenes of diplomatic negotiations. But as I steadily made progress in my combat with depression, my mind began to grasp the potential of his European diary. I realized that I must do a great deal of research work before I could finish this worthy project. Consequently, I spent many long, tedious hours poring through maps to find the obscure names of various cities and towns in the disputed border area and frequently sought advice from Pam Millard, the librarian of the Central Library in Sacramento. She was most helpful in my endeavors and went out of her way to find the information I needed for my book. Without her help, my second draft might have taken longer to be finished.

In my second draft, I selected all the entries that contained the new government policies to improve China's strength that my great-grandfather shaped. Although I don't think his suggestions were ever implemented by the Manchu government after his untimely death, I discovered that several of his policies have been borrowed by the modern Chinese government. One good example was his South American emigration policy (January 16, 1891). I clearly remember that in the late 1950s, my sister in China wrote to me that my father was diligently studying Spanish in order to be able to immigrate to South America. I was overjoyed and looked forward to being reunited with my parents again. Of course, such dreams never materialized, and my father subsequently perished during the Cultural Revolution.

I further translated all the crucial negotiations of the boundary dispute over Pamir (involving Britain, China and Russia) and in the Yeren Mountains (involving Britain, Burma and China). Several place names were hard to locate even with the help of both Professor Douglas Howland of DePaul University and Professor Lau Yee Cheng of the Chinese University of Hong Kong because, as Professor Howland thoughtfully suggested, these place names suffer from the confusion of being secondhand transliterations of Russian or English transliterations. The best example is the location of Xima: it turned out that there were three places with this name along the border.

Those diary entries I left out contain either the histories of all the nations in the continents of both Europe and the Americas or the minute details of the manufacturing technology of either some machinery or a new weapon. I regret not going through the first two years more thoroughly before soliciting publishers for my book, since I may have missed some good passages from those years.

I am grateful to Professor Douglas Howland, who edited and anno-tated the text and who encouraged me to write this preface and to trans-late sixteen additional entries. I am also grateful to Simon Winder, senior editor at St. Martin's Press. Without his insight, this translation of my great-grandfather's diary might never have seen the light of day in my lifetime. I also must thank Professor Lau Yee Cheng of the Chinese University of Hong Kong, who took time out from his busy teaching schedule to give me help on the basis of his respect for and admiration of my great-grandfather. And I would like to express my deepest grati-tude to the late Professor Fairbank of Harvard University, who gave me the endorsement I sought for my manuscript. Little did I know when I wrote to him that he was on his deathbed, yet without the slightest hes-itation, he gave me, a complete stranger, the assistance I needed for this project. He was truly a great man, and I cannot help but feel tears brim-ming in my eyes every time I think of him.

I also would like to express my deepest gratitude to my grandfather, Hsieh Tze Ming. Without his diligent work and devotion, some of my great-grandfather's overseas writings would never have been published. I sincerely hope that he may heave a sigh of relief in heaven that his astronomical chart in 1929 for his unborn grandchild was correct: a granddaughter can be as effective as a grandson to carry out one's wishes. To my father, Hsieh Sun Tien, I would like to give thanks for the large sum of tuition fees he has invested in me. To my Chinese tutor, Professor Wang, I owe the training that he gave me in the Chinese clas-sics, without which I would probably be like many of my contempo-raries who cannot comprehend the meaning of the Chinese classics. And thanks also to my two English tutors, Mrs. Lena Evans Chang, an Oxford scholar and professor at St. John University in Shanghai, who inspired me to express my feelings in writing, and Mr. Gregory, the edi-tor of the English publishing house in Shanghai before World War II, who drilled me hard in English grammar with his old Eton textbook. I sincerely hope that both of them are still in this world and would like to hear from them should they happen to read this.

I would also like to express my appreciation to David Perlman of the *San Francisco Chronicle,* my teacher at the 1983 Writers' Workshop in Squaw Valley, who was the first one to recognize the value of my book project, and to James Vesely of the *Seattle Times* and formerly the editor of the *Sacramento Union,* who was kind enough to schedule me for an interview with Sue Mote, whose article appeared in December 1986.

And last but not least, I would like to thank the staff of the Central Library during my part-time employment there. Pam Millard helped me with my letter to Professor John K. Fairbank, and she, Ruth Ellis, Janice Abe and Sandy Pelose all helped me with my research. Teddy Lehner, my supervisor, allowed me to have a flexible working schedule so that I could continue working on this translation without any hindrances. I know that I have missed the few names of those who have since been assigned to other libraries, and I hope they will understand that I have a poor memory for names.

—Helen Hsieh Chien
December 1992

Introduction

$\mathcal{I}$n the century since Hsieh (Xue) Fucheng published the first install-ment of his massive *Diary of an Embassy to Four Nations,* historians have remained somewhat indifferent to Hsieh and his work.[1] Aside from entries in the standard compilations of Qing Dynasty (1644–1912) biographies, little else has been written about him—not for reasons par-ticular to the character of Hsieh or to his life's work, but rather because of prejudices associated with his era. Born on the eve of the Opium War with Great Britain and dead by the outbreak of the Sino-Japanese War, Hsieh's life coincided with the great failure of the Imperial Chinese state in the nineteenth century. Accordingly, historians both in China and in the United States have viewed timely and innovative scholar-officials such as Hsieh with a perspective clouded, at best, by ruined optimism. Chinese historians, so often informed by a dogmatic Marxism, and their American counterparts, informed by an equally dogmatic modernization theory, marginalize Hsieh as a would-be reformer—one whose plans and exhortation ultimately came to nought. In both of these versions of modern Chinese history, the failure of nineteenth-century reform has meant that scholars such as Hsieh who dedicated their careers to improving Chinese government and society have been brushed aside in favor of a concentration on greater forces such as nationalism, liberalism and communism. Such a simplistic interpretation of Hsieh's life and work unduly distorts the historical processes evident in his *Diary,* where he is engaged in rethinking China's relationship to a larger world and recounting his participation in actualizing that change.[2]

Hsieh Fucheng was born on April 12, 1838, in the city of Wuxi, in the eastern and coastal province of Jiangsu, a region up the Yangzi River from Shanghai and long known for its tradition of scholarship. Like his father before him, Hsieh succeeded at the civil service exam, but his entry into the imperial bureaucracy was complicated by the chaotic Taiping Rebellion then raging throughout much of central and southern China. Throughout his career, Hsieh would remain concerned with the difficulties of peasant life in rural China and in particular with the eco-nomic and social problems that not only encouraged the spread of secret societies but also gave rise to rebellion against imperial authority.

Indeed, his first professional opportunity came in response to a memorial that he presented to Zeng Guofan, the heroic official credited with the defeat of the Taiping rebels, in which he suggested methods by which Zeng might suppress the Nian Rebellion then afflicting Anhui Province, to the west of Jiangsu Province. Zeng invited Hsieh to join his staff in 1865.

In 1875, responding to an imperial edict inviting suggestions on improving the welfare of the state, Hsieh presented a memorial to the throne in which he outlined six proposals for new administrative priorities. He urged the court to promote men of talent to posts in foreign relations, to imitate key Western technological advances such as railroads and telegraphs, to encourage and protect new business corporations among merchants and the people, to promote tea exports, to develop mining industries and to expand the imperial navy.[3] While this nexus of proposals remained the core of Hsieh's reform plans for the next two decades (see pp. 129, 135), it had the more immediate effect of bringing Hsieh to the attention of like-minded officials—the "Foreign Affairs Clique"—in Peking, the imperial capital. As a result, he was invited to join the staff of the most powerful official involved in China's Westernization plans, Li Hongzhang, and in that capacity, Hsieh composed in 1879 what is still considered the first substantial proposal for comprehensive reform.[4]

Prospects for reform were at a critical stage by 1879. China had lost the first Opium War to Britain in 1842 and the second to Britain and France in 1860; as part of the 1860 settlement, the Chinese government had committed itself to Westernizing its diplomatic procedures. The International Office was established in 1861 (see p. 11, note 10), and under its auspices, a school was founded to train future Chinese diplomats, translators and interpreters in European languages. The directors of this school, which was known as the Tongwen Guan (or "Office for Unified Language"), simultaneously took this opportunity to conduct courses in Western learning, although not without a great deal of protest and interference by more conservative elements in the court. For some officials in the Chinese government, who were reassured by the defeat of the Taiping and Nian rebels and the reassertion of state control over former rebel territories, the general sense of well-being existing by 1879 persuaded them that the recent decade represented a laudable "restoration" and mitigated earlier pressing needs for reform. The treasury had been stabilized, good men were filling the ranks of government and the Europeans were pacified now that the first Chinese ambassador to

Britain had taken up his London post in 1877; in short, a satisfactory amount of progress had been accomplished.

As an advocate of comprehensive "improvement" (*gailiang*) or "reform" (*bianfa*), Hsieh demonstrated with his 1879 proposals a penetrating grasp of the economic development of Western Europe and the United States. He understood that industrial capitalism had grown out of mercantilism, and his call for reform thus focused on three key aspects of that process. In the first place, Hsieh advocated the expansion of commerce and industry. Given the British and Western European taste for Chinese tea and textiles, Hsieh believed that the Chinese government should actively promote the producers and merchants involved in these main industries. By encouraging profits from this trade, the wealth of Chinese merchants would increase and in turn would foster the wealth of peasants in the countryside. In the second place, knowing that industrial expansion depended on technology, Hsieh urged the Chinese government to take an active role not only in building transportation and communication systems like those of the West—including railroads, steamships and telegraph lines—but also in fostering the technology necessary to imitate Western techniques of producing iron, rail cars, ships, newspapers and so on. And third, since the development of technology depended on a specific form of knowledge, Hsieh advocated the study of Western science and the establishment of new schools intended for that purpose.

The controversy at the heart of Hsieh's proposals was his reevaluation of a critical idea, profit (*li*), which inherently challenged the intellectual orthodoxy of the Imperial state. As Confucius and his follower Mencius had declared centuries earlier, the pursuit of profit was contrary to the pursuit of benevolence. Where the latter was the right and good aim of government, profit was the nefarious goal of parasitic merchants who, for the better welfare of society, were appropriately kept under strict official control near the bottom of the social ladder. Hsieh was proposing a new theoretic relationship: that the profit of merchants would enhance the wealth and strength of the empire as a whole. The Imperial Court, however, was hesitant to sanction such a revision of orthodoxy, even though Hsieh pointed out that unless Chinese themselves actively sought to profit from their international trade, the British and other foreigners would continue to reap most of the profits from trade with China (see pp. 47-48). Hsieh felt that China should protect what was rightly her own.[5]

A further point of contention confronting Hsieh's proposals was the purported need for Westernization. Ideologically orthodox members of the court reasoned that since the Chinese empire had maintained itself for centuries without Western ways, there was simply no justification for any change. One could find historical precedents for occasionally sending an ambassador overseas, but that was sufficient. In opposition to this stand, Hsieh and other advocates of reform argued, first, that the "Tao" or "Way of Heaven" underwent periodic alterations independent of the present and orthodox understanding institutionalized in the civil service examination system. As Hsieh put it in his 1879 proposal, "After several hundred years, the Way of Heaven changes slightly; after several thousand years, it changes greatly."[6] By way of evidence, Hsieh pointed out that mankind in the time of early antiquity lived more like animals than like present-day men; having made the transition from dwelling in holes and pits to living above ground in houses, Hsieh reasoned, it seemed clear that major shifts in the Way of Heaven for mankind had actually taken place in the past and could certainly recur. The orthodox position was subject to historical change wrought by Heaven itself.

A second argument, which we see occasionally in the *Diary* before us (p. 22), was that Western ways had originated in China. Although the sage-kings of old had chosen not to follow the path that the West had borrowed from China, the present crisis legitimized a shift to the values of profit, practicality and technology, which, after all, were originally elements of Chinese civilization. Although one might speak of reform as "Westernization," this process was but a recovering of indigenous Chinese civilization.

Hsieh was a prolific scholar. His collected works include fourteen volumes of essays, twelve volumes of official papers, six volumes of notes, the 1879 book on foreign affairs and reform and his sixteen-volume *Diary of an Embassy to Four Nations*. Hsieh had the first six volumes of the *Diary* published in 1892; they cover the first fourteen months of his trip abroad as ambassador to England, France, Italy and Belgium from January 31, 1890, to April 8, 1891. Ten more volumes were published posthumously in 1898; these cover the years from April 9, 1891, to July 1, 1894. Given that each of the sixteen volumes is roughly sixty pages, the whole amounts to nearly 1,000 pages of text, or, when translated into English, well over 3,000 pages. Consequently, choices have been made in abridging this translation. Instead of Hsieh's many personal encounters in Europe, this translation highlights his impressions of European culture. Instead of treating each of Hsieh's days equally, this translation emphasizes his major diplomatic undertakings.

Like travel diaries in most cultures, Chinese diaries give evidence of the attempt to overcome one's sense of dislocation produced by the mere fact of being in a foreign space. One's sense of self is challenged not only by different physical surroundings, but also—and perhaps more so—by different social surroundings produced by different "kinds" of human beings with different physical features, languages and customs. The traveler's sense of dislocation arises precisely from the fact that these unfamiliar people share these alien features; after all, it is the traveler who is objectively different. In this context, Hsieh's *Diary* provides a daily means of establishing continuity; in effect, the diary is a defense against the foreign and serves to guard Hsieh's sense of self from the estrangement produced by the challenge of another order.[7]

Stylistically, two features provide this continuity. One obvious feature is the diary format. The daily entries begin with the date according to the Chinese lunar calendar (see page 3, note 1), often followed by a mention of the weather that day, and then follow with a description of the day's activities. This seemingly perfunctory notation of date and weather by the author is part of an effort to mitigate the difference between familiar and unfamiliar space. By referring both to one set of objective (and hence universal) coordinates, this notation establishes a time-and-place continuum for the trip. Second, the psychological point at which these diaries begin and end works to maintain continuity with the familiar. Most Chinese diaries of official travel overseas begin *before* the author arrives at his destination. That is, the author commences his diary as an author, at a point prior to his becoming a traveler, with an account of the circumstances that led him to undertake his trip. The effect produced is that the diary blurs the distinction between author at home and traveler abroad. Correspondingly, most diaries finish *after* the return to China, so that the author, no longer a traveler, is in a position to make his final day's entry as an author in familiar surroundings again. Hsieh's *Diary* begins and ends at home.

Like most of his contemporaries, Hsieh wrote his travel diary in part to fulfill his obligations as an ambassador. The Imperial Court, to whom such diaries were typically offered, welcomed these texts as useful sources of information on foreign places and often paid to have them typeset and printed as public documents. But Hsieh's diary is more ambitious than most. In addition to the anticipated accounts of his travels, Hsieh's activities in residence at the various embassies reflect his active engagement with the new world of Europe. Not at all the random jottings of a marginal figure overshadowed by greater historical forces, his descriptions of Europe and Europeans were the material informing his contemporaries' impressions of that distant continent. Hsieh includes a great deal of information intended to expand his countrymen's understanding of foreign history and the world situation. These details, he hoped, would enhance their study of foreign affairs and, in turn, inspire domestic reform.

Hsieh was, for example, a penetrating and knowledgeable observer of life in nineteenth-century Europe, and his juxtapositions of China and Europe are the very substance of the history of intellectual development. He makes constant analogies in order to grasp the nature of the West and calls upon his reader to consider the differences dividing the respective cultures of Europe and China. Hsieh draws arresting comparisons between Chinese and Western theories of astronomy (p. 124), energy (p. 184) and the fundamental elements of physics and chemistry (pp. 99-100). He evaluates Western manners and customs (pp. 110-111) and returns to the subject of Christianity as a vehicle to orient his reader to life in Western society (p. 108). That Hsieh was open-minded in his considerations of government and society—which he examined from the point of view of human nature—is evident in his evaluation of the changing political systems of the West (pp. 113-114). He had read of the downfall of Napoleon III and had himself witnessed the ongoing commotion in the French General Assembly.

At the same time, Hsieh includes a remarkable amount of pertinent background material for his readers. He spent his first months in Britain and France examining the files stored at the embassies in order to familiarize himself not only with the history of Chinese relations with those nations but also with the history of China's "foreign service" itself—the International Office, which was established in 1861. Many valuable documents are reprinted verbatim in Hsieh's text, and these add a uniquely historical dimension to Hsieh's account of his own work from 1890 (pp. 28-29). Furthermore, Hsieh includes extensive discussions of the history of peoples and lands—not only those that entered into his diplomatic work, such as Burma, Tibet and Turkestan, for example, but also those in which he took a purely intellectual interest, such as the nations of South America. As he saw it, the Chinese needed to recover their curiosity about foreign lands in order to foster a spirit of exploration, which, when applied to practical political problems, might encourage a knowledge of China's frontiers and a desire to defend them from foreign aggressors (pp. 130-131).

During the 1880s, Hsieh served as Intendant of the Ning-Shao-Tai Circuit in Zhejiang Province and then as Surveillance Commissioner in Hunan Province; in 1889 he was appointed to the post of ambassador to

England, France, Italy and Belgium. In essence, he was fulfilling one of the proposals he had advocated fifteen years earlier: that men of talent be appointed to positions dealing with foreign affairs. By 1889, Hsieh's many publications had earned him a serious reputation with Chinese officials, and the British were pleased to have an acclaimed scholar serving as Chinese ambassador. Like his celebrated predecessor Zeng Jize (see p. 26, note 16), who had served as the second Chinese ambassador to Britain (1878–1885), Hsieh lived up to British expectations of the Chinese gentleman and scholar, and this reception facilitated the primary tasks facing him: to maintain diplomacy on a footing of equality and, in the process, address four major problems irritating China's relations with Britain.

One of these perpetual thorns in Hsieh's side was the British and French outrage over the treatment of foreign missionaries in rural China. One article of the 1860 peace accords (following the second Opium War) allowed Christian missionaries to reside and proselytize throughout China. Although French and German Catholics were most militant about demanding these rights, British Protestant missionaries also ventured into the Chinese countryside, where resentful mobs occasionally tried to force missionaries out, provoking the deaths of foreigners and the destruction of church property. Hsieh probes these incidents for connections to secret societies; he seems certain that these are not spontaneous but rather conspiratorial incidents. From his point of view, local magistrates responsible for maintaining order were caught between two loyalties: on the one hand, certain local leaders who sympathized with the mob action, since it was directed against the new foreign privileges; on the other hand, the central government, who wanted such action stopped in order to avoid further confrontations with foreign powers. Hsieh, of course, sided with the central government, and he had the job of assuaging British anger over the ongoing incidents. Although few British subjects were actually the targets of such violence (pp. 73-74), the British government vociferously supported French and German claims in the interests of European solidarity.

A second area of diplomatic activity, which followed from the same legal principle of extraterritoriality that applied in the missionary cases, was Hsieh's effort to assert official Chinese representation of overseas Chinese communities in the British colonies of Hong Kong, Singapore, Australia and various South Sea islands. Significant numbers of Chinese laborers were exported annually from Hong Kong and were often forced to work under conditions approximating slavery (pp. 40-41). Hsieh insisted that China had a right to establish consulates in those places in order to represent and protect her subjects. Moreover, highly successful Chinese business communities had been established in colonies such as Hong Kong and Singapore. Because Hsieh believed that those business-men had a role to play in China's Westernization, he was especially interested in protecting overseas Chinese. Hsieh was both forceful and successful with this project, for within two years of his arrival in London, Britain had agreed to the establishment of new Chinese consulates in Hong Kong and Singapore (pp. 78-79).

The protracted negotiations over the Burma-Yunnan border dispute were a third diplomatic matter that consumed a great deal of Hsieh's attention as ambassador. An uncertain area of high mountains, steep valleys, dense jungles and little-known tribal peoples, the border between Britain's new colony of Burma and China's longstanding province of Yunnan erupted in 1875 into a violent confrontation remembered as the "Margary Affair" (p. 74). A British explorer, Augustus Raymond Margary, was ambushed and murdered by unknown assailants on the Yunnan side of the border in February of that year. Although the problem was contained and eventually settled (see p. 47, note 21), both Britain and China continued to aspire to a clearly defined border in that remote region. After much circulation of confused maps and reports, recorded in detail in Hsieh's *Diary*, a treaty was concluded on March 1, 1894 (p. 194), only three months before Hsieh left Europe.

Less successful was Hsieh's fourth major piece of diplomatic work, the similarly protracted negotiations with both Britain and Russia over the boundaries separating British India and interests in Afghanistan from Russian Turkestan and Chinese Turkestan (the new province of Xinjiang). Chinese-Russian treaties, going as far back as the mid-1600s, had defined respective spheres of interest in Turkestan, but the new age of colonization and British interference in Chinese-Russian relations served only to complicate matters. Although the Chinese had had their fill of dealing with the distant Islamic kingdoms in the Pamirs and Khokand, consigning them to a kind of self-rule in the 1830s, the scholar-general Zuo Zongtang had in the 1870s waged a successful pacification campaign in Xinjiang, and the Chinese court was determined to maintain China's position there as Britain and Russia faced off along a grand frontier through Persia, Afghanistan and Bukhara. Hsieh's three years of negotiations in London failed to yield the desired agreement, and the process faltered when he sailed for China.

Hsieh Fucheng's *Diary of an Embassy to Four Nations* is likely the last work that he completed in his lifetime. He returned to Shanghai on July 1, 1894, a day commemorated by the final entry here, where he died only twenty days later.

Douglas Howland
Chicago, 1992

Notes

1. The Chinese character used to write our subject's surname has two pronunciations. Although nowadays it is usually transliterated as "Hsueh" or "Xue," British diplomatic records indicate that Hsieh Fucheng spelled his surname in English as "Sieh." In the diary and in the text of this introduction, we have used the spelling "Hsieh," but notes below use the accepted spelling "Xue."

2. There are three standard biographies of Xue Fucheng: *Qingshi liezhuan* [Qing History: Collected Biographies] (Shanghai: Zhonghua shuju, 1928), 58: 54b-57; *Beizhuan jibu* [Supplement to Biographical Collections], ed. by Min Erchang (1931; reprinted Taibei: Siku quanshu zongshu quan yinyong, 1959?), 13: 1-7a; and *Eminent Chinese of the Ch'ing Period (1644-1912),* ed. by Arthur W. Hummel (1943; reprinted Taibei: Chengwen Publishing Co., 1970), 331-333. See also two essays: Huang Zitong, "Xue Fucheng de sixiang" [The Thought of Xue Fucheng], in *Zhongguo jindai sixiangshi lunwenji* [Collected Essays on the History of Modern Chinese Thought], [by Feng Youlan, et al.] (Shanghai: Renmin chubanshe, 1958), 51-65; and Zhong Shuhe, "Zhuzhang kaifang de mudi shi weile jinbu—guanyu Xue Fucheng *Chushi siguo riji*" [On Progress As the Motive of Enlightening—regarding Xue Fucheng's *Diary of an Embassy to Four Nations*], in the reprint of the first six volumes of Xue Fucheng, *Chushi siguo riji,* collated by An Yuji (Hunan: Renmin chubanshe, 1981), 1-15.

3. "Ying zhao chenyan shu" [Outwarn Phrases in Response to an Imperial Decree], in Xue Fucheng, *Yongan quanji* [The Complete Works of Xue Fucheng] (N.p., 1884-1898), 1: 1-29.

4. *Chouyang chuyi* [A Humble Discussion of Plans for Foreign Affairs], in Hsieh, *Yongan quanji,* 15: 1-47.

5. Ibid., 34-45.

6. Ibid., 46a.

7. See Douglas Howland, "The Japanese Borders of the Chinese Empire" (Ph.D. diss., University of Chicago, 1989), 114-163.

Part I

Sixteenth Year of the Guangxu Emperor (1890)

11TH OF THE FIRST MONTH [JANUARY 31, 1890][1]

In the Fourth month of the fifteenth year of the Guangxu Emperor, I, Fucheng, received by decree official confirmation of my appointment to the position of Envoy Extraordinary of China to England, France, Italy and Belgium. My petition to visit my ancestors' gravesites in Wuxi was subsequently granted, so I had official permission to spend two months there starting on the 25th day of the Fifth month.

I left the imperial capital on the 1st of the Sixth month. During the trip to Wuxi, I made two short stops at Tianjin and Shanghai and arrived in Suzhou[2] on the 23rd of the same month. Since there were not enough rooms in my ancestral home to accommodate my entire family, I arranged for them to stay at the temporary official housing of the city.

During that time my elder brother was gravely ill; he had suffered a severe stroke and had lost his ability to speak while he was in Beijing waiting for the soon-to-be vacant position of Imperial Censor. Accordingly, I had to submit a resignation on his behalf to the Imperial Court to release him from duty. He was brought home on the 15th of the Sixth month. When I reached Wuxi on the 28th of that month, he was failing rapidly. He subsequently passed away on the 2nd of the Seventh month.

After his death, I made all the funeral arrangements and then visited several of my ancestors' gravesites in the countryside. By the end of the Ninth month, I began to make preparations for my trip abroad and set my date of departure for the first day of the following month. Unfortunately, I suddenly caught malaria and was confined to bed for an entire month. Before I fully recovered, both my feet became infected and were painfully swollen, which required further medical treatment. Compelled to meet my obligations, I nevertheless left my sickbed and arrived in Shanghai on the 14th of the Eleventh month. A variety of social obligations in the city took a serious toll on my newly regained strength, and I was subsequently stricken with the flu,

---

1. Because the Chinese recorded time according to a lunar calendar, all of Hsieh's daily entries are understood to refer to lunar dates. Hence we will dispense with "lunar" and instead simply indicate his daily entries by, for example, "First month." The reader, however, should not take this to mean "January." On the rare occasions when Hsieh does refer to the Western solar calendar, we, of course, use Western month names.

The Chinese counted years according to the reign name of the emperor on the throne. The Manchu Prince Zaitian (1871–1908) became the Guangxu Emperor on January 15, 1875, according to Western reckoning. Hence, 1875 corresponds to the first year of the Guangxu Emperor.

But there was also a second method of counting years. By combining ten signs for Earth with twelve signs for Heaven, the Chinese generated a cycle of sixty years; each year, therefore, had a name formed from two signs. Hsieh's diary begins in the *geng-yin* year (the name for 1830, 1890, 1950, 2010, and so on), or, to be more specific, the sixteenth year of the Guangxu Emperor (1890).

2. A major city of Kiangsu Province adjacent to Wuxi. (Trans.)

which nearly cost me my life. For five days, I was unable to keep down even a drop of water and was not expected to live. But a competent doctor was found for me, and he truly saved my life.

After another month of complete bed rest, I booked another passage on the French ocean liner *Irrawaddy*, which set sail today. In the early morning I boarded the ship with my wife and my second daughter. My entourage included one advisor, seven aides, five interpreters, two military attachés, two footmen, two cooks, two tailors, one barber and three maids. Several additional aides and interpreters from Guangdong Province will join us at Hong Kong.

The *Irrawaddy* is a comparatively large ocean liner, and the captain of the ship holds an officer's rank in the French navy. All the members of the crew are enlisted men who are undergoing mandatory navy training. This is a remarkable idea, and we must keep it in mind for the training of our own navy recruits in the future.

14TH OF THE FIRST MONTH

It turned out to be a nice day after heavy rain in the morning, and we reached Hong Kong during the hour of *si*.[3] Hong Kong, once a desolate island, was conceded to Britain during the reign of the Daoguang Emperor. Now it's a bustling city boasting of two million people among whom there are but three thousand foreigners. Hong Kong has become a haven for criminals from both Fujian and Guangdong provinces as the local Chinese officials lack the jurisdiction to arrest them. Several of my predecessors have fought vigorously for our right to install a consulate there, but to no avail. I must keep this in mind and strive again at the appropriate time for our legal rights as a nation.

15TH OF THE FIRST MONTH

Two interpreters from Guangdong Province came aboard today. I sent

---

3. At the outset of his diary, Hsieh refers to the time of day in the Chinese fashion. The twelve signs for Heaven (see note 1) also served to mark divisions of the day into "hours" or "watches." Their rough correspondences are as follows:

zi	11:00 P.M.–1:00 A.M.	wu	11:00 A.M.–1:00 P.M.
chou	1:00–3:00 A.M.	wei	1:00–3:00 P.M.
yin	3:00–5:00 A.M.	shen	3:00–5:00 P.M.
mao	5:00–7:00 A.M.	you	5:00–7:00 P.M.
chen	7:00–9:00 A.M.	xu	7:00–9:00 P.M.
si	9:00–11:00 A.M.	hai	9:00–11:00 P.M.

Later in the diary, Hsieh comfortably uses the Western system of clock hours.

one of them with one of my aides to the Hong Kong Governor's Office to announce my arrival. The governor sent a small steamer for me at noon. When the boat reached shore, we were greeted by a battalion of eighty British soldiers with a band and a fifteen-gun salute. I rode to the governor's Office in a sedan-chair and was received warmly by Governor William Des Voeux.[4] After exchanging pleasantries, the governor confided to me that he is currently in poor health. He expected to return home on the next French ocean liner as he had served almost two years in Hong Kong. After I returned to the ship, the governor came aboard in the afternoon to return my call. I offered him wine and fruit, and we chatted for a few minutes before he took his leave.

16TH OF THE FIRST MONTH

This morning Counsellor Huang Zunxian[5] came aboard with his son and servant. The ship left Hong Kong in the afternoon and sailed out into the sea.

During my short stay in Shanghai, Zhao Jinglain had asked me to write a foreword to the forthcoming translation of *Natural Science* by an English scholar, John Fryer.[6] Fryer has spent the last twenty years in China translating and thereby introducing many Western books to our culture. I wrote the foreword and sent a copy to Fryer. Today, in the warm sun and mild breeze, I edited the piece again and include it in this diary:

> Natural science is, in China, the foundation of civilization; in the West, the impetus for wealth and power. So both East and West share a common origin.[7]
> In our ancient society, people at all levels were encouraged to pursue new discoveries, such as the wheels for the cart, the sails for the ship and the arrows for the bow. Consequently, these new inventions became sources of power for kings and

---

4. Sir William Des Voeux was governor of Hong Kong from October 1887 to May 1891. (Trans.)

5. Huang Zunxian (1848–1905) began his diplomatic career as counsellor to the first Chinese ambassador to Japan (1877–81). He then served as consul general in San Francisco (1881–85). His third assignment was the present trip to Europe with Hsieh Fucheng, but, as we read in the course of Hsieh's *Diary*, he soon was appointed consul general to the new post in Singapore, where he served from 1891 to 1894.

6. John Fryer (1839–1928) was perhaps the single most important translator of Western scientific books into Chinese in the nineteenth century. He started his career at the Jiangnan Arsenal in Shanghai (founded in 1865 by Ding Richang) but later left it to work independently.

7. In his *Diary*, Hsieh repeatedly compares Chinese and Western knowledge and technology with an eye to verifying their common origins. Here we have the first instance of his belief that Western civilization originated in China, a notion familiar to scholar-officials in the nineteenth century. Some asserted that the great floods in the legendary time of King Yü cut Europe off from what had been a unified Chinese world. Others theorized that the ancient Chinese classics, lost to China during the infamous burning of books by the First Emperor of Qin (213 B.C.), were taken to Rome, where they provided the foundation for Western civilization.

emperors. In later centuries, such basic, practical knowledge was taken for granted by our people, and no encouragement was given to inventors for further new development. As a result, the technology of our past generations drifted into foreign lands and served as the foundation of their future scientific inventions. The Westerners further studied this basic knowledge, competed fiercely among themselves and produced never-ending changes and advances. However, these achievements of the West should not be regarded as sheer luck; we must admire the energy and resilience of those people who have relentlessly pursued the development of these new and practical ideas throughout the centuries.

The world has been at peace for many years now. Men of both East and West are frequently traveling across the ocean to different continents and exchanging ideas with each other. Many Western scholars began to take the initiative in studying the writings of our ancient sages. And our own learned men are also developing an interest in the rapid progress of new Western knowledge in areas such as astronomy, geology and mathematics. Even though it appears that there are a variety of new fields in Western technology, the theory in each scientific discovery remains similar to the past concepts of our ancient culture.

Mr. Fryer, an English scholar who has spent some twenty years in China, is well versed in the Chinese language. Over the years, he has introduced many English books into our culture through his translations. Now he is taking a step further by collecting the basic knowledge of general science and compiling it into a book. It is certainly not an easy task; in the past few years, he has devoted all his time to tedious research and has spent many long hours editing. He has diligently explained the details of each scientific subject in his own words. In my opinion, he is truly a remarkable scholar. With great admiration and deep respect, I regard his book as an unprecedented contribution to China for many generations to come.

18TH OF THE FIRST MONTH

Nice weather and smooth sailing. The ship is cruising southward toward Saigon. A huge whale appeared periodically at the ship's right hull some ten yards away. Once, it leaped up three to four feet, playfully spurting water. I have heard several theories about the sudden appearance of a whale. One suggested that the whale comes to feed on the small fish that tend to follow the trail of the ship for food scraps thrown overboard. Another story told of an Indochinese prince of ancient times who was saved from drowning by two whales, which lifted him up above the water. Therefore, the whale is traditionally regarded as a deity by the natives, who do not dare attack the fish under any circumstances.

19TH OF THE FIRST MONTH

The ship entered the Saigon harbor in the early morning. I went ashore and rode in a carriage sightseeing and then visited the zoo in the park. All the natives there are of Muslim faith, and both men and women go barefoot. After the French conquest some fifty years ago, Indochina was divided into four districts, each of which is now controlled by a governor. The present governor general (formerly the governor of Saigon) administers government operations by traveling throughout all four districts. Since he is currently visiting Hanoi, I went to pay my respects to De Lanessan,[8] the governor of Saigon. The governor sent a carriage, led by one of his military officers, to accompany me on my trip to his office. I was first led into the office of the Governor General and then ushered into the office of Governor De Lanessan. After my subsequent departure, Governor De Lanessan came aboard the ship to return my call. He appeared to be a nice person; however, I understand he is relatively new at his post. Perhaps he was unfamiliar with the protocol, as he didn't welcome me with the regular gun salutes. I really don't think he intended to slight me.

In the afternoon, Zhang Puling, the president of the local Chinese Chamber of Commerce, invited me to a banquet in my honor. Mr. Zhang came to Saigon some thirty years ago and has since become a prosperous merchant. He has ten sons, two of whom have returned to China to take their examinations in the family's native province. Zhang is a sincere person and consistently takes care of the needy in the local Chinese community.

22ND OF THE FIRST MONTH

In the first hour of early morning, the ship anchored near Singapore to wait almost two hours for the tide before entering the harbor. Chinese Consul Zuo Binglong came aboard with his son. Both of them wore clothing made of light gauze. As I understand, the weather there remains hot and humid all year long. Zuo is a man of extraordinary ability and has been stationed there for some nine years. He is fluent in foreign languages and can communicate directly with the local foreign officials. Before noon, Mr. Zuo sent a carriage for me, and I went to the banquet he prepared in my honor.

After dinner, I went to see Governor Smith at his office. Smith is an old China hand who has spent some twenty years in Guangdong Province. He informed me that I would be saluted by cannon during my departure from the island.

In Singapore there are various consulates of different countries. All foreign countries except China have installed consulates in both Kuala Lumpur and Penang. Consequently, the overseas Chinese at these two locations must seek help at the Singapore consulate whenever they encounter problems. This situation has to be corrected, and I made a note of that.

---

8. Jean-Antoine De Lanessan (1843–1919). (Trans.)

In the afternoon, Chen Jinzhong, consul of Siam and a former prominent merchant of Fujian Province, came to see me. His family has made its home in Singapore for several generations, and he himself has now become a millionaire. Both his grandfather and his father served as the Chinese consul in Siam. He is also a philanthropist and founded the first institution of higher learning for the Chinese on the island. Over the years he has donated tens of thousands of taels of silver for the cost of defending China's coast.[9] Unfortunately, he cannot speak Mandarin and thus had to communicate with me through an interpreter.

The ship left Singapore in the late afternoon. As it slowly cruised through the harbor I perceived white smoke bursting from the mouth of the cannon but was unable to count the number of shots on account of the great distance.

27TH OF THE FIRST MONTH

Calm sea and smooth sailing. The ship cruised through the Bay of Bengal and reached Colombo, the capital of Ceylon, four hours later. There are six different nationalities living on the island. In addition to the natives, there are Indian, Portuguese, Dutch, Singaporean and British people. This is due in part to the fact that many years ago there was a native king who surrendered first to the Portuguese invaders, then to the Dutch and ultimately to the British. The native religion is Buddhism; however, after the multiple invasions, other religions such as Islam, [Protestant]Christianity and Catholicism were all brought to the island.

There are three famous temples in Ceylon. I paid a visit to one of them, since it was located only seven miles from the ship. In front of the temple the river is covered by a uniquely constructed bridge, which is actually a fleet of small boats tied together. Since we went across the bridge by carriage, we were charged ten cents. As we stepped into the temple, we were asked to remove our hats. At the entrance hall, we confronted a statue of the Buddha in repose that is some 150 years old. At another hall sat a statue of the Buddha flanked by his two attendants; this statue was 2,000 years old. I recall that in Chinese history, Ceylon was known as the nation of lions and the place where Shakyamuni Buddha entered Nirvana. A tall, imposing pagoda, which contains the ashes of the Buddha's body, stands nearby. Several monks were seen selling copies of Buddhist scriptures written on bay

---

9. The *liang* or "tael" was a standard measure for the weight of silver used as money. It was roughly equivalent to an English ounce, and one tael of silver was legally worth 1,000 copper coins. At the same time, however, largely because of China's participation in world trade, nineteenth-century Chinese also used a silver coin, the *yuan* or "dollar." It was roughly equivalent to 7/10 of a tael and was mixed with copper at a theoretical ratio of 9 to 1.

leaves and tied together with string. I bought a few copies from them. In the courtyard, there stands a huge Bo tree some forty feet in height, which is more than 2,000 years old. The natives call the tree the Holy Tree, because it is said that the Buddha was born there.

8TH OF THE SECOND MONTH

Clear sky but windy as the ship entered the Red Sea. The temperature remains at sixty-nine degrees. This is an unusual weather pattern for this area and is due to a cool northern wind blown in from Europe. I had a long talk with my aide, Huang Zunxian, who once served as the Chinese consul in San Francisco. According to him, the annual drafts that the overseas Chinese send home often total as much as hundreds of millions of dollars. It's for this reason alone that the American authorities established a quota for Chinese immigration. With the recent rapid increase of the Chinese population in Australia, the British may take the same measures to curb the Chinese population explosion there.

9TH OF THE SECOND MONTH

The ship reached Egypt. A small steamer came by and collected the fee for the ship's entry into the Suez Canal. The amount of money collected annually can be as high as £8,400. As I understand, the upkeep of the canal is very expensive.

10TH OF THE SECOND MONTH

The ship cruised at a slow pace for fear of colliding with other vessels and made several stops on account of the busy traffic. The temperature soared to eighty-six degrees. It's humid and uncomfortable on board.

11TH OF THE SECOND MONTH

The ship entered the Mediterranean Sea in the afternoon. There was a light fog, and the ship almost lost its way. In the evening we reached Alexandria. Today happens to be the birthday of the emperor of Turkey. A rainbow of flags was hoisted atop each vessel for the celebration.

14TH OF THE SECOND MONTH

The ship sailed by Sicily and passed Naples, which is known to be a beautiful city. In the evening we were hit by a heavy storm. The noise of the machinery in the engine room and the sound of broken dishes amid the constant thrashing of the waves raged all night. It created a frightening experience for everyone on board.

15TH OF THE SECOND MONTH

The storm cleared up in the morning. In the evening, strong winds hit the ship again. The majority of the passengers became seasick and vomited, but I remained well throughout the ordeal.

16TH OF THE SECOND MONTH

The ship anchored at Marseille, which is located 43.13 degrees north of the equator and 411.07 degrees from Beijing. A bustling seaport, Marseille was initially discovered and built up by the ancient Greeks long before it developed into one of the largest cities in France.

Counsellor Chen Jitong from the Chinese embassy in France came aboard and took care of everything for me. We were taken to the Hotel de Marseille and registered in room 26. It is a seven-storey building, every floor of which is kept immaculately clean. The city of Marseille is better built than the Shanghai French Concession and is nearly as large as Paris.

17TH OF THE SECOND MONTH

Two officials from the Labor Department came to fetch me for a tour of the harbor. Both were personal friends of Chen Jitong. I asked Chen and Huang to accompany me on the tour. We boarded a small steamer to cross to the newly constructed embankment. The officials led me through the engine room, and I watched its operation in awe. We then went to the shipyard and ended the tour by ascending to a chapel on the hill, where I had a bird's-eye view of the city.

18TH OF THE SECOND MONTH

We boarded the train for Paris.

19TH OF THE SECOND MONTH

There was heavy rain in the morning, but it cleared up as soon as we reached Paris. I went to the embassy and met my predecessor, Liu Ruifen. An altar had been erected in the courtyard, and we both prostrated ourselves to pay homage to His Majesty the Emperor. After a few hours of discussion about embassy affairs, I was taken to a restaurant and had dinner there.

20TH OF THE SECOND MONTH

Ambassador Liu is staying at a hotel in Paris, and I went to pay him a visit. Ambassador Hong Jun [the ambassador to Germany], who is presently visiting Paris, was also there. All three of us had a long chat.

22ND OF THE SECOND MONTH

I received the official brass seal from Ambassador Liu and gave him the wooden pass, which will be returned to the International Office in Beijing.[10]

25TH OF THE SECOND MONTH

I asked both Military Attaché Chen Jitong and Interpreter Wu Zonglian to remain at their current positions at the embassy.

Today, there was a heated debate at the French Parliament between the senators and the ministers of foreign affairs over the issue of treaty agreements between Turkey and France. Such controversy, as I understand, may jeopardize the future of the present government.

28TH OF THE SECOND MONTH

Both the prime minister and the foreign minister of France resigned, and I obtained a list of names of the new cabinet.

1ST OF THE INTERCALARY[11] SECOND MONTH

Interpreter Wang, who was the candidate for the post of military attaché,

---

10. The Zongli geguo shiwu yamen (Zongli yamen), or Office for the Comprehensive Management of International Affairs (International Office), was a product of the peace accords of 1860 that followed the Second Opium War (1858–60). It was established in 1861 by Yixin (1833–98), the first Prince Gong, to manage China's foreign relations, but it also undertook a number of important Westernization activities. It created and managed the Tongwen Guan, an institute for foreign language learning, Western studies and the translation of Western books; it oversaw the Maritime Customs Office and the Office of the Northern Ports and it supervised diplomatic service and programs for overseas students. As we see in Hsieh's *Diary*, the International Office was also involved in the development of Western manufacturing and technology, largely because of the interests of Li Hongzhang. In 1901, it was absorbed into the new Ministry of Foreign Affairs (Waiwubu).

Diplomatic posts followed certain established procedures for office protocol. Each official post had its own seal of office, which authenticated an official's documents. When one commenced one's travel to a new post, one was given a wooden pass (originally to pass a border guard post), which was turned over to the official being replaced. He would then transfer the seal of office to the new diplomat. The function of the wooden pass, of course, was to verify that one truly was the newly arriving official invested with the authority of the Imperial Court.

11. Irregularities in the lengths of lunations meant that the length of a given lunar month varied. To make up for progressive discrepancies in the lunar year, the Chinese periodically added an intercalary month (*runyue*). The principle is similar to the Western "leap day" of February 29. Note that another, an intercalary Sixth month, occurs in the eighteenth year of the Guangxu Emperor (1892).

died today. He had studied in America for eight years and was fluent in the English language. During the voyage he caught the flu in Ceylon and became seriously ill when we reached Marseille. He was subsequently brought to Paris and placed under the care of physicians, but they were unable to save him.

It's truly a pity that he had to die on foreign soil so far away from home. What a waste of such a talented young man!

Today I paid a visit to the foreign minister of France.

4TH OF THE INTERCALARY SECOND MONTH

At four o'clock this afternoon, President Carnot of France sent a double horse-drawn carriage, with Minister Mollier and a brigade of cavalry, for my trip to the Versailles Palace. I arrived there with Attaché Chen and Interpreter Wu at five o'clock. A military band played music at the front gate when I made my entrance. The president stood at attention with his hat in hand while I read aloud the imperial greetings and subsequently submitted my portfolio. He personally accepted these official documents and then expressed his appreciation before he retreated.

5TH OF THE INTERCALARY SECOND MONTH

Since China established an embassy in France, six ambassadors have been consecutively assigned to the post. Over the years, the accumulation of official documents there has become overwhelming. Among the files there are many of great importance. Consequently, I have taken time out to read one or two files each day and make notes on the most essential ones for future reference. I discovered that the current president of France was voted into office in the thirteenth year of the Guangxu Emperor [1887].

7TH OF THE INTERCALARY SECOND MONTH

Today I visited the leader of France's Upper Parliament and then the ambassadors of both Italy and Turkey.

The French Parliament leader promised me that he will help all he can with any future problems.

The Italian ambassador claimed to have once served as the prime minister and then as the foreign minister of his country. When he received his appointment to his present post, he was seriously contemplating retirement. It appears that he must now wait until a multitude of foreign-affairs problems are resolved before he can retire from official duty. He also mentioned that, to his understanding, all the past and present Chinese ambassadors to both England and France have been prominent Chinese scholars; he therefore regards them with the highest esteem.

The Turkish ambassador confided in me with tears in his eyes. He contended that both England and France are threatening the future of both our countries with their superpower weaponry, and in today's world there is no justice as far as territorial disputes are concerned. The nation that is best equipped with powerful cannons and fast battleships can devour any large portion of territory at will, and thus all this talk of international law is sheer nonsense.

8TH OF THE INTERCALARY SECOND MONTH

This afternoon I visited the British embassy, the Lower House of the French Parliament, the Spanish embassy and the Russian embassy.

The British ambassador appeared to be a sincere person and is known to be a scholar. The leader of the Lower House also assured me that he will do everything he can whenever there is a dispute between our two countries. The Spanish ambassador had once served as the foreign minister of his own country; he also expressed his wish to retire as soon as he sets all foreign affairs on the right track. The Russian ambassador, a man of advanced age, loves to talk, but he appears to be sincere and honest.

9TH OF THE INTERCALARY SECOND MONTH

This afternoon I paid visits to the embassies of both Austria and the Vatican. The Austrian ambassador is courteous and sincere; the ambassador of the Vatican delivered the same message as the Buddhist priests of China and was dressed in the same attire as well.

12TH OF THE INTERCALARY SECOND MONTH

This afternoon I paid a visit to the wife of the French president, and we exchanged greetings for half an hour. Then I went to the German embassy. According to the German envoy, even though the seventy-five-year-old Premier Bismarck has officially retired, the Kaiser still rests responsibility for the nation on his shoulders. As far as the German envoy knows, there will not be any change in policy in the immediate future.

13TH OF THE INTERCALARY SECOND MONTH

After lunch I went to the Oriental Museum. In the Chinese room I recognized two jade seals, one green and the other white, which were evidently taken from the Yuanming yuan in Beijing.[12]

14TH OF THE INTERCALARY SECOND MONTH

There are twenty-eight provinces in Vietnam, geographically divided into southern and northern provinces. The majority of the southern part, which is wilderness inhabited only by primitive tribes, has been in the hands of France for a long time.

In the first year of the Tongzhi Emperor [1862], France occupied three provinces of northern Vietnam and then negotiated a peace treaty with the Vietnamese. In the eighth year of the Guangxu Emperor [1882], France attacked Hanoi and conquered the rest of Vietnam. Since that time Vietnam has been a colony of France.

23RD OF THE INTERCALARY SECOND MONTH

I took my interpreter and ascended the newly constructed Eiffel Tower by elevator. When I reached the top, I felt as if I were floating on clouds high above the earth.

24TH OF THE INTERCALARY SECOND MONTH

I went to the Wax Museum and was amazed by the vivid likenesses of the figures in various poses. As I understand, this art form was developed by an old woman and became extremely popular in Europe less than a century ago.

My next visit was to the art gallery, where battle scenes between Prussia and France are vividly displayed on large oil paintings that span the four walls of a single room, with light filtered through the ceiling. As I entered the room, I saw the military forces of both countries engaging in fierce battle in and around forests and over the valley with winding streams, high ridges and a backdrop of castles and fortresses. A multitude of soldiers are seen firing muskets, waving banners and lighting or towing the cannons. There are crumbling walls, gutted houses and fallen bodies strewn where the cannon-balls exploded. Fighting men with broken limbs lie either on their backs or with their faces down on the ground, and underneath their bodies the earth is saturated with pools of blood. It's truly a gruesome scene to behold! Yet with the painted moon shining brightly above in the sky and thick layers of

---

12. The Yuanming yuan (Garden of Perfect Clarity), or Old Summer Palace, was the summer palace enjoyed by the Xianfeng Emperor (r. 1851–1861). During the Second Opium War, it was looted and then burned down by British and French commanders as a personal punishment for the Chinese emperor.

green grass on the ground, one can't help but wonder whether one is actually standing in the midst of a battleground or in this one single room of the art gallery.

As I touched the wall lightly with my fingers, my mind finally came to the realization that this horrible sight was but an illusion of the past. Because this fine artist of the West has projected a past image into such a present reality, the battle scene of twenty years ago may be perceived as a nightmare in human history.

4TH OF THE THIRD MONTH

I submitted my credentials and then intended to leave France for England. However, I was unable to follow this original plan immediately because all the children of my predecessor, Ambassador Liu, had the measles and were not supposed to be exposed to cold air.

Three days ago, I sent ahead my aides to England, and today my family and I left Paris by train. After some 200 miles of traveling we went boarded a ferry that took us across to Dover. We then traveled some seventy-five miles by train and reached Victoria, where I found Ambassador Liu waiting for my arrival. We left the station by carriage for the trip to the embassy.

5TH OF THE THIRD MONTH

I received all the official documents of the embassy and asked three of the officials there to remain in their positions at my service. One is an advisor of the first rank, an Englishman by the name of Margary; one is an interpreter of the second rank named Zhang Sixun; and the third is named Wang Wenzao.

9TH OF THE THIRD MONTH

Today is the day for Ambassador Liu's departure. I set up an altar in the courtyard, and we both prostrated ourselves in homage to His Majesty the Emperor. Thereafter, I went to the train depot with Ambassador Liu and saw him off.

11TH OF THE THIRD MONTH

I paid a visit to the British prime minister, Marquis Salisbury, who is also that country's foreign minister. Also present were Deputy Foreign Minister Grey and the assistant to the foreign minister, Sandison. Marquis Salisbury made his name known while he was serving as foreign minister during the war between Russia and Turkey in the fourth year of the Guangxu Emperor [1878]. During the crisis he dispatched the royal navy to patrol the coast of Turkey. This timely action curtailed the force of Russian aggression. Now Salisbury serves as the prime minister of Britain as well as the foreign minister. I shook hands with him and chatted a while before we parted.

13TH OF THE THIRD MONTH

I was rather dubious when I first heard Chinese officials who had served abroad singing the praises of the system of government in the West. But having toured Parliament, the schools and the prisons from Paris to London, I am totally convinced.

I also heard much praise of the sincerity of the American people and came to the conclusion that the people of such newly established countries are like newborn infants. Unaffected by old and stultifying habits, they naturally express their innate sincerity. The European countries were established several centuries after China, so their people appear to be in their prime and tend to be eager to explore new territories.

15TH OF THE THIRD MONTH

The Western people are true believers of their predominant religion, Christianity. The essence of this religion preaches the same message as Confucianism: high moral conduct and love for one's neighbor. However, both their Old Testament and their New Testament are filled with tales of superstition so incredible that even a small child cannot believe them to be the truth.

I have talked to Western scholars on several occasions and have found them to be in total agreement with the philosophy of Confucius. When I expressed my opinion of Christianity, they all agreed with me but would not openly criticize the doctrine. However, they hinted broadly that once the natural sciences are fully developed, their religion will eventually be cast away.

17TH OF THE THIRD MONTH

Two days ago the British Foreign Office sent a letter to the embassy confirming that I would be presented to the Queen of England at three o'clock this afternoon at Windsor Palace. I took Margary and Counsellor Huang with me, and we traveled to the railway station by carriage. The deputy foreign minister, who was apparently waiting for our arrival, came to meet us at the train depot and led us to the train. After traveling for some thirty miles by rail, we alighted from the train and found a double-seated carriage sent by the queen. After two miles in the carriage we arrived at Windsor Palace and were subsequently led to the Great Hall. We were served dinner and wine. Several court attendants, acting as our hosts, joined us during the meal.

After dinner we were brought into a small court where the queen was sitting on her throne. I paid my respects by bowing low, and Counsellor Huang handed me the portfolio containing a letter from our emperor to the queen as well as my credentials and my own written tribute to the queen. I stood and read aloud the contents and then presented them all to the queen. Her Majesty extended greetings and expressed her concern over the long voyage I had recently undertaken. Margary acted as interpreter for both of us. I subsequently made another bow and retreated.

The letter from His Majesty the Emperor to the queen of England was as follows:

> The emperor of China extends greetings to the queen of Britain, empress of India. By divine mandate, I wish to take the initiative to renew our friendship and to reconcile the differences between our countries by sending to your honorable nation my envoy, Hsieh Fucheng. He is presently a candidate for minister of third rank and is currently in the uniform of minister of the second rank.[13] I have entrusted him with this letter, which should be looked upon as a testimony of our true friendship. I personally vouch for the honesty and integrity of Hsieh Fucheng, whose administrative capability is beyond reproach. He will readily negotiate between our two nations in the future in terms both fair and thorough. I implore you to put your trust in this man so that he may accomplish the mission of upholding the long-lasting peace and friendship between our two nations in which I have the utmost confidence.

My own tribute to the queen was expressed in the following words:

> Ambassador Hsieh Fucheng wishes to pay his respects to Her Majesty, the queen of Great Britain, empress of India, whose benevolence to her subjects and ability as a great ruler are widely known throughout the world. I, your servant, request the honor of presenting you with this portfolio as a testimony of peace and beg you to accept the good will of my emperor so that both our nations may enjoy prosperity for ten thousand years to come. Most obligingly, I remain at your Majesty's service.

The queen's reply went as follows:

> I extend my greetings to your emperor of Imperial China. I have previously expressed my desire to have a learned man from your country serve as the envoy to

---

13. Officials in the Chinese bureaucracy were classed into nine ranks, from one down to nine. Each rank, however, had an upper and a lower division, making in effect a system of eighteen ranks.

England and am pleased to know that you are a noted scholar and the author of many books in your own country. I am delighted to welcome you as the envoy from your country. The good will of your emperor, as expressed by you, coincides with my own hope of maintaining everlasting peace and prosperity between our two nations. My heart is gladdened by such prospects.

After the audience, we were led on a tour of the palace. I was very impressed by the beauty and magnificence of the architecture. As I walked along the passageways, I admired the portraits and statues of former kings and queens, outstanding prime ministers and famous generals, all of which are either hanging on the walls or displayed on pedestals.

21ST OF THE THIRD MONTH

The crown prince of England held a party for the gentlemen of the court on the 17th of this month at St. James Palace. I attended the party with ambassadors from various countries. Today the queen also gave a party at Buckingham Palace that included the ladies as well. All the ambassadors were presented to the queen first, and we paid our respects by bowing, which meant merely lowering one's head down a few inches. Presented after us were the prime minister and his cabinet members. Titled ladies were the last to be presented; there were more than a thousand ladies at the party. When they were presented, they bent down on one knee. As they were retreating, the queen tended to shake hands only with the duchesses and the marquesses. All the ladies' skirts had trains several feet long dragging along the floor. I was told that the ladies of the highest rank wear the skirts with the longest trains.

22ND OF THE THIRD MONTH

I paid a visit to the Russian ambassador at his embassy. He is most courteous and appears to be a sincere person.

24TH OF THE THIRD MONTH

Today I paid visits to the French ambassador, the German ambassador and the Italian ambassador. All three ambassadors hold first-rank portfolios.

25TH OF THE THIRD MONTH

I paid visits to the ambassadors of both Austria and Turkey, accompanied by Margary. At the Turkish embassy, I asked the Turkish chief envoy about the progress Turkey has made in the past few years. He kindly gave me all the details about his own country.

According to him, Turkey has lost a large amount of territory in both Asia and Europe since the war with Russia. The four newly independent countries in Europe—Greece, Rumania, Serbia and Bulgaria—were all former colonies of Turkey. And the viceroy of Egypt, which was formerly a protectorate of Turkey, declared his territory autonomous after the Berlin Treaty between Turkey and Russia and subsequently heavily borrowed money from the British. To protect their interests, the British set up a management organization in Egypt and participated actively in Egypt's internal affairs. Thus the sovereignty of Turkey was flagrantly violated, and Egypt fell into the hands of Britain.

26TH OF THE THIRD MONTH

Further study of the Turkish ambassador's information revealed that Turkey didn't lose the war. Although the Turkish soldiers of Muslim faith were brave beyond the call of duty, Turkey was compelled to accept a truce under pressure from both Britain and France. The ambassador warned that China may encounter similar pressure; as the Western foreign powers gain strength in Europe, they will eventually threaten the future sovereignty of both China and Turkey. He stressed that China and Turkey must combine their strengths and build an united front that will benefit both our countries. In my opinion, his statement reflects the words of the Chinese proverb: "People who suffer from the same illness are sympathetic to each other."

I summoned Attaché Ma Qingchen for a conference. He explained that the reason that there is no treaty existing between China and Turkey is simply that there is no trade between the two countries. He asserted that the Gulf of Turkey is the one and only route by which the Russians can launch their naval force into the Mediterranean Sea and that Turkey has the right, according to international law, to stop Russia's maneuvers. For this very reason, Britain, France and other European nations have chosen to sign treaties with Turkey.

It may be advisable for China to sign such a treaty with Turkey if China is allowed to share the same privilege in the gulf as the European nations. However, if a trade mission is included in the treaty, future problems may surface due to such commitments. I consider Ma's analysis reasonably sound.

27TH OF THE THIRD MONTH

The ambassadors of Turkey, Italy and Russia all returned my courtesy call and paid me a visit today.

Consequently, I dispatched an urgent telegram home to the Imperial Commissioner of the Northern Ports.[14] The telegram stated as follows:

> Korea's proposal for foreign loans should be discouraged. Since there is no guaranteed security for such loan payments, the results may be devastating to Korea as well as to China. Therefore, I implore you to grant me the permission to alert all foreign powers so that they may advise their merchants not to accept loan proposals from Korea.

Official documents for the offices of both Britain and France were prepared accordingly.

29TH OF THE THIRD MONTH

It has been reported that Russian activity in gold mining along the border at Irkutsk has increased dramatically in recent years. Natives near the border on the Chinese side constantly hear the distinct sounds of picks and shovels when they are traveling through the mountain range on their way to the frontier. The Russians make a habit of sneaking into Chinese territory during the night and daringly digging in the mine or panning the sand in the river for gold. When daylight comes, they simply return to their own territory with the loot.

30TH OF THE THIRD MONTH

Initially, the Russians had no gold mine on their own soil. During the latter part of the Ming dynasty (1368–1644), Russia seized parts of the Ural Mountains, thus engendering conflict over mining interests between the two countries. Consequently, Russia established a mining company there. During the course of 300 years, Russia gradually took over the entire eastern and western portions of Siberia after an abundance of gold was discovered in the Ural Mountains. Over the years, the Russian government has focused all its attention on developing the mines and has subsequently passed special tax laws for private entrepreneurs to operate mining companies in Siberia.

---

14. The Beiyang tongshang dachen, or Office of the Commissioner of Trade for the Northern Ports, was established in 1870 and largely designed for Li Hongzhang, who filled it for twenty-eight years (1870–98). As holder of this office, Li was also given the appointment of Governor General of Zhili Province. This allowed the Office of the Northern Ports to: 1) manage Zhili Province; 2) manage the trade of the three coastal provinces of Zhili, Fengtian and Shandong and 3) manage the coastal defense and foreign affairs of the same three provinces. Although nominally under the direction of the International Office, the Commissioner of the Northern Ports had direct access to the Imperial Court, because unlike other commissioners, Li was given the title of Imperial Envoy (*qinchai*). It was by the authority of this office that Li sponsored the development of shipping, telegraphs, railroads and other Westernization projects between 1870 and 1898.

1ST OF THE FOURTH MONTH

The key to the prosperity of all the nations on both the European and American continents lies in their relentless search for knowledge to improve their industrial technology. Their capability of being major world powers of the world depends solely on the application of newfound technology, which, incidentally, has been initiated only in the last seventy years. There are truly no other great achievements that have been developed in the West other than its industrial technology. However, as far as the *discovery* of new technology is concerned, such technology has been locked in the universe by the Creator since the beginning of time, sooner or later to be released on this earth. It is the way of nature to provide no special favor to any particular people. Chinese scholars possess as much intelligence as their Western counterparts, but they are traditionally compelled to pursue literary endeavors whereas the Western pundits are free to study in their own chosen fields. Therefore, there is no sufficient reason for the Westerners to believe that they possess intelligence superior to ours.

In ancient times, the great minds of China consistently recorded the movements of heaven and the activities on earth. Apparently, people in the West adopted these fundamental principles and over the ages improved their industrial technology. It is time now for us Chinese to embark on such pursuits and to reveal more secrets of the universe. The results may astonish all the people in the West.

2ND OF THE FOURTH MONTH

I went to the Buckingham Palace ball at ten o'clock tonight with an entourage of four people. We watched the dancing and returned to the embassy at midnight.

3RD OF THE FOURTH MONTH

The birthday of the queen of England falls on the 24th of May, according to the Western calendar. A three-day celebration has been planned for the occasion, and today is the first day of the festivities. Marquis Salisbury invited all the chief envoys and their second-ranking officers from all the embassies to a party at his house on behalf of Her Majesty the Queen. The king of Belgium was also present.

When the party broke up at ten o'clock in the evening, we were taken to another tea party at the Foreign Office that was hosted by the Marquis himself.

10TH OF THE FOURTH MONTH

Scholars in the West acknowledge the vast influence of early Chinese inventions. The following evidence has been discussed: the origin of the newspaper may be traced to the tradition of our journals and official records; chemistry was definitely derived from our alchemy; the postal system was taken from the records of Marco Polo; the printing process was picked up from the invention of Fong Dao; the application of natural gas for lighting can be traced to our discovery of the fire well in Sichuan Province and the civil-service examination may have been modeled after our scholastic examination. As far as the compass, gunpowder, mathematics and astronomy are concerned, the impact of these inventions is widespread in the West. However, while the Western world steadily seeks to improve on these ancient discoveries, China was content with the early results and ceased to venture any further.

22ND OF THE FOURTH MONTH

In the early hour of *si* [9:00 A.M.], I rode in a carriage with an entourage of four people plus a cook to the train depot. We traveled to Dover and boarded a steamer for Belgium. After a four-hour voyage, the ship reached the harbor of Ostend. We traveled again by train to the depot in the north of Brussels, the capital, and then continued our journey by carriage to a hotel, arriving in the hours of *you* [5:00 P.M.]. The hotel, located at the back of the palace, is an exquisite, three-storey building.

23RD OF THE FOURTH MONTH

The Russian consul in Shanghai stopped at the hotel and paid me a visit. He spoke Chinese fluently, as he had spent some twenty years in Shanghai. He stated that he was on his way home for a holiday and was pleased to make my acquaintance in Belgium.

In the afternoon, a tour of the museum was arranged on my behalf. My interest was aroused by two strange-looking fossils, each of which was nearly thirty feet long. The heads and feet of both the creatures resemble those of a mammal, but the tails appear to be finlike, and the necks extend as long as a giraffe's. These fossils were unearthed from a coal mine, and it's believed that these creatures lived on this earth several thousand years ago.

On the way back we passed through a huge forest that covers seven square miles. The forest was characteristically different from those in England and France. In those countries the trees are more widely spaced, but in Belgium the trees are planted more closely together.

24TH OF THE FOURTH MONTH

I visited the Foreign Office and had the opportunity of meeting Minister Hainant and Deputy Minister Lambermont.

Both of these names are the surnames of these two officials. According to Chinese tradition, a man is introduced by his given name and family name together, whereas the Manchus and Mongols are called by their first names only. It appears that the men of the West are introduced by their family names only.

Hainant comes from an ancient noble family whose principality has since been annexed into Belgium. However, the descendants still retain the family name and the title of Marquis.

The present marquis was elected to Parliament and was then appointed one of the cabinet ministers. Since he has a poor memory, which prevents him from taking an active part in the administration of foreign affairs, the responsibilities of the minister fall into the capable hands of Lambermont, the deputy minister. The only duty of the marquis now is to sign his name to the official documents. Lambermont doesn't appear impressive at first glance; however, his knowledge of international affairs is astonishing. He prefers to study problems thoroughly and then deal with them one by one in his slow-paced, gentle way. He is also known to enjoy popularity among the gentry and serves as president of all the clubs in the capital. In the three years since he was named to his present position, Belgium's Foreign Office has become known as the most efficiently administered ministry in the Western world.

During our visit Lambermont mentioned that twenty-five years ago, when the present king of Belgium was then the crown prince, he followed him on a voyage to China. As the ship was sailing into Shanghai harbor, news of the former king's death reached the ship, Subsequently, the prince ordered the ship to return to Europe. Lambermont expressed his lifelong regret over this incomplete voyage, which prevented him from visiting China. He indicated that he lost a good opportunity to study the great culture and history of China. Lambermont further contended that Belgium's munitions industry is progressing as rapidly as those in England and France, and if China was interested in purchasing arms, he would do his best to assist China in negotiations with the industrialists in Belgium. He can obtain an 80 to 90 percent discount on all merchandise, which should be beneficial to both our countries. Also, he suggested it would be more convenient for China to set up an embassy in Belgium, or at least a liaison office, which may well be sufficient. He further stated that their ships will be responsible for all the deliveries if

China makes purchases from Belgium. He mentioned that the Belgium Chamber of Commerce is interested in establishing a company in Shanghai, and both Australia and Italy are willing to participate in a joint venture by subsidizing shares of the cost for the annual operation.

A tour was conducted for me that started at the law building. This magnificently built structure, which cost the Belgium government a tidy sum of money, was completed last year. As I understand, it took the architect sixteen years to complete the design before he could begin to draw the blueprints. Regretfully, he died before construction began on the building. Consequently, a statue of the architect was erected at the front of the building in his memory.

The tour then continued to the Parliament building. I found the structure less grand in design than those in England and France. Nevertheless, it's well kept and arranged in a more orderly fashion. We then went through an ancient fortress and an ancient church, whose designs suggest a strong Greek influence. We ended the tour at a crudely built, ancient castle that was 1,200 years old.

25TH OF THE FOURTH MONTH

Today's tour started in the morning at the Verviers Textile Mill. The mill employs more than 2,000 women, but the majority of the workers are given raw materials to weave at home. Less than 100 women work at the mill itself. The finished products include clothing materials, handkerchiefs and shoulder wraps, all of which are priced extremely high. They absolutely will not sell in China. I understand that all the women in Europe value these products highly. They invariably bring lucrative profits for Belgium in the European market.

The tour then proceeded to a garden at the summer palace of the king. There were singing birds and fragrant flowers, deep woods and rolling hills. Amid such beautiful scenery stands a statue of the former king, Leopold I, on a stone pedestal. We ended the tour at the cathedral; the former king is buried in its courtyard. To the right of the courtyard there is a large cemetery where the rich and famous are buried. In the evening we visited a wax museum and then went to watch some Arabian dancing.

26TH OF THE FOURTH MONTH

I received a letter from the Foreign Office indicating a two o'clock audience with the king. A double horse-drawn carriage with a court official was sent to the hotel for my trip to the palace, and I brought along counsellors

Chen and Wang. When we reached the palace gate, several court officials were waiting for us, and each took turns shaking hands with us. The minister of the Foreign Office was also on hand to greet us. We were subsequently led into the court; the king was standing in the east wing. As I entered, bowing, His Majesty removed his hat and returned my bow and then proceeded to shake hands with me. I read aloud my own written tribute to the king and then presented to His Majesty the portfolio that contained my credentials. His Majesty received them and then responded to my tribute verbally. He then entered into conversation with me in the most sincere manner. After talking to me for a considerable length of time, he turned his attention to my two staff members and exchanged a few words with each of them before we took our leave. Afterward, a court official took us back to the hotel by carriage.

27TH OF THE FOURTH MONTH

A former manager of the Seraing steel mill came to see me at the hotel. He is over seventy years old and retired. Initially, the mill was operated on a small scale, but it underwent an extensive expansion after he took over its management. Today, this large mill specializes in manufacturing mine shafts and railroad tracks.

An official from the Belgium embassy in Beijing came to pay me a visit at the hotel. He speaks fluent Chinese and told me he has served two terms in Beijing. He's presently on a leave of absence and will return to China in the fall. Later, I remembered that I had met him twice last year in Beijing.

28TH OF THE FOURTH MONTH

A meeting was arranged for me to visit the king's brother, who is about fifty years old and deaf. He is an extremely friendly person and showed great interest in the clothing of China. He asked numerous questions on the subject and examined our attire closely.

Tonight, His Majesty the King gave a banquet. Earlier, I had received an invitation from the palace that also included Counsellors Chen and Wang. We arrived at the palace by carriage at six o'clock. After a few minutes, the king appeared. He removed his hat and shook hands with us. Also present were his brother, the prime minister and the foreign minister and his staff. The total number of the party, including the hosts, was twenty-four. Dinner was served at an extraordinary long table and the food tasted delicious. A most gracious host, His Majesty kindly advised me that I shouldn't force myself to eat anything I don't really care for, as it may harm my health. He mentioned that he had noticed during one dinner party we both attended in England that I had difficulty in partaking of the food.

After dinner the king walked hand in hand with his brother and led us into another room. We were served drinks while standing; hosts and guests formed small groups. Lambermont engaged me in conversation on the subject of international affairs. He stated that natives in both Old Gold Mountain [San Francisco] and New Gold Mountain [Sydney] are growing restless, and he won't be surprised if, several decades later, they rise up and declare independence. By that time both America and Britain may lose control of their colonies and the power of world dominance. Then China may find herself with two more new nations to deal with, which may prove troublesome. He further stated that of all the prime ministers in the world, Bismarck is first in the league and Imperial Commissioner Li of China[15] should be ranked either second or third. He asserted that he had heard of the various accomplishments of Li and was impressed with his future plans for China He further claimed that Li is a great minister. Lambermont also mentioned the former Ambassador Zeng[16] as an outstanding diplomat in foreign affairs and expressed his regret over Zeng's short stay in his country and sudden disappearance from the diplomatic scene. He continued that he had heard recently that Zeng had passed away and offered his condolences. He then praised China's profound culture, the size of her population and her abundance of resources. He stressed that, with the help of Western technology, China could conceivably become a world power, but at the present time China needs international diplomacy. However, he emphasized that there is no need for China to forget her own proud past. He scoffed at Japan, who, in her ambitious endeavor to emulate the West, has discarded her traditional Japanese clothing to suit the style of the West. All the Westerners think the Japanese look ridiculous in their Western attire. He suggested that China should blend her traditional political system with those of the West by absorbing the West's strong points and discarding the weak ones.

Before we took our leave, the king shook hands with me and said movingly, "I wish you the best of health during your present European stay and implore you to do a thorough study of European culture and political sys-

---

15. Li Hongzhang (1823–1901) was a central official in the Chinese government during the last third of the nineteenth century. He rose with his patron Zeng Guofan during the defeat of the Taiping Rebellion in the late 1850s and early 1860s. By the end of his career, he had held several significant positions and titles, two of which Hsieh uses in his *Diary*: Grand Secretary (*Zhongtang*); and Imperial Commissioner (*Qinchai dachen*). The disastrous Sino-Japanese War of 1894–95 began the decline of Li's favor with the Empress Dowager and the court.

16. Zeng Jize, better known as Marquis Zeng (1839–90), was the son of Zeng Guofan (see note 15) and had a highly successful career as the Chinese ambassador to England, France and Russia between 1878 and 1885. His premature death was considered a tragic loss by reform-minded officials both in China and in Europe.

tems for the duration of your post. I'm looking forward to the day when your reputation as a great diplomat will be widely recognized throughout Europe."

Deeply touched, I stood at attention and expressed my sincere appreciation before we took our leave.

29TH OF THE FOURTH MONTH

At three o'clock in the afternoon, I led my small entourage from Brussels and boarded the train for Paris. The train made two stops at the border and all the passengers rushed out to the custom office to have their luggage checked. But we diplomats are not required to do so, and thus we merely sent an envoy to show our passports. We reached Paris at seven o'clock in the evening and arrived at the embassy by carriage at nine o'clock.

2ND OF THE FIFTH MONTH

At 11 A.M. we boarded the train for Calais and then crossed the channel. We arrived in London by train at 7 P.M. and reached the embassy there shortly thereafter.

4TH OF THE FIFTH MONTH

I've made a habit of studying the embassy records at leisure. I learned that an imperial decree of the 24th of the Third month of this year carried the following message:

> Li Hongzhang petitioned His Majesty the Emperor to have the achievements of past envoys recorded, compiled and submitted to the Historiographical Office so that the biography of each envoy can be subsequently compiled based upon these materials.

Zeng Jize was the first to be nominated for this honor, and I therefore informed the British Foreign Office of this news. They responded with enthusiasm and claimed that Marquis Zeng deserved such an honor.

5TH OF THE FIFTH MONTH

An English engineer who is presently employed as the vice president of a textile mill in China's Hubei Province wrote to the embassy requesting some steel parts for the construction of a mill by another engineer in Wuchang [the capital of Hubei Province]. The total amount of the order comes to £10,015. After a round of negotiations, £500 were deducted from the original order, and the materials will be shipped to Hubei within a few months.

10TH OF THE FIFTH MONTH

A report of the exchange of portfolios with Belgium was dispatched. It included a recommendation for an award for Interpreter Wang.

11TH OF THE FIFTH MONTH

It has been more than two months since I first arrived in London. During a break from my busy social obligations, I have found time to read the old official documents that have accumulated over the years in the embassy and to outline those files of great importance. According to an old document, the queen of England celebrated her fiftieth year on the throne in the year of Ding-hai [1887]. The International Office prepared and submitted a gift list to His Majesty the Emperor for approval. It was subsequently returned with the seal of approval in vermilion ink. A tribute was sent with the gifts to the Imperial Court of England accordingly. The gift list including the following items:

1. One jade centerpiece
2. One teakwood box containing one jade incense burner, one jade box and one jade vase
3. One jade mountain carving with stand
4. One pair of porcelain jars
5. One porcelain fruit tray with a blue flower design on a white background with a stand
6. Two wall hangings of white satin embroidery
7. Fourteen circular wall hangings of white satin embroidery
8. Two barrels of jasmine tea

Another entry from the same year is as follows:

> The British Foreign Office made a request on behalf of the British military band to the War Ministry in China through the embassy for the lyrics of the Chinese national anthem. Liu replied that China has only one piece of music that has been transcribed into European music for the convenience of Western musical instruments. It's known as "Universal Harmony." This particular piece of music was therefore sent with a letter. The lyrics were written by Marquis Zeng.

12TH OF THE FIFTH MONTH

According to embassy documents from the Third month of Yi-you [1885], Marquis Zeng, in a direct dispatch to the International Office, gave a complete report regarding the British occupation of Korea's An Island to the northeast of Jizhou Province. After lodging a protest with the British

Foreign Office, Zeng received an answer from Foreign Minister Earl Granville through a clandestine channel. The British claimed that they were obliged to take over what they called Hamilton Island as a temporary measure against Russian aggression. Consequently, Britain expressed her willingness to negotiate with China so as to protect China's interests on the island. Britain contended that she harbors no ill will or wishes to downgrade China's position on an international level.

After checking the position of the island on a Chinese map, we concluded that in future negotiations over that particular island, the name of "Hamilton" should be used in all legal documents.

Further study revealed that the island occupies a strategic position crucial to both Britain and Russia. In the dispatch, Zeng concludes that since China cannot prevent either of these two foreign powers from occupying this island, it's better for China that the island remains in the hands of Britain. It will invariably halt the Russian invasion of international waters and thus stop further aggression. And since Britain expressed a willingness to negotiate an agreement to maintain China's special privileges on the island, we should agree on a face-saving basis.

Copies of another document reveal that in the Third month of Bing-xu [1886], an embassy envoy was sent to the British Foreign Office to deliver the following message:

> The Russian ambassador in Beijing has repeatedly made inquiries at the International Office regarding the British occupation of Hamilton Island. He stressed that if Britain was allowed to occupy this particular island, then Russia is likely to occupy another place within Korean territory.

Our vice minister gave Russia the following answer:

> Imperial Commissioner Li and the British ambassador have entered into negotiations regarding the withdrawal of British forces from Hamilton Island. Britain claimed that she has no desire to remain on the island if China can guarantee that no other foreign power will occupy the island. However, if China cannot keep such a promise, Britain will call a conference with Russia and other European powers so that an agreement can be reached to keep other nations away from the island. As soon as such a conference date is set, Britain will be more than willing to sign the agreement and withdraw her occupation force from the island.

13TH OF THE FIFTH MONTH

According to further copies of old documents, in the Eighth month of Ting-ha [1887], Imperial Commissioner Li addressed the king of Korea in the following special dispatch:

Korea is a dependency of China, and therefore the exchange of formal documents between the officials of both countries has always been conducted according to traditional rules. Recently, your country has sent several envoys on special missions to the countries in both the East and the West. As Your Majesty probably knows, China has long stationed well-qualified ministers as envoys in all these countries. We expect your envoys to keep in close contact with them. From now on all the envoys of Korea, regardless of title or rank, should follow protocol by using the traditional stationery with printed titles under the direction of our envoys in all their correspondence with foreign countries. And our envoys will follow tradition by using vermilion ink on these official documents.

Later, in the Eleventh month, a petition for further negotiations was submitted to His Majesty the Emperor. Following an imperial decree, negotiations with the Korean king produced the following three major points:

1. When a Korean envoy reaches the country of his destination, he should be led to the Foreign Office of that country by the Chinese envoy stationed there.
2. During social functions he should stay behind the Chinese envoy in the receiving line.
3. Matters of importance should be discussed confidentially with the Chinese envoy first. This is the established protocol that a dependency must follow, and no other countries should participate in the discussion.

15TH OF THE FIFTH MONTH

According to documents in the embassy records, in the winter of Yi-you [1885], Marquis Zeng and the British foreign minister conferred on the boundary and commercial rights of Burma. The boundary issue was first on the agenda as the trade rights could not be discussed until the boundary was clearly drawn. Deputy Minister Grey stated that the disputed region stretches from the east of the Lu River, also known as the Salween River, in the south of Yunnan Province, to the south of Burma, joining the Mekong River in the east. Within that area, there are the kingdoms of Nanzhang and of several other tribes of Dan people.[17] Grey stressed that China is free to include this region in her domain and to act as the protector of the kingdom of Nanzhang. Marquis Zeng's advice to the International Office in Beijing was that since Britain is willing to return Nanzhang and the tribal territory to

---

17. The kingdom of Nanzhang lay in what is today parts of Burma (Myanmar) and Laos, but it is frequently translated as "Laos" in nineteenth-century documents. The Dai (or Dan) people are ancient relations of the Thai people presently in Thailand. There is still today a Dai Autonomous Zone in Yunnan Province in China.

China, we should accept the offer without further delay. He also suggested that we should inform the leaders of the region that they must send tributary missions to China at regular intervals and should proclaim clearly to the world the status of this region in order to prevent future dispute. At the same time, the marquis protested the loss of Bhamo, which appears to be the territory that the governor of Yunnan Province refers to as Xinjie. It is situated to the west of the Yunnan border, beyond the Dragon River and on the upper stream of the Nu River, known in the West as the Irrawaddy River, which flows into the lower stream of the Dragon Cloud River. The marquis suggested that if China regains this strategic point as a commercial seaport, we could not only strengthen our boundary but also collect a lucrative tariff there. However, after the British occupation of Burma, the place became a major point of debate between the two political parties in the British Parliament when the strategic value of the area was discovered. Britain may therefore change her mind about surrendering Bhamo to us.

Later, Deputy Foreign Minister Grey confided in Margary that Britain will follow the earlier agreement and that China may retain suzerainty over all the Dan tribes, including those under British control. He mentioned further that the British officials in Burma surveyed the Menan River to see if it was possible for China to open a commercial port there.

16TH OF THE FIFTH MONTH

This evening I visited the Lantern Festival with Attaché Zhang. The festival was held by the Botany Society. We then strolled to the gallery at the Royal Academy, where oil paintings were on display. Thereafter, we went to the Kensington Museum and attended a tea party, which was hosted by the London Post Office to commemorate the fifth anniversary of the issue of money orders.

17TH OF THE FIFTH MONTH

According to documents in the embassy record, in the spring of Bing-xu [1886], the British foreign minister responded to Marquis Zeng's inquiry:

> Lord Salisbury had once recommended that either a pope or a lama should be put on the throne in Burma so that diplomatic relations may thus be established and maintained by the end of a decade. The viceroy of India was entrusted with the undertaking of a thorough study of this subject, and he came to the conclusion that it is not feasible. Consequently, the minister who had been previously stationed there will be given the responsibility of governing Burma. Normal relations should soon be developed, and China shall resume suzerainty over the Dan tribes east of the Salween River.

I received your last letter and understand that China is accepting our offer. As for the territory west of the river, we cannot surrender the area along the west of the Irrawaddy to Bhamo. However, we have made a subsequent request to the viceroy of India that the territory of an anchorage be given to China as her new commercial port. We are presently expecting an answer from the Burmese minister and look forward to discussing the possibility of a joint venture in a commercial undertaking between Burma and China.

20TH OF THE FIFTH MONTH

According to the *History of the Latter Han*,[18] there was a kingdom of Dan that bordered the Byzantine Empire, so Dan tribes have existed on this earth for a long time. To the east of the Dan tribes is the kingdom of Laos, which, according to the ancient history, was listed among the nine tributary nations.

21ST OF THE FIFTH MONTH

Three days ago a personal invitation from the queen of England was delivered to me requesting my presence at the Buckingham Palace Ball. Regretfully, I had to decline due to pressing business at the embassy.

Today I received another invitation requesting my presence at St. James Palace, where all the other ambassadors will be present. I accepted the invitation and went to the party. During the course of the evening I had the opportunity to converse with a British official who had once traveled through the Tianshan Mountains along the northwestern Chinese border.

A letter reached the embassy from the International Office in Beijing concerning Brazil's recent solicitation for China's recognition of the newly established republic. The letter further stated:

> This office is well aware of the practice among European countries that a nation may change its political system from a monarchy to a republic. Nevertheless, if all the foreign powers have not yet reached a decision, this office will not act in haste to recognize Brazil as a republic. Please conduct a complete investigation of the British attitude toward Brazil so that we may take appropriate action.

After a thorough investigation I discovered that only a few of the Brazilian army and navy officers have declared a political takeover, having forced the

---

18. The *Hou Han Shu*, or *History of the Latter Han*, was one of the early official dynastic histories of China. Hsieh quotes many such works in his *Diary*. Typically, a new dynasty undertook the writing of the history of the preceding dynasty; this was done by the central government's Historiographical Office. Consequently, such histories carried great authority.

Official histories included sections on barbarian peoples for two specific purposes. In the first place, the Chinese kept a record of tribute missions from distant lands and could claim a degree of sovereignty over those people based on the historical record. And in the second place, such information was the foundation of Chinese knowledge of geography.

former monarch off the throne a year ago. So far, only France and the United States have recognized the republic of Brazil, as both these countries maintain a republican system themselves. Even though the British Foreign Office has shown a certain measure of courtesy to the Brazilian ambassador, the queen has never granted him an official audience. I forwarded this information to the International Office in Beijing and recommended that we delay recognition of Brazil as an independent republic.

25TH OF THE FIFTH MONTH

Sixty nautical miles equals sixty-nine-and-a-half land miles. Nautical miles are used only in a captain's log during a voyage. Such is the regulation of measurement in England. As for the measurements in other European nations, they remain unknown to me.

27TH OF THE FIFTH MONTH

According to documents in the embassy record, in the Third month of Ding-chou [1877], the former ambassador, Guo Songdao, stated the following in a memorandum to the emperor:

> Chinese people bear a deep-rooted resentment toward the missionaries of the West. In recent missionary cases at Hunan, Fujian, Anhui and Sichuan provinces, the escalation of mutual slaughter between the missionaries and the local populations was completely due to such resentment. Local officials were unable to mediate these disputes according to the law of the land because they clearly lacked the basic understanding of Western religion.
>
> In the early years of the present dynasty, during the reign of the Yongzheng Emperor [1722–1735], the building of Catholic churches was forbidden whereas the construction of Muslim mosques was allowed; this was based on the principle that practicing one's religion is the right of all people, but forceful conversion is an infringement on the rights of our people. However, in the ninth year of the Xianfeng Emperor [1859], the sanction was lifted by decree. French missionaries began to abuse their rights by protecting their own converts, who were obviously engaging in unlawful activities. Consequently, these Catholic converts continued their abuse and later even challenged the authority of the local officials. In many instances, murderers were allowed to hide in the church for protection. Therefore, once a Catholic church is built in a city, town or village, local residents immediately feel the pressure and realize they can no longer pursue their former peaceful existence. Thus the power of the Catholic missionaries has expanded to such an uncontrollable state that they have become a menace to each community in every province. Such abuse of church power is most predominant in Sichuan and Guizhou provinces. Whenever the people of these two provinces hear the name of the Catholic church, they immediately explode with rage. It is all the fault of the Catholic church, and these missionaries deserve to encounter such resistance from our people.

This humble servant implores Your Majesty to issue a decree instructing the governors of every province with explicit rulings on all missionary cases so that they may post your decree in all cities and towns they govern with words such as the following:

> Discrimination against Chinese church people should be restrained. Any cases involving either a missionary or Chinese converts should be decided in a just manner and as defined by the law of the land. If there is a hint of discrepancy, close examination and correction should be immediately undertaken. If a foreigner is involved in the case, he should be sentenced by the law of the Western world, whereas his Chinese accessory should be convicted by the law of the land even though he professes to be a member of the church.

This servant heard that the preachers of the Catholic church are known as "spiritual fathers" [priests] and those of the Protestant church are known as "shepherds" [pastors]. The preachers are believed to be learned men with a deep belief in helping the poor. Those who preach in China are all priests, and the success of their missions depends solely on the number of converts they recruit. Apparently, unsavory characters or even criminals in the local communities are recruited into the priesthood as long as they can bring enough converts into the church. But the more criminals the Catholic church accepts into their order, the less chance they will have to recruit reputable and true believers from the local communities. Since respectable citizens feel ashamed to associate with the Catholic church, they tend to stay away from the missionaries. In the last twenty years, the Catholic church has accepted many undesirable characters into their order, and the local residents look upon the church with disdain and disgust.

This humble servant begs Your Majesty to call a conference of all the ambassadors through the auspices of the International Office so that some agreements can be reached. The church must run a character check on local members before they can be accepted into the order of the Catholic church. This move will certainly ease the anger of the local communities and create good will toward the Catholic church. Thus years of hostility and distrust between the church and the local people may finally be resolved.

An additional note may be added in the forthcoming decree: If the local residents unreasonably destroy church property, they must be fined for the cost of the repair. As for personal conflicts between the converts and the local residents, each case should be weighed individually with care so that a fair judgment can be made concerning both parties involved. A definite date must be enforced in the payment of a fine in order to eliminate further incidents. In view of the mounting missionary cases, right or wrong in each conflict must be clearly defined.

4TH OF THE SIXTH MONTH

I have previously stated that it is customary in the West for men to be addressed by both their family name and their given name together. Now I have discovered that they tend to place their family name *after* their given name.

5TH OF THE SIXTH MONTH

Improving relations with China has become a favorite subject of conversation among British and French officials. They no longer regard China with utter contempt, which was the Western attitude of earlier years. The first reason is the battle in Vietnam, where the French failed to gain any concessions from China and lost more men than they expected. Other nations began to take notice of the strength of China, whose army fought bravely against the French invasion. Secondly, there has been a steady flow of Chinese scholars reaching the West in recent years. They have familiarized themselves with Western culture and have closely examined the benefits and perils of international commerce. It is they who have improved China's relationship with the West. Thirdly, China has strengthened her naval defenses along the coast, a well-publicized event that has achieved most satisfying results. Fourthly, Chinese students who have been sent overseas by our government have proved to be the best students in the European schools. The Western world has been impressed by the superior intelligence of the Chinese and has finally realized that China is not a backward country. We should therefore take the initiative and make good use of it. From now on, if an unexpected incident occurs, we should act with absolute calm and negotiate with extreme care; the future of our country depends upon such diplomacy.

7TH OF THE SIXTH MONTH

I had previously placed orders of machinery for both steel and textile mills on behalf of General Zhang. The original plan was to divide the machinery into five sets to be shipped to Guangdong Province at different times so as to fit the schedule of completion of each mill. However, I was informed recently that General Zhang has been transferred to Hubei Province and that the sites of the mill have not yet been determined. I immediately wired General Zhang and alerted him to the fact that new machinery of such intricate design may rust in the open air and therefore the transportation date should be rescheduled as soon as possible. Unfortunately, two sets of machinery as well as the building materials have already been delivered.

8TH OF THE SIXTH MONTH

The British deputy commissioner of Darjeeling, India, came home on leave and paid me a visit. I conversed with him at length and found out that Sikkim, the small kingdom between Tibet and India whose southern corner is adjacent to Darjeeling, is what we call Zhemengxiong. The British have taken control of the government and installed a British official there.

10TH OF THE SIXTH MONTH

According to Western scholars of geology, minerals are embedded in the earth's crust and have been since the beginning of time. They cannot be planted like farm crops. It is my contention that with the increasing productivity in mining and the insatiable demands of the world's masses, these resources may be exhausted in the future.

The supply of lumber in China is the best example of such abuse. During the time of the Warring States [453–221 B.C.], every feudal lord had the local forest at his disposal and therefore used all his manpower to build palaces and villas for his own pleasure. Now on the mainland of northern China, there is not one single tree in an area of a thousand miles. And when the palace of the Ming dynasty [1368–1644] was being built, lumber had to be shipped in from the southwestern provinces of Guizhou, Hunan, Sichuan and Yunnan.

Gold is another good example. In the ancient text "The Tribute of Yü,"[19] the lands of Jing and Yang offered three measures of gold as tribute. Upon his marriage to the Marchioness Xuanping, Emperor Hui, the second emperor of the Former Han dynasty [206 B.C.–A.D. 8], offered her family 20,000 catties of gold, which is equivalent to 320,000 taels of gold in present measurements. Yet when Emperor Ping, the second-to-the-last Former Han emperor, chose his empress, he had to resort to the use of copper coins. Evidently, gold was already in short supply at that time.

11TH OF THE SIXTH MONTH

I learned from today's paper that Britain will cooperate with the United States in a joint venture in building an airship. If both these countries pool their resources and succeed in designing an airship, I will not be surprised to see the flying chariot of Qigong[20] rising above the clouds and sailing on the wind.

---

19. Yü was the third of the ancient sage-kings, according to early records such as the *Classic of History*. Yü was commissioned by the second sage-king, Shun, to tame the floods, and for his success and exemplary behavior, Shun passed over his own son, whom he deemed unworthy, and granted Yü the empire. Yü thus became the founder of the first of the "Three Dynasties," the Xia (see note 25). Hsieh Fucheng makes occasional references to the sage-kings of antiquity, Yao, Shun and Yü, who are heroic figures of legend and were possibly actual persons.

20. The land of Qigong is first mentioned in the *Classic of Mountains and Oceans*, an ancient geography now considered little more than legend and fable. The story that the people of Qigong had flying chariots seems to have come later and can be traced to the Jin period (fourth century A.D.) "encyclopedia," *Bowuzhi* (A Treatise on the Natural World). The renowned poet Su Shi (1037–1101) of the Song dynastic period (960–1279) mentioned the story in a poem.

12TH OF THE SIXTH MONTH

According to documents in the embassy record, in the Second month of the year Yi-you [1885], the International Office held a conference at the Hanlin Academy at the request of the Imperial Censor, Xie Zuyuan. He recommended that the Imperial Court sponsor trips for officials abroad. A summarized version of his statements follows:

> To acquire a basic knowledge of foreign nations, one must travel through their territories. Many foreign visitors, in addition to spreading their religious messages, have acquired useful information while traveling through our country. They have quietly memorized the route to each city, secretly drawn maps of every mountain and river, precisely calculated the correct figures for crop yields and carefully tested the coal and iron deposits from underground. They never wasted a minute of their traveling time.
>
> Our pressing needs at present are to watch every move of the enemy; to understand the laws of foreign lands; to comprehend the analysis of raw substances, drawings of blueprints and the manufacturing processes of Western industry; to learn their practices of warfare in both army and navy; and to improve in areas such as tariffs, tea production, sericulture, shepherding and mining.
>
> I appeal to you, Your Excellency, to instruct all our ambassadors to send their embassy personnel out to tour the country to which they are assigned and to record whatever information they can gather during their travels. They must enlist the help of our students who are studying in each country in order to learn the technology of Western industry. However, enforcement should be administered with encouragement, so that satisfactory results will follow.
>
> There is much talent among the ranking officials at the Hanlin Academy. Their interests vary from manufacturing processes to calculation, land surveying to military strategy. The successful candidates must be chosen on the merits of perseverance, patience, diligence and ambition. I implore Your Excellency to petition for a decree from the emperor so that the Hanlin Academy may submit the names of talented scholars to the International Office for further interviews. After being approved by decree, these chosen officers will then be sent overseas.

13TH OF THE SIXTH MONTH

According to documents in the embassy record, in the year of Ding-hai [1887], the International Office, after receiving confirmation by imperial decree of the overseas project, drafted a regulation of fourteen points:

> 1. In order to economize, funds for the project should be subtracted from the money allocated to the diplomatic corps. Fourteen thousand taels of silver will be appropriated annually for the project, and each tour should consist of ten to twelve officials in addition to the interpreters.
>
> 2. Officials of ministries other than the Hanlin Academy are permitted to participate but must take a written examination. The date of the examination

will be announced by the International Office as soon as the lists of recommendations from all the ministries have been received and processed. The accurate recording of minute details will be the focus of the examination.

3. Officials of the Imperial City who rank in the fourth degree and above, or those who hold crucial posts in the government, should petition the emperor for a temporary leave of absence.

4. Officials who rank below the fourth degree may receive 200 taels of silver each month during the trip and are permitted to hire a personal interpreter at a monthly salary of 50 taels of silver.

5. Round-trip sea fares plus train fares are included in the government grant. Each official is entitled to a second-class ticket and allowed to bring with him a personal servant; however, the servant's wages must be paid by the official himself, although a third-class ticket may be issued to the servant by the government. Short trips of either boat or carriage fares should be itemized in a list, which will be subsequently submitted to each ministry or consulate.

6. The duration of each tour is set for two years, which includes traveling time. Those who wish to remain after the time limit may stay a year and a half longer at their own expense, and those who wish to return at an earlier date are allowed to do so.

7. Each official is allowed to receive six month's salary in advance, up to 1,000 taels of silver. If additional money is needed, he may ask for a loan at his own ministry.

8. Sea fare and carriage fares should be recorded in separate categories in each official's account book, which can later be submitted to the government for reimbursement.

9. Any inquiries about detailed points of interest or necessary expenses in each country the official intends to visit must be made before the tour begins.

10. While traveling, officials must keep a record of the strategic points of each locality and its defense operations in general by detailing for future reference: internal distances, customs, politics, the location of cannons and the various manufacturing factories for steamships, torpedoes and munitions.

11. As to the various fields of knowledge (such as language, astronomy, mathematics, chemistry, physics, electricity, optics, engineering and natural science), each official should choose one subject according to his interest and record all the details in a notebook, which should be submitted to the International Office for future reference.

12. Each official should report the subject he has studied and explain the structures of the machinery in his report after his return. The best writer will be chosen on the basis of these reports and will receive an award from the International Office. Each writer should clearly indicate in his report the name of either the ambassador or the consul under whose guidance he has undertaken the tour.

13. Each official should start his tour as soon as possible. He should not waste time fraternizing with his peers or seeking pleasure, as both these activities will limit the time devoted to official business.

14. If the official should have a parent of advanced age or in ill health, he may be excused from the overseas tour by submitting the necessary facts as an explanation. If either parent of the official dies at home during his tour, he must complete his trip but may ask for an extended mourning period after his return.

17TH OF THE SIXTH MONTH

There are several theories regarding the ancestors of the Russian people. It is understood that they first made their presence known in China during the 11th year of the Jiaqing Emperor [1806] in a memorial by then Governor General of both Guangxi and Guangdong provinces, Wu Xiongguang. He reported that natives of the kingdom of Russia arrived at several seaport towns and engaged in trade there. After spending considerable time in research, I have discovered solid evidence supporting the theory of those scholars who claim that the Russians are truly the descendants of the Tufan people. Furthermore, this also happens to be the theory of the Western scholars, who are known to pursue their research work with painstaking effort.

Russia rose to power as a nation during the period of the Tang dynasty [618–907], during which time Tibet was in decline. Presumably, several tribes in Tibet left their country and fled into the wilderness of Europe. Then the tribes were separated and scattered from the territory southeast of the Baltic Sea to the territory northeast of the Black Sea and the Caspian Sea and west over the Ural Mountains. There were several tribes involved in this expedition and the forebears of the Russians were just one of those tribes.

Later, in the Ming dynasty [1368–1644], the forebears of the Russians managed to make a crossing over the Ural Mountains and capture the court of Rumania in the European part of Russia. In later decades, the Russians invaded Central Asia and annexed the territories of Omask and Bukhara.

18TH OF THE SIXTH MONTH

In the first year of the Jiaqing Emperor [1796], an allied force of Russia and France 70,000 strong prepared to launch an attack on British-controlled India but halted the operation when both countries encountered unexpected problems at home. Seven years later Napoleon attacked Prussia, and Russia sent out her army to join the invasion. Again, both nations made plans to invade India, and Russia even went so far as to send an envoy to Persia negotiating a passage for the crossing of the allied force into India. Nevertheless, due to the sudden unrest in Europe, that plan was also dropped. After France lost the war to Prussia, the Black Sea Treaty was subsequently annulled. Since then, Russia has extended her power into Central Asia and taken many Muslim tribes into her fold. If Russia succeeds in procuring the help of Persia, the west of India will not know peace for many years to come.

There are five routes for Russia to enter India; however, Persia holds the key to equilibrium. And whoever becomes Persia's friend will win in the end. From the information gathered through recent discussions, it is known that

Britain obviously contrived to seek an alliance with Persia by using that country as a fortress against India. The problem Britain faces presently in protecting India is similar to the problem China encounters in protecting Korea. If Britain and China can combine their forces, their suzerainty over both India and Korea may be strengthened. Therefore, Britain is presently striving to improve diplomatic relations with China.

20TH OF THE SIXTH MONTH

News from Hubei Province reveals that rich iron ores have been found in the county of Dazhi. Mining operations are underway, and five commissioners have been appointed. Their job is to advise the peasants either to sell their land to the government or to buy shares of stocks in the mining company. All the peasants have responded with enthusiasm and have invested in the mining company.

21ST OF THE SIXTH MONTH

A comparison of the total import tariff figures in the fifteenth year of the Guangxu Emperor [1889] with those of the fourteenth year shows an obvious decrease. However, a comparison of the export figures of the two years shows a considerable increase. China is definitely on the rise again.

22ND OF THE SIXTH MONTH

According to the documents in the embassy record, in the Sixth month of the twelfth year of the Guangxu Emperor [1886], the Governor General of Guangxi and Guangdong provinces, Zhang Xiangshuai, proposed in a memorandum a detailed survey of overseas Chinese on the South Sea Islands. By imperial decree, Wang Ronghe, a military officer and candidate for army captain, and Yu Wei, a scholar and candidate for prefect, were both sent to the Philippines, the Sulu Archipelago, Singapore, Malacca, Penang, Rangoon, Saigon, Sydney and other small islands to conduct the survey. The following is their report:

> Singapore is a manifestation of great wealth, with its multitude of stores and acres of rich farm land. Notwithstanding British control of the island, the Chinese own 80 percent of the businesses whereas the Westerners own 20 percent. The largest group of Chinese businessmen came from both Jun and Qian counties in Fujiang Province and the rest from both Zhou and Guan counties in Guangdong Province. The total number of Chinese on the island is 150,000.
>
> In recent years the British set up an office to take care of Chinese immigration. However, the devious black-market recruiting practices of Chinese laborers and the dishonesty in both trading and lodging remain clearly evident on the island.

25TH OF THE SIXTH MONTH

Officials in Sydney, Australia, made a suggestion to China that a Chinese consulate should be established there. The British governor in Melbourne also expressed interest in inviting Chinese officials to participate in the local annual Chinese race meet and the Chinese navy to patrol their coast. The Chinese immigrants in the two provinces, Adelaide and Queensland, were so overwhelmed by the presence of Chinese envoys that they organized an elaborate ceremony to welcome them. However, in southern Australia, the Chinese population is less than 3,000 people because the tax levied on rice, the staple food of the Chinese, is extremely high: £9 per ton of rice plus the additional, annual personal tax for each individual. In Sydney, there are 4,000 Chinese merchants and laborers, and within the province of Victoria there are 6,000 plantation workers and tradesmen. An extra £10 has to be paid by the Chinese who wish to travel from Sydney to Melbourne and £30 to go to Queensland.

26TH OF THE SIXTH MONTH

At every trading post in the South Sea Islands, Chinese form the skeleton structure of each business community. The Chinese there are either traders or indentured laborers working on plantations or in mines. The Chinese population reaches an overwhelming number of three million. However, the Chinese didn't arrive at the islands as free men but as slaves. All of them have gone through the slave market of the British-controlled seaports. And the Dutch plantation owners, unlike their British counterparts, tend to keep the Chinese slaves throughout their natural lives. There are three ways to keep the Chinese slaves in line: 1) beating, 2) luring the slaves to gamble in their privately owned clubs and 3) restricting the activities of the slaves. The yearly export of Chinese laborers exceeds 100,000, all of which are exported through several seaports along the South Sea coast. Nevertheless, Hong Kong remains the center of the trade. And to keep the profits on their own islands, the British have opened an office in Singapore to protect their Chinese laborers.

28TH OF THE SIXTH MONTH

An altar was erected at the embassy for the ceremonial ritual of our emperor's birthday. I led my staff in offering incense as homage, and we prostrated ourselves toward the direction of China. At night, small rainbow-colored lanterns were tied on the fence around the embassy. Following our instructions, the local gas company managed to twist some tubes into four

Chinese characters to represent "ten thousand years (for) the Son (of) Heaven." When they were lit, bright light streamed down the street for several miles. Crowds gathered around the embassy and applauded loudly.

1ST OF THE SEVENTH MONTH

News from Guangdong Province states that the garrison stationed there is busy drilling daily along the coastal forts, and steps have been taken to repair the foundation of the eroding cannon site so as to meet Western standards.

The Whompoa shipyard in Shanghai has completed the construction of the first battleship, and their plant in Fujian Province has finished building a steamship, which they have named *Dragon Fury*.

4TH OF THE SEVENTH MONTH

In Tibet there are 20,000 lamas in the three major temples, yet their army consists of only 3,500 men equipped with bows and arrows. Their treaty with Britain allows British subjects to travel through Tibet at will. In the thirteenth year of the Guangxu Emperor [1887], Margary of Britain made an attempt to enter Tibet with an army of 3,000 men. The International Office, in view of the Burma incident, contacted the British ambassador, and they both agreed to halt the entry of the British army and forbid missionaries to preach in Tibet. Unfortunately, the news didn't reach Tibet in time, and the Tibetans mounted a cannon at the foot of the mountain by the border after they heard that the British army was entering their territory.

Consequently, the viceroy of India claimed that the Tibetans were invading Sikkim and had to be driven off immediately. The British ambassador appealed to the International Office, and a special dispatch was issued to the minister at the Tibetan outpost. A subsequent order was thus given to the Tibetans, but it was ignored. In the following year [1888], Indian troops drove the Tibetan garrison from Sikkim. One month later, the entire Tibetan army of 3,000 men attacked a British army camp in Sikkim. The battle lasted ten hours. Ultimately, the Tibetans retreated with heavy casualties. Evidently the Tibetans, unaware that Sikkim is no longer independent but has become a British protectorate, thought they were helping Sikkim to fight off the British army. Consequently, another treaty was drawn between Tibet and India, and peace finally resumed between these two countries.

5TH OF THE SEVENTH MONTH

Yesterday a decree by telegram reached the embassy instructing me to deliver a greeting to the queen of England on behalf of His Majesty the

Emperor, because the British ambassador had at an earlier date offered a birthday greeting from the queen to our emperor.

Today at three o'clock I went to the Foreign Office as instructed and was received by Under Secretary Grey, who promised to convey this message to Lord Salisbury, who will personally deliver it to the queen. Last month the French foreign minister, who went to the Chinese embassy in France, also bore a birthday greeting from the French president to His Majesty the Emperor. This message was sent directly to the International Office in Beijing. Today another telegram bearing the same instruction as the earlier one arrived at the embassy. I instructed my staff in the Chinese embassy in France to have the message delivered to the Foreign Office there.

The treaty between Tibet and India was signed on the 26th of the Second month of this year in Madras. Four copies were translated into both Chinese and English. Two copies were directly delivered to the Imperial Court of China. After being stamped with the imperial seal, one copy was sent to the International Office and then handed to the British ambassador, who subsequently mailed it to England.

Yesterday the British minister of revenue paid me a visit with an interpreter and delivered the said treaty to me. Consequently, I made an appointment with Under Secretary Grey to exchange copies with each other.

6TH OF THE SEVENTH MONTH

I studied the correct procedure for negotiations and discovered a detailed history of foreign etiquette:

> During the reign of the Kangxi Emperor [1662–1722], foreign officials who came to the Chinese Imperial Court were allowed to stand beside the emperor and did not need to prostrate. During the reign of the Yongzheng Emperor [1723–1736], the pope sent an envoy to the Imperial Court. His Majesty the Emperor allowed the envoy to pay his respects according to the Western tradition and even shook hands with the envoy. In the fifth year of the Qianlong Emperor [1740], a British envoy, by previous arrangement with court officials, was granted the special privilege of paying his respects according to Western tradition. During the banquet held in honor of the envoy, the emperor personally offered a cup of wine to the British envoy. During the reign of the Jiaqing Emperor [1796–1820], the British again sent an envoy to China. However, no previous arrangements had been made regarding court procedures. When the envoy and his assistant arrived at the palace gate on horseback from the seaport of Tongzhou, the emperor was already presiding in the Great Hall, and they were told to follow Chinese tradition while being presented. The chief envoy pleaded illness so that he could be excused. When His Majesty the Emperor asked the assistant envoy to take the place of his superior, he also claimed to be sick. The emperor was visibly annoyed and canceled the banquet that was to

have been held in the envoy's honor. A letter censuring the envoys' misbehavior was thus composed for the king of England and was given to the envoys upon their departure. Afterward, His Majesty the Emperor summoned the Governor General of Guangdong and Guangxi provinces, Sun Yuting, to court and inquired about the reason behind the envoys' misdeed. The Governor General explained the difference in etiquette between the two countries, and the emperor was apparently relieved.

All these anecdotes were recorded in the journals of several scholar-officials of that period, when a visit from a foreign envoy was considered a rare event. As I understand, the performance of prostration before the Chinese emperor was widely discussed in several English newspapers. The conclusion reached was that no Englishman should be subjected to this form of humiliation.

7TH OF THE SEVENTH MONTH

According to documents in the embassy records, in the seventh year of the Guangxu Emperor [1881], the International Office, by the decree of His Majesty the Emperor, divided the star-shaped, jewel-studded badges into five categories so that the imperial court may present foreign dignitaries with these gifts according to their ranks.

The first badge of the first category, which would be a gift for a foreign dignitary such as the sovereign of a nation, is a solid gold, square badge, 3.3 inches by 2.2 inches, with a pearl set between twin gold dragons stitched on a piece of golden red sash with a ring on the top. The second badge, for either a crown prince, a prince, an aristocrat or an ambassador of the first rank, is the same size and shape but with a piece of coral set between twin silver dragons with the ring on a piece of bright red sash.

In the second category the solid, round badges range from 2.2 inches in diameter down to 1.6 inches in diameter, with a curved piece of coral set between twin silver dragons on a piece of purple sash. Among these gifts, the first group are for ambassadors of the second rank; the second group for consul generals, first-rank advisors or military advisors; and the third group for navy commanders, generals or training officers of military schools.

In the third category, the badge is a square, turquoise feather base set with blue jade between twin gold dragons on a piece of blue sash. These are for deputy consuls, lieutenant commanders, lieutenant generals or interpreters.

In the fourth category, the badge is also of turquoise feather base set with a blue stone between twin green and gilded silver dragons on a piece of brown sash. These are gifts for military officers only.

In the fifth category, the badge is of silver with a piece of imitation gem set between twin turquoise feather dragons on a piece of moonlight-white sash. These are gifts for merchants and engineers.

8TH OF THE SEVENTH MONTH

Sikkim, with a population of 7,000 people, was once a small kingdom under the protection of Tibet but was later taken over by the Gurkhas as their principality. After an unfortunate incident involving two British travelers, the south of Sikkim—including Darjeeling—was put under the control of a deputy governor appointed by the viceroy of India. When wild tea bushes were discovered on the hilly terrace of Darjeeling, the small trading center exploded into a booming town. Envious of the unprecedented wealth, the Sikkim king asked for the return of Darjeeling. Consequently, the British offered an annual rental fee of several hundred taels of gold. Since then the annual rental fee has risen to several thousand taels of gold.

9TH OF THE SEVENTH MONTH

A foreign officer in the Chinese navy under the Office of Northern Ports, Williams, was initially a British navy officer. He has served in the Chinese navy for a considerable number of years. Recently, he was deeply concerned that his prolonged absence from the British navy would jeopardize his future naval career in his own country. My predecessor, Ambassador Liu, sent a message on William's behalf through the British Foreign Office to the British navy ministry pleading for the security of William's position in the British navy and informing them that the Chinese navy dearly needs to keep Williams on its force. A similar instance involved two other Navy Academy instructors who came to China in the tenth year of the Guangxu Emperor [1884]. When they reached their time limit for a leave of absence last year, a special arrangement was made through the British Foreign Office. The names of these two officers were subsequently placed on a list of British navy officers who had been stationed in China for only seven days so that their names would not be sent down to the reserve list. Also, another British navy officer, Rogers, instructor of the torpedo division of the Chinese Navy Academy, holds a three-year contract with a monthly salary of 350 taels of silver. The technicians there also have three-year contracts, but their monthly salary is only 150 taels of silver.

12TH OF THE SEVENTH MONTH

This afternoon I went to the British Foreign Office and exchanged the treaties regarding Sikkim and Tibet.

The International Office in Beijing is presently preparing a memorial for the future policy regarding the protection of Korea.

22ND OF THE SEVENTH MONTH

Every nation of the Western world maintains a parliament as part of its political institution. However, the American variety too strongly emphasizes popular rights, whereas the French system encourages unruly commotion. England and Germany appear to have set up the best example of a parliament system.

I'm not too familiar with the German parliamentary procedure, but I made a careful study of the English system, as ambassadors are allowed to sit in the gallery of the English Parliament. Last month I personally attended one Parliament session.

28TH OF THE SEVENTH MONTH

In the ninth year of the Guangxu Emperor [1883], Hennessy, the former governor of Hong Kong who is now the newly appointed governor of Malaysia, wrote to Marquis Zeng requesting the placement of a handmade, gilt gold vase upon the shrine of Confucius, the Exalted Saint and ancient teacher. The Marquis mailed the gift to Imperial Commissioner Li, who subsequently dispatched a special envoy to deliver the vase to the temple of Confucius.

1ST OF THE EIGHTH MONTH

In the year of Bing-xu [1886], thirty students were sent overseas for the third time. The allowance for each student came to 300,000 taels of silver.

4TH OF THE EIGHTH MONTH

In the eleventh year of the Guangxu Emperor [1885], the overseas guidance counsellor presented a report to Marquis Zeng on the ability and achievements of those students whom he had accompanied on both overseas trips.

6TH OF THE EIGHTH MONTH

In the twelfth year of the Guangxu Emperor [1886], Chen Endao, lieutenant commander of the battleship *Ding Yuan* in the North Sea, volunteered to learn basic mapmaking by joining a British naval survey team aboard a British ship sailing from the Mediterranean Sea through the Indian Ocean into the South China Sea. During the voyage he exhibited rare courage by tying himself to the flag pole during a rainstorm under orders from the captain so as to conduct an accurate survey.

8TH OF THE EIGHTH MONTH

Preparing Chungking as a foreign trading post and halting the entry of the foreign steamer into the upstream of the waterway were the reasons for a memorial from the International Office. The main points were as follows:

> In the Sixth month of the thirteenth year of the Guangxu Emperor [1887], Ambassador Wilson of Britain informed this office that a British merchant has purchased a small steamer, which he intends to sail from Nanchang to Chungking. The merchant made the attempt to purchase a permit according to a provision of the Chefoo Convention,[21] which would provide him with protection of the local authorities along the waterway. Since the treaty clearly states such a provision, there is no legal means of avoiding issuing the permit. Sanction was thus given by this office, which authorized the Governor of Sichuan Province to set up a conference with his staff and the British consul at Nanchang so that new regulations may be drawn up to launch the sail of the said steamer. The governor has since telegraphed this office several times and expressed his concern over the disturbing mood aroused among his populace after this authorization was made public. He warned repeatedly that the steamer must not be allowed to sail into the waterways of Sichuan Province. Later, Hart, the Commissioner of the Customs Office, acted as mediator and amended the provisions of the treaty with regard to the sailing of foreign vessels into the interior. The British merchant was thus advised to use the regular method of renting a Chinese vessel to ship his cargo from Nanchang to Chungking and to abandon the plan of using his own steamer.
>
> Understandably, foreign trade has gone on for a relatively long time. If we promise to open up Chungking as a foreign trading port, it would be more convenient for the foreign merchants there to conduct their business. However, the foreign merchants are planning to establish trading companies in the city, and consequently it shall not provide us with any future interest. Therefore, it would simplify the matter further if we could keep foreign vessels out of the waterway. Nevertheless, this matter must be settled once and for all. We have instructed Hart to contact the foreign merchant by telegram expressing our willingness to purchase his steamer at the price of 120,000 taels of gold. This expenditure

---

21. The Chefoo Convention (or Yandai Treaty) was concluded in September 1876 to settle the Margary Affair and other outstanding issues between Britain and China. A British captain Margary had been ambushed and killed while exploring the Burma-Yunnan border. In addition to arranging 1) the dispatch of an apology mission to Britain and the payment of 200,000 taels to Margary's survivors and 2) the preparation of a code of etiquette to be used by the Chinese government and foreign diplomats, the Chefoo Convention also opened new ports to foreign trade and attempted to equalize British and Chinese shipping rights and tax liabilities along the Yangzi River. It was not ratified by the British government until 1885, but it did have the important consequence of sending Guo Songdao as China's first ambassador to Britain.

should be deducted from the embassy funds as a loan in order to settle this pressing matter.

The British commissioner has since forwarded the amended specification of the Chungking issue in the treaty to this office. After a conference with the Imperial Commissioner of the Northern Ports, some appropriate changes have been made. And after several more conferences with the British commissioner, it has been determined that these specifications should be classified into several points. One point is to clarify whether foreign merchants will lease Chinese vessels or use foreign-owned vessels built according to the structure of Chinese ships so that the problem of being harassed by hostile Chinese vessels in the waterway will be resolved. Another important point is that the foreign steamship owners must hire Chinese hands exclusively, so that the livelihood of Chinese people along the river will not be harmed. Yet another point is that if Chinese steamers begin their sail along the Chungking thoroughfare, British steamers should also be allowed to enter the waterway. Therefore, as long as our own steamers stay away from the waterway, the British cannot find an excuse to launch their steamers there. The rest of the specifications are set down in the same vein and appear in good order as following:

1. Chungking is sanctioned to be a trading post. The British can either lease Chinese vessels or launch their own for their commercial shipping purposes.

2. If the vessel carries an amount of cargo from Nanchang to Chungking similar to that carried from Shanghai to Nanchang, the tax and shipping fee will be imposed according to the treaty and the regulations of the Yangzi River.

3. For the safety and protection of each vessel and the passengers on board, the vessel must abide by the law and carry a permit, fly the proper flag and provide separate cargo lists indicating which cargo will be carried beyond the point of Nanchang. Additionally, the machinery parts of each cargo must be kept together if the cargo must be separated during transportation.

4. Those British merchants who lease Chinese vessels must make their payments in either Nanchang or Chungking. Those who use privately owned vessels sailing under the British flag should also abide by the treaty rules and pay their bills with the shipping currency. All these vessels, whether they are leased or privately owned by the British merchants, must obtain permits and banners from the custom office. Those vessels that possess neither shipping permits nor custom office banners shall not receive any profit from their trade. Chinese vessels are strictly forbidden to fly the British flag.

5. When Chinese steamers are allowed into the river, the British steamers may also follow suit.

6. These amendments should be followed as strictly as those provisions specified in the Chefoo Convention.

10TH OF THE EIGHTH MONTH

According to documents in the embassy records, in the eighth year of the Guangxu Emperor [1882], Marquis Zeng sent dispatches to both the International Office and the Office of Northern Ports regarding a letter from former Governor Hennessy of Hong Kong. In the letter Hennessy stated that he had written to a cardinal, who is also the foreign minister of the Vatican, about a conference he once had with Imperial Commissioner of the Northern Ports Li regarding the persistent conflicts between the Chinese populace and the Chinese Catholic converts. Hennessy suggested that if the Vatican wishes to regain the excellent relationship of earlier years with the Chinese government, the pope should send an emissary from the Vatican to Beijing in order to manage Catholic affairs there.

Marquis Zeng deemed it a farsighted proposal. He further stated that missionary cases have risen to a record high in recent years because the missionaries are allowed to erect their own churches and to preach their religious messages in every province. Under the protection of France, the Catholic church began to abuse its rights in every manner possible. In fact, the French are known to treat the Catholic population in their own country with harshness, yet they go out of their way on foreign soil to protect the interests of their Catholic priests. It's obviously a scheme that they are employing to blackmail the Chinese government. It's understood that the pope controls the Catholic population in each nation by faith, whereas the government of each nation rules them by law. Therefore, by weighing these two powers, the authority of the pope is significantly higher than that of the French government in comparison. *If we deal with the pope directly,* without the intervention of aggressive foreign nations, we can resolve these unfortunate cases through reason and compassion. It would benefit us in future negotiations.

The Marquis further suggested that some 100 years ago the British established the East India Company and brought opium to China. Later, compulsory trading imposed by the British resulted in a war, which subsequently led to a peace treaty. In the treaty, the profit of commerce and the privileges of the missionaries were not clearly defined. According to the treaty, the Chinese Catholic converts are put under the protection of the French, which now proves to be hindering the progress of the Catholic missionary work. During the reign of Napoleon III [1852–1870], this provision was fully enforced, but things were not running as smoothly as they expected. In recent years, the number of converts has fallen behind. Before the French intervention, the number of Chinese converts reached was in the millions. Now, there are merely 400,000. Our ministers tend to think that Western religion fared poorly in China, and even the British ambassador claimed that the

Christian missionaries have wasted a good deal of money in China with only a handful of converts in return. In short, every foreign intervention only hinders progress of the missionary work. So far, the Catholic church has lost 5,000 Chinese converts. As for the additional 4,000 Chinese Christian converts, they are but Christians in name only and have no true faith in the religion.

11TH OF THE EIGHTH MONTH

A dispatch from the International Office, which was sent on the 14th of the Fifth month to Imperial Commissioner of the Northern Ports Li, informed me of a memorial that Imperial Commissioner Li had submitted recently on behalf of Navy Commander Ding Ruchang:

> While Navy Commander Ding was reconnoitering through the South China Sea, he noticed that the overseas Chinese are treated reasonably well on islands such as Singapore; however, they are discriminated against and suppressed on islands where a Chinese consulate is not available. Requests for protection of these Chinese communities have been overwhelming and should not be ignored. After a careful survey, it has been learned that the largest number of islands under the control of Britain, which have the largest overseas Chinese communities, are located within the vicinity of Singapore. Since the Singapore consul receives no portfolio to represent the Chinese on other islands, he finds himself helpless to assist them with their problems. Therefore, this office is preparing a memorial proposing to rename the Singapore consul as a consul general and to place several vice consuls on the surrounding islands. To fill a vice consul's position, an overseas Chinese who is also the resident of that particular island should be chosen.
>
> This office realize that we must discuss terms and apply for permits from the British foreign ministry if we wish to install additional consuls on her colonies. Therefore, we implore Your Excellency to forward an excerpt of this dispatch to the British Foreign Office and to discuss the possibilities within the context of present conditions. It should prove beneficial to all overseas Chinese if this negotiation is successful.

12TH OF THE EIGHTH MONTH

I studied the treaties that China has signed with foreign powers and discovered that while provisions were written for the establishment of foreign consulates on our own soil, no mention was made about Chinese consulates on their land. This is obviously the result of our ignorance of foreign culture, and we have therefore been deceived all these years. My predecessor, Minister Guo, was instrumental in the establishment of the Singapore consulate as he pushed many issues with the British Foreign Office in grilling debates by correspondence. Marquis Zeng made an attempt to establish a consulate in Hong Kong, but after several exchanges of letters, the British

Foreign Office gave the excuse that the power to make such an agreement lies not with their office but with the Office of Colonization. Further negotiations produced yet another excuse, this one claiming that the military and civilian matters cannot both be settled within one ministry.

I conferred with my aides and reached the following conclusion:

> While it is acknowledged that the overseas Chinese community in Singapore needs the protection of a consul, Hong Kong also appears in dire need. Hong Kong serves as the gateway to all foreign trade, and therefore all cargo must pass through there before it can be shipped into each province of China.
>
> The three major problems we now have with Hong Kong are 1) extradition, 2) contraband, and 3) international water boundaries. Presently, a Chinese man who commits a crime can easily slip into Hong Kong. Since there is no consul on the island, Chinese police officers from Guangdong Province cannot legally arrest the fugitive even if they are sent to Hong Kong by Chinese authorities. All criminal prosecution in Guangdong Province is therefore hampered on account of this unique status of Hong Kong. It's for this reason alone that a consulate must be installed there.
>
> There are two more places that in my opinion also require the installation of consulates: Australia and Burma. Since negotiations over each place appear burdensome and impractical, Margary suggested that one official document to the British Foreign Office should be prepared to put forward the proposal to install consulates in all British colonies. It should state clearly that according to international law, China has the right to install consulates in any British colony. Furthermore, other nations, such as Japan and Siam, have already installed consulates in Hong Kong; therefore, Britain's consistent refusal of China's proposal is discriminating. Margary further suggested that if we concentrate on stating our desire to maintain normal international relations with Britain, the British Foreign Office may run out of excuses for rejecting our proposal. And once they accept our proposal, they cannot stop us from dispatching consuls to wherever we please. I fully approved of his idea and subsequently asked him to prepare an official document in English, which will then be dispatched to the office of the British prime minister, Lord Salisbury, who is also the foreign minister.

13TH OF THE EIGHTH MONTH

Margary presented me with the finished text, which has been translated into Chinese so that I may verify the contents. The statement is precisely to my liking; however, the differences between the Chinese and English languages is obvious in the structure of the writing. While it may appear clearly stated in English, some sections sound redundant in Chinese.

16TH OF THE EIGHTH MONTH

I sent Counsellor Ma Qingchen to the British Foreign Office to inquire about the installation of consulates on the South Sea islands. Before he left, I instructed him to convey my personal message to the British Foreign Office: I will neither be discouraged by a barrage of refusals via correspondence nor swayed by persuasion into accepting other alternatives. If Britain rejects this proposal, I shall consistently protest on the basis of reason and relentlessly pursue our objective until it is met.

Ma met with Sandison, the assistant to the prime minister, and asked about our proposal, which, as he understood, the British Foreign Office had received at an earlier date. Their conversation went as follows:

Sandison: According to the peace treaty between Britain and China, no provision was made for the installation of Chinese consulates on British colonies. Negotiation on this issue at earlier dates has therefore been consistently rejected.

Ma: In the peace treaty, a provision is made for the installation of British consulates on Chinese soil, which we can certainly apply to the territories of Britain as well. It will surely complicate the matter further if additional provisions are added. Furthermore, Britain and China are presently enjoying a cordial relationship, and if this case is not resolved, the friendship between our two countries may be jeopardized. Such disagreement certainly is not healthy as far as the relationship between our two countries is concerned.

Sandison: It is possible for China to establish consulates in any place she prefers. However, Hong Kong, with its large Chinese population, is too close to Guangdong Province. Installing a consulate there may pose a threat to British authority. Also, in Australia, the relationship between the British settlers and the Chinese immigrants is strained. New regulations have been implemented recently to remedy the situation. As a result, resentment may be easily aroused. These two places definitely can't be included in the terms of the treaty.

Ma: Australia can be put off for future negotiations; this is totally acceptable. As I understand, the document that our embassy dispatched to your office places an emphasis only on Hong Kong because the increase in fugitive cases and smuggling operations is affecting the provincial administration of Guangdong Province. Furthermore, both Japan and Siam have installed consulates in Hong Kong, and to exclude China from this privilege is truly unjust. Therefore, my mission here today is to remind you that a healthy international relationship between our two countries depends upon the outcome of this issue.

Sandison: China is a newly developed country and her consuls tend to overstep their boundaries. Such a step will not be beneficial to either of our countries.

Ma: The Chinese consul in Singapore, Zuo Binglong, had his share of problems with the local British authorities at first. But now he has developed a familiarity with Western traditions and has cultivated a comprehensive understanding of the differences between the British and Chinese communities on the island. A considerable amount of time has passed since any complaint accusing him of mismanagement has been lodged at our embassy. I think my superior will be more than happy to recommend him for the Hong Kong post so that everything will run smoothly, according to your rules.

Sandison (after a long pause): Your recent proposal has been brought to the attention of Lord Salisbury. Our plan is to have a conference with the Ministry of Colonial Affairs before we make a decision.

Ma (confiding to Sandison in private): As I understand, China is determined to establish a consulate in Hong Kong. If Britain refuses this proposal, our ambassador will make his presence known in this office three or four times each day, or perhaps even six or seven times, until this problem is resolved. He will not give up easily. By then I'm afraid that Britain may not be able to find any excuse to reject our proposal. Hong Kong currently has consulates from almost every country. What harm can come to Hong Kong by adding one more consulate? Accepting this proposal can only improve the relationship between our two countries; there's no valid reason for your office to reject it. I would like to tell you a Chinese proverb: "Accepting a cup of wine given as a reward is better than taking the cup of wine as a penalty." Don't you think it's better for you to drink this cup of wine as a reward?

Sandison agreed and promised he will do his best to advise Lord Salisbury to accept this proposal after conferring with the minister of colonial affairs. After being told that the answer would come through in two weeks' time, Ma took his leave.

18TH OF THE EIGHTH MONTH

The International Office sent a letter to the embassy regarding the government-sponsored tours abroad. A summarized version follows:

Nearly all the participants have submitted their journals as well as the translations of the essential industrial manuals to this office. Fu Yunlong of the Ministry of War recorded his travels through Japan and other countries in eighty-six volumes with detailed illustrations. This outstanding work demonstrates his attention to detail as well as the extent of his knowledge. It also shows his keen observation skills and diligent research. Also, Liao Yousun of the Ministry of the Interior and Liu Qitong of the Ministry of War both offered a wealth of information pertinent to current affairs.

With the exception of those who haven't yet reported back to the International Office in Beijing and those whose whereabouts are presently unknown, all returnees should be rewarded accordingly for their reports. Among the group both Fu Yunlong and Liu Qitong requested a transfer to the Office of the Northern Ports.

28TH OF THE EIGHTH MONTH

Siam began to pay tribute to China after the reign of the Qianlong Emperor [1736–96]. During the reign of the Xianfeng Emperor [1851–61], the envoy leading the tributary mission was robbed, and thus the practice was abandoned. Although it was not the true intention of the Siamese king to avoid such tribute, the fear of a penalty prevented the resumption of these missions after such a long period. In the Third month of the fifth year of the Guangxu Emperor [1879], Siam claimed to have received an official notice from China indicating that the tributary missions must be resumed. Since the notice was delivered to Siam by the *British* envoy, however, it may not be genuine. A rumor has gone around this year that British gunboats were seen cruising along the Siamese coast under the flag of China demanding that Siam make up back payments for their Chinese tributary missions.

The king of Siam told his ministers that the real reason behind his reluctance to resume such practices is that he objects to the format of the tributary document, which calls for prostration. Since Siam has now adopted Western customs, he feels uncomfortable with such terminology. Generally speaking, the king is prepared to comply with the request for back payment but has hesitated for fear of jeopardizing his close relations with Britain.

5TH OF THE NINTH MONTH

I received a telegram from the International Office back in China informing me that the title of minister of the Imperial Court has been awarded to me by Imperial decree as of the 2nd of the Ninth month.

6TH OF THE NINTH MONTH

There are three mountains in Fujian Province: Black Stone Mountain, Nine Immortals Mountain and Shield Mountain. Natives there firmly believe that the interlocking mountain ranges are the vein of a dragon that can cast a spell on the local residents if any houses are built atop these three mountains.

In the first year of the Guangxu Emperor [1875], a missionary built a church there. Instantly a torch was placed to it, and it burned to the ground. This case nearly touched off an international incident. Now, the gentry of Fujian Province have joined together and presented a petition to the government. They have suggested that since the area of the three mountains is exempt from taxes, the local magistrate must assume the responsibility of preventing any further land sales or leases to missionaries. The ambassadors of every foreign nation should thereby be notified so as to convey this message to their respective foreign ministers.

11TH OF THE NINTH MONTH

In Peru, a consul was temporarily stationed at the office of the Chinese trade commissioner. After the negotiations regarding indentured laborers are finalized, he may be officially placed at the gulf of the sea to halt the slave trade.

7TH OF THE TENTH MONTH

The Singapore consul asserted that the Penang Isles, Malacca and all the other small islands are under British rule. The number of Chinese people on all these islands totals 600,000, and therefore, more Chinese officials should be posted there to protect them. This matter should be negotiated with the British Foreign Office, and a request must be made to appoint the Singapore consul as consul general. He will then have the power to post consuls on all the surrounding islands.

8TH OF THE TENTH MONTH

In Port Arthur, the construction of a large shipyard is in progress. A French developer received a contract in the fall of 1886 worth more than a million ounces of gold. It took four years to finish the project.

Opium has devastated the health of the Chinese population. In recent years, a majority of Indian people have also become addicted. Even some Americans and Japanese are now smoking opium, and so are the French, although those French who have developed such a dependency usually reside in Indochina or Tokyo. At one time, they tended to be discreet about their habit, but now they have come out into the open, and their daily consumption almost exceeds that of the Chinese, reaching as high as one to two ounces a day. There are many soldiers in the French garrison who have also become addicts, and they claim that Indochina's foul weather is the reason for their dependency.

10TH OF THE TENTH MONTH

I conducted a ceremony with my staff in the embassy garden in honor of the birthday of the Empress Dowager Cixi. We prostrated toward heaven.

14TH OF THE TENTH MONTH

Japan and the Western countries are planning to make changes in the old treaty with China as follows:

1. Japanese demands may not be necessarily met.
2. The positions of foreign administrators will be eliminated.
3. Westerners will be allowed to live in the interior of China.
4. A joint conference of all nations will determine further increases in import taxes at the customs office.
5. Westerners are not allowed to purchase property.
6. More seaports will be opened up for trade.
7. The duration of the treaty should be limited to twelve years.

19TH OF THE TENTH MONTH

A letter from the minister of the British Foreign Office, Lord Salisbury, acknowledged my letter requesting the installation of Chinese consuls in various British colonies. His letter stated that certificates will be issued to all Chinese consuls; however, some areas for the present time have to be given more consideration before such certificates can be granted.

20TH OF THE TENTH MONTH

I consulted Ma on the letter from the British Foreign Office and wondered whether "unidentified areas" refers to both Hong Kong and Sydney. Ma replied that it likely applies to Sydney, since they already have given consent to the placement of a consul in Hong Kong. Consequently, in my reply, I commended the British Foreign Office for their fairness in dealing with this matter and informed the minister that China will first place two consuls in both Singapore and Hong Kong. The candidates for these positions have been chosen and are presently waiting for orders from our International Office. The present consul at Singapore, Zuo Binglong, will be transferred to Hong Kong, and the second in command at the consulate here, Counsellor Huang Zunxian, will replace Zuo at the Singapore post. Huang will also take on the additional duty of dealing with the affairs of Kuala Lumpur, Penang and all the other neighboring islands by assuming the responsibilities of consul general. If it is necessary to install additional deputy consuls on the islands, the names of qualified personnel will be submitted in the near future. A few days later, the British Foreign Office acknowledged my letter and raised no questions. It appears that all the problems have been resolved.

3RD OF THE ELEVENTH MONTH

A telegram from the International Office informed me of a recent Imperial decree that has been issued to all members of the Grand Council:

> Since the signing of the treaties with the European nations, a steady stream of international communications has understandably nurtured our friendship with all these nations. It's a pleasure to know that our ambassadors are trustworthy and assertive in the improvement of international relationships. In the first two months of the past year there were several occasions for celebration. By decree of the Empress Dowager, the International Office and other ministries have invited foreign dignitaries to dinner parties in order to cultivate friendship.
>
> I have ruled this country for over two years now, and therefore each ambassador in Beijing should be granted an audience.[22] By the precedent set in the twelfth year of the late Tongzhi Emperor [1873], a date of audience for each ambassador should be scheduled annually as a token of courtesy. In the first

month of next year the International Office will designate the dates of audience for each ambassador after submitting a memorial at an earlier date for my approval. After the audience, a dinner party honoring the ambassador will be held in the International Office. From now on, the first month of each year will be set aside for such occasions. This will also apply to all ambassadors in the future. If there is a national celebration, our foreign guests should also be included. The International Office should send a memorial at an earlier date in order to prepare dinner parties for embassy personnel after such celebrations. This decree is to express my pleasure in our continuing efforts to improve relationships with the European powers. As far as the procedures of the ceremony are concerned, the International Office should submit a plan at an earlier date.

I would like you to inform the foreign ministries of Britain, France, Italy and Belgium of my message and also to telegraph Ambassador Hong in order to convey this message to the foreign ministries of Russia, Germany and Austria, as well as Ambassador Cui in order to inform the foreign ministries of America, Japan and Peru.[23]

6TH OF THE ELEVENTH MONTH

Since Germany and Italy began to give protection to their own missionaries, France's deliberate aggression has considerably lessened. This change of attitude may wipe out the past unfair practices of cover-up and abuse, thus maintaining peace in the future.

In the Seventh month of Ding-hai [1887], the International Office dispatched the following orders to the governor of each province:

> On the 20th of the Sixth month in the fourteenth year of the Guangxu Emperor [1888], the German ambassador confirmed an agreement that had been made a day earlier at the International Office. It stated that if a German Catholic priest carries a passport issued by the German embassy, he is entitled to the same privileges as those of the French Catholic priests, who carry passports issued by the French embassy. The International Office has since accepted the proposal and has made an official record of priests with French passports. Furthermore, the Italian ambassador notified us that the Italian passport with the seal of approval stamped by the Chinese government is valid; those issued to tourists by other countries should also be looked upon as valid. This office has accepted their proposal and expects these orders to be carried out accordingly.

---

22. The Guangxu Emperor came of age in 1889 and began ruling on his own. However, his maternal aunt, the Empress Dowager Cixi, continued to assert her influence in the court and forced the Guangxu Emperor into retirement in 1898 when he attempted to carry out a program of Westernizing reforms.

23. Hong Jun (1840–93) served as ambassador to Russia, Germany, Austria and Holland from 1887 to 1890. Upon his return to China, he served as vice premier of the Board of War until his death. Cui Guoyin served as ambassador to the United States, as well as to Peru and Japan, between 1889 and 1893. Unfortunately, little is known about him other than the diary of his ambassadorial service.

11TH OF THE ELEVENTH MONTH

A former Belgian ambassador to Mexico paid me a visit at the embassy. His family had been in Mexico for three generations and had acquired a large amount of land. I subsequently inquired about the political system and the economy of that country and discovered that the British have invested some £4 million to boost the economy of Mexico.

24TH OF THE ELEVENTH MONTH

The International Office sent the following message:

> On the 18th of the Seventh month of this year, Ambassador Wilson of Britain personally came to this office and offered congratulations to our emperor for His Majesty's forthcoming wedding. He presented a gift of a grandfather clock on behalf of the queen of England.
>
> A memorial was drawn up and submitted to His Majesty the Emperor, and a dispatch was simultaneously sent to Ambassador Wilson with a personal note of thanks on behalf of His Majesty the Emperor. The note will be mailed to our embassy in England so that our ambassador can personally deliver the letter to the British Foreign Office. This Imperial letter will soon be dispatched through the Department of Military Strategy. Please make a note of both the arrival and delivery dates of that letter.

26TH OF THE ELEVENTH MONTH

The general manager of the Great Eastern Company, Bundy, his assistant Hess and the general manager of the Great Northern Company's London branch held a conference with me at the embassy concerning a comprehensive plan to develop China's telegram system. Bundy, a man in his seventies, is well respected in his field and is credited for the invention of coated lines that can be run under water.

27TH OF THE ELEVENTH MONTH

A telegram from Imperial Commissioner of the Northern Ports Li announced the death of the Prince Regent's wife.[24] Although the emperor is in mourning, his subjects have not been instructed to do likewise. Later, another telegram from the International Office arrived announcing the passing of the Prince Regent. I was instructed to go to the Foreign Office to acknowledge the condolences that the queen of England had sent to His Majesty the Emperor through the British embassy in Beijing.

---

24. The wife of the Prince Regent (Yihuan, the first Prince Chun) was the natural mother of the Guangxu Emperor and a younger sister of the Empress Dowager.

Afterward, I had a meeting with the staff, who advised me to send death notices to all four foreign offices in Europe and to fly the flag at half-mast according to European custom.

2ND OF THE TWELFTH MONTH

This afternoon I took several members of my staff to Dover and sailed across the Channel to France. London has been enveloped in dense fog for the past two months, and the city is in almost total darkness, even in the daytime. Tens of thousands of people suffer from coughing spells. I am not accustomed to such a climate and was anxious to leave. In London this morning, the sky was covered with a thick cloud of fog, but as soon as we journeyed some ten miles away from the city, it cleared up, with not a cloud remaining in the sky. After several days of such foul weather I felt exhilarated. We reached France with the sun shining brightly high above our heads; however, the weather there is a trifle colder than in London.

8TH OF THE TWELFTH MONTH

A telegram from the International Office informed me that the funeral date of the Prince Regent and his lady will be the 16th of this month and instructed me to observe that day as a day of mourning at the London embassy. I was further instructed to alert the ambassadors in Germany and Russia.

10TH OF THE TWELFTH MONTH

The Western governments provide their people with care that can be compared only to the wonderful ancient political system before the era of Three Dynasties.[25] The reason for their success in maintaining a democratic process lies with the Christian faith they follow. And in my opinion, there are strong similarities between the Christian faith and the teachings of our ancient sages. However, there are several deficiencies in their system: the strength of their party leaders, who can force the king to abdicate; the individual rights of children, who have the right to refuse to live with their own parents, and the rights of women, who can leave their husbands for a lover. All these are clearly a violation of the teachings of our ancient sages.

---

25. The "Three Dynasties" was somewhat of a "Golden Age" in Chinese legend and history and an age presumably ruled by the perfect virtue of the ancient sage-kings. Although the existence of the first dynasty, the Xia, remains to be independently verified, the second dynasty, the Shang (c. 1600–1100 B.C.), and the third, the Zhou (c. 1100–249 B.C.), are confirmed in both archaeological and historical records.

12TH OF THE TWELFTH MONTH

The letter of His Majesty the Emperor reached the queen of England via the International Office early this month. The matter had already been taken care of according to the instructions.

15TH OF THE TWELFTH MONTH

According to the *Times*, the consul of the Netherlands listed the total number of Chinese indentured servants in Singapore and the other surrounding islands three years ago as 164,000. Last year the number was reduced to 150,000. The reason behind this sudden decrease may be the recent development of diplomatic relations between China and the Netherlands. This year the Dutch consul in China informed Chinese officials that the Netherlands is providing Chinese indentured servants a direct route from Swato[26] to Singapore. It clearly indicted that the Netherlands needs Chinese laborers to survive. Since it is compulsory for Chinese laborers to became Dutch citizens before they are allowed to work on the islands, the Dutch colony absorbs a large number of Chinese who, over the years, lost interest in returning home. It has become increasingly clear to me that a Chinese consulate must immediately be established there. If the Netherlands refuses our proposal, we should retaliate by terminating all their labor contracts, and they will invariably comply with our demands. If we continue the present round of negotiations via correspondence, we will never be able to establish our consulate there.

30TH OF THE TWELFTH MONTH

In Europe weapons are so varied and efficient that the powerful nations of Britain, France, Germany, Italy, Spain, Russia and Austria are vigorously competing with each other to improve or invent more powerful weapons, which conceivably will exhaust all their resources.

To my knowledge, such an arms race began thirty years ago, but these nations have been engaging in warfare for decades. After the arms buildup, however, confrontations between the nations have decreased considerably and have seldom developed into war. The reason is obviously fear. They are frightened that once a war starts, there will be enormous sacrifices on all sides. In the end no one will be able to claim total victory. This is a frightening interpretation, and I shudder at such a thought.

---

26. A seaport in Guangdong Province. (Trans.)

Part II

Seventeenth Year of the Guangxu Emperor (1891)

1ST OF THE FIRST MONTH

I led our embassy staff in the New Year celebration ceremony by prostrating toward the southeast of the embassy courtyard as a token of greeting to the Imperial Court of China.

2ND OF THE FIRST MONTH

The Chinese construct words according to the visual shape of each character, whereas Westerners form words according to the audible sound of each letter. The Chinese pronounce words through the throat, the tongue, the lips and the teeth, whereas Westerners speak either between the throat and the tongue or between the lips and the teeth. Frequently, the Chinese can't find the proper letters to match the phonetics of the Western language. Therefore, it's hard to match word for word when translating between these two languages. Even the best translator can convey only the general meaning of the original text.

6TH OF THE FIRST MONTH

There is an observatory located in the north of France. Last night I went there with my staff. It was a fifty-minute ride by carriage. The director of the observatory, Marchand, who had spent a number of years in China, was a most gracious host to our group. We were shown star maps from various countries, including a large scroll of a Chinese star map, which was probably charted during the Yuan dynasty [1271–1368], and a huge globe manufactured during the reign of Louis XIII. Next we were led to the planetarium, and I had the opportunity to observe the Old Man constellation [Ursa Major], which appeared as luminous as the moon. Later, through another telescope, I viewed the Heavenly Dog Star [Leo], which is even brighter than the Old Man.

9TH OF THE FIRST MONTH

A question was put to me regarding gravity and heavenly bodies: "If the earth has been hanging in space secured merely by the force of the sun's gravity since the beginning of time, can this heavy object with a circumference of 90,000 miles be further supported by the gravity of the sun in the future?"

I gave an answer based upon the theory of Western astronomy: "We human beings on this earth are accustomed to seeing objects falling on the ground. We should realize that the true cause of their fall is the pull of the earth's gravity. Therefore, even if the circumference of the earth is the staggering figure of 90,000 miles, the earth will remain afloat as light as a feather in space."

13TH OF THE FIRST MONTH

The successful colonization of the African continent by the European nations in the last thirty years must be attributed to the European nations' inexhaustible sources of funds, their passion for challenges, and their tolerance of new ideas.

In a recent discussion with Westerners I discovered that Weihaiwei appears to possess a better strategic location than Port Arthur. The Office of the Northern Ports must be urged to chose Weihaiwei as the site of the naval base and Port Arthur as the site of the shipyard.

15TH OF THE FIRST MONTH

Westerners tend to regard Kaiser William I of Germany as a second-rate monarch and claim that the growing prosperity of Germany as a nation has been achieved by the combined talents of several ministers, among whom the most outstanding is Prime Minister Bismarck.

I totally disagree with such a shallow assessment. Talent is not required to be a competent sovereign. As long as a monarch can discern the special talents in his subjects and trust them with responsible positions in his councils, he has done his job well and deserves all the credit his ministers earn.

16TH OF THE FIRST MONTH

The population of China is the largest on earth. In China there is not one single piece of land that has not been cultivated. With the ever growing population, hundred of thousands of men will be out of work and unable to support their families. With hunger in their hearts, the only way they can survive is to engage in unlawful practices. This in turn generates unrest and killing, which invariably reduces the population. The question of how to break this vicious circle by peaceful means and to solve this problem of overpopulation has been on the minds of many statesman for centuries. After a painstaking study of world geography I have found a remedy for China's overpopulation problem. The American continent is in the initial stages of cultivation, and the combined territories of Brazil and Mexico cover an area as vast as China. Yet their present population is merely 20 percent of China's population. The climate in both these countries is mild and similar to that in China, and both countries are hospitable to foreigners. We should take advantage of this good opportunity to sign contracts with these two countries for our laborers and to establish consulates there for their protection. In the contract we must clearly demand fair treatment for our people even after their work is finished so that they will not be subjected to the humiliation of mistreatment and deportation, which the American authorities have recently imposed on our people. Under the protection of our consulates our people will not be threatened by the natives and will be able to purchase land, build houses and raise families there. After several generations, their descendants may even invest in China on account of their heritage. In all likelihood, we will be building a new China outside of Chinese territory so that our people may prosper in years to come. This move will strengthen our nation, feed our people, reduce our national deficit, increase our productivity and change our national image. Therefore it's essential to implement such a policy as soon as possible.

18TH OF THE FIRST MONTH

Imperial Commissioner Li's letter stated that Ron Williams, chief instructor of the Chinese Naval Academy, has resigned after his requests were repeatedly denied and that the Academy is in the process of hiring a replacement. The letter also stated that Williams, in his letter of resignation, pointedly criticized the Academy policy of exclusively hiring Fujian natives to be captains of all the battleships.

20TH OF THE FIRST MONTH

The International Office informed me by letter that British ambassador Wilson recently paid them a visit regarding a Chinese merchant who desires to become a British subject. The merchant, Cai Dexi, was originally from Fujian Province and now permanently resides in Haichen. The British embassy claimed that since Cai was born in Singapore, he is automatically a British subject and that despite the fact that he has never applied to change his citizenship, he has to pay taxes as a British merchant. The prefect of Amoy refused to comply with the naturalization process. Wilson therefore proposed that our government should standardize the procedure for naturalization. Since there was an earlier agreement as such, the proposal was accepted accordingly.

27TH OF THE FIRST MONTH

Sandison of the British Foreign Office contacted my aide, Margary, by letter regarding a Chinese document that he thought might be of some significance. I told Margary that if he found the document valuable, he should bring it back and leave it with Zhang so that Zhang may make another copy by hand. Shortly afterward, Margary came to Paris and told me that in the storage room of the British Foreign Office there was a box wrapped in yellow silk that had been stored there for some seventy years. The box is believed to have originally come from China, but the contents have remained unknown all these years. When the box was opened, a large piece of bamboo was found inside. Neatly tucked inside the hollow hole of the bamboo was a letter dated during the reign of the Jiaqing Emperor [1796–1820]. The letter, addressed to the king of England, was written by the Chinese emperor in three languages: Chinese, Latin and Manchurian.

The letter contains the same story I read in the journal of Wang Yiwu about a British envoy who refused to be presented to the emperor when he found out he had to prostrate himself. However, this story continued beyond the departure of the envoy. According to this letter, it appears that after the emperor angrily dismissed the British envoy without offering gifts to the king of England, he later regretted his action and subsequently summoned the governor of Guangdong and Guangxi provinces to Beijing for an explanation of the bizarre behavior of the British envoy. When he fully understood the cultural differences, he immediately sent gifts to the king of England through an English merchant with a letter of explanation. The gifts, which consisted of a white jade scepter, a bag of green jade beads, two large embroidered purses and eight small ones, were placed in the box with the letter.

I found the letter to be composed in the most eloquent tone, and I am convinced that the king of England would have accepted the apology if he had only opened the box.

28TH OF THE FIRST MONTH

Today I received a telegram from General Xiang, who heads the steel manufacturing division in Hubei Province and who has recently built two steel mills there. He requested the purchase of some tools for the machine repair shop. A second telegram followed with a request for the purchase of a fire engine for the textile factory there.

1ST OF THE SECOND MONTH

Since I left China, I have presented my credentials to three nations: England, France and Belgium. The reason I haven't yet gone to Italy is that both the king and the foreign minister tend to leave Rome during the summer. When I arrived in England last year and visited Belgium, it was already summer, and in the following months of autumn, there were several urgent negotiations that required my immediate attention and thus prevented my leaving England. Therefore, I was unable to go to Paris until the end of this year. While there, between socializing with the French officials and attending to official business, there was not too much time left for me to go to Italy. When spring finally arrived this year, I caught a cold and suffered from a cough as well. I've since gotten over the cold, although the cough lingers on. However, I felt the trip to Italy could no longer be postponed and took a train through France for Rome with Margary and several other members of my staff.

6TH OF THE SECOND MONTH

I had a meeting with the prime minister, who is also in charge of foreign affairs and bears the title of Marquis. I mentioned that some 600 years ago in China, many visiting Italian scholars were given high-ranking positions in the Imperial Court, and therefore the good relationship between China and Italy that both countries have enjoyed over the years is much longer than those between China and other European nations. The Marquis replied that this proves China never misses a real talent. He further stated that these past events had brought honor and pleasure to his country. Then I left to pay a visit to the deputy minister, who bears the title of Count. He is a refined gentleman who possesses great knowledge in international affairs. We had a long talk.

13TH OF THE SECOND MONTH

When I was in Shanghai, I heard about a Chinese institute in Naples, Italy, that was initially funded by the Kangxi Emperor [1662–1722]. Recently, the king of Italy has made plans to deprive the church of its ownership by nationalizing the institute. In my opinion, this matter requires a serious discussion with the Italian Foreign Office. I visited the institute and had a meeting with Director Guo and several other members of the institute. It appears that during the reign of the Kangxi Emperor, an Italian priest, who was skilled in oil painting, served in the Chinese Imperial Court for some fifteen years. Upon his departure from China, he was given a large amount of silk and several horses. Five Chinese students followed him to the West. After his return to Naples, he raised the funds to build the Chinese institute. There are now twenty-two Chinese students as well as students from Turkey and Greece studying at the institute. In the last few years the Italian government dispatched two officials from their Ministry of Education to share responsibility for school administration with two outside priests, and they intend to take over the property gradually. The priest of the institute brought the grievance to the court, but the case has not yet been reviewed.

I sent one of my staff, Ma Qingchen, to the Foreign Office of the Vatican, and was told that over the years the Vatican has been contributing money to the institute; therefore, the case is closed and the institute will be nationalized.

Today, Director Guo came to see me. He had cut his hair and was wearing the cloth of the church. He stated that the tuition fee for each Chinese student there is 1,200 francs and is paid for by the bishops of every province in China. I asked him about his background. He said he had been a student at the institute for twelve years. He returned to China for thirteen years and then came back to the institute as the principal. I asked about the number of Chinese Catholic converts in China; he replied that there are five million. After spending a reasonable amount of time thinking about the problem, I decided that the property of the institute rightly belongs to the church as there is no solid evidence of Chinese funding. As I understand, the government of Italy has been confiscating church property for a long time. Apparently, it's their right to do so; such practices cannot be changed overnight. However, for the protection of the Chinese students' rights, I feel I should offer help. I gave Guo my word that I would contact the Italian Foreign Office and discuss this matter further with them.

19TH OF THE SECOND MONTH

The prime minister of Italy paid me a visit, and we talked a little longer this time. He may not be a bright man, but he certainly has a warm personality. The parties on both the left and the right are pleased with the prime minister, who was elected two months ago.

21ST OF THE SECOND MONTH

A double horse-drawn carriage was sent for me on the day when I was to be presented to the king of Italy. Margary, Wu and I were driven to the gate of the palace and then led to the inner court. The king extended warm greetings and talked to me for half an hour. His Majesty mentioned the historically good relationship between our two countries and praised the excellent judgment that our emperor had had in selecting a scholar like myself to be the ambassador to Italy. Then His Majesty asked me additional questions: How long have you been in Europe? Are you kept busy in England and France? Has China completed her railroad construction? I answered all these questions and presented my credentials. The king removed his hat and received them with a bow. I withdrew bowing, and the king shook hands with me again saying: "Now I've another good Chinese friend."

22ND OF THE SECOND MONTH

In keeping with Western practice, an appointment was made for me to be presented to the queen of Italy. I was again led into the palace. The queen looked graceful and spoke in a gentle tone. After a few words I retreated with a bow, and the queen answered with a bow.

24TH OF THE SECOND MONTH

I received a letter from Ambassador Hong, who asked me to meet him in Rome, as he was traveling to Genoa, where he was scheduled to depart for home on the third of next month.[27] I informed him by letter that I had completed my official business here and would return to Paris. It would be more convenient to meet him two days later in Berlin, as I may easily reach there by traveling across Switzerland.

Furthermore, I have heard that Germany has recently become a powerful nation, and I truly would like to tour through this country.

25TH OF THE SECOND MONTH

I arrived in Frankfurt, once the site of many embassies. I have noticed that the behavior of Germany's people is not like the behavior of people in other European countries. This is due to the effectiveness of their police and the spirit of the German people. I changed trains for Berlin and arrived at the Bavaria Hotel. Ambassador Hong was already there. I paid him a visit, and we talked well into the night before I returned to my hotel.

26TH OF THE SECOND MONTH

Comparatively, Germany is not as rich as England or France, but the streets are extremely clean. German people are very polite and do not make fun of our clothing. When they meet us on the street, they remove their hats and bow. I've never met such courtesy before.

I didn't have time to go sightseeing and merely went around town by carriage through the boulevards and by the gates of the palace. Ambassador

---

27. Hong was replaced by Xu Jingchen (1845–1900), who remained ambassador to Russia, Germany, Austria and Holland until 1896, when the job was divided into two. Xu remained ambassador to Germany until 1898, and Yang Ru (?–1902) became ambassador to Russia, Austria and Holland (1896–98).

Hong took me to a wax museum and then to a banquet in a large restaurant, which he held in honor of his successor, Ambassador Xu Jingchen. All the embassy people were invited, including the staff of the former ambassador. I enjoyed the food there tremendously, and the party lasted until midnight. Thousands of miles across the ocean, far away from our own country, all thirty of us had this opportunity to get together and truly have a good time.[28]

28TH OF THE SECOND MONTH

We left Berlin around noon. When the train reached French territory, we changed trains because the rail tracks there are laid differently.

8TH OF THE THIRD MONTH

From the official Chinese papers, I learned that on the 25th day after the lunar New Year, His Majesty the Emperor received the ambassadors of various countries at the Hall of Purple Light. The German ambassador acted as the leader of the group.

26TH OF THE THIRD MONTH

I left Paris with my staff at noon by train. After crossing the Channel we boarded an English train; they run much faster than the French trains.

29TH OF THE THIRD MONTH

Britton, the newly appointed American ambassador to China, had frequently expressed his view when he was a member of Congress that the United States should stop the flow of Chinese laborers into America. China has given official notice to the American government of its unwillingness to accept him as the new ambassador to our country. However, by that time, Britton had already reached San Francisco. The State Department summoned him back to Washington but expressed no surprise at our demand. In their view, if China is not willing to accept the ambassador they send, it's perfectly within China's rights to do so.

17TH OF THE FOURTH MONTH

Yuan Shuangqiu of the Interior Ministry wrote me the following letter:

---

28. This banquet gained a measure of notoriety when satirized by popular writer Zeng Pu (1872–1935) in *Niehai hua* (A Flower in a Sea of Woe), completed in 1905. Zeng likely heard of the banquet through his French literature and philosophy teacher, Chen Jitong, whom we see in Hsieh's *Diary* as counsellor (and military attaché) to the Chinese embassy in Paris.

For many years General Xiang of Guangdong Province has made several attempts to install a consulate in Hong Kong without much success. And now, Your Excellency has successfully resolved this issue. You have certainly accomplished a great achievement.

The recent placement of a British official in Kashgar, in our opinion, may curb Russia's ability to monopolize all the trade there. And with India close by acting as a watchdog, we will be reasonably safe for years to come. Both Russia and Great Britain are world powers, and neither of them dares to make the first move. Xinjiang Province[29] may remain on solid ground for the time being despite the power struggles of these two nations.

As for the tariff problem with Britain, I suggest that we replace the old agreement drawn up in the seventh year of the Guangxu Emperor [1881], which specifies that the province is excluded from tax revenues. This will bring more money to our country, and no harm can possibly come from this minor change in the agreement.

Recently, we have been discussing in our office the possibility of establishing a consulate in Kashgar. However, in my opinion, you should make the proposal after you hear from the British Foreign Office. Please be advised, Your Excellency, that you must refrain from speaking your own mind on this matter of great importance. Extreme caution should be exercised; nevertheless, it's your responsibility as to when the negotiations get underway.

22ND OF THE THIRD MONTH

I received a letter from the counsellor at our French embassy. It concerns the renewal of a ten-year-old contract that was due a month ago. He stated that the present French Parliament has been considering letting the contract remain as it is because over the years it has helped considerably to promote business in both our countries. He further stated that if there are any minor changes China would like to make, he shall prepare the contract accordingly.

The problem of the Chinese institute in Italy was finally resolved between the church and the Ministry of Education. The institute is required to pay 12,000 lire and return some furniture to the church.

24TH OF THE FOURTH MONTH

According to the Western calendar, today is May 30th, the birthday of the queen of England.

25TH OF THE FOURTH MONTH

I received a letter from Vice Minister Xu Xiaoyun that read as follows:

---

29. Xinjiang Province is located in the northwestern frontier. (Trans.)

Last year, British Ambassador Wilson came to the International Office to express the British Foreign Office's interest in placing a British official in Kashgar. The request was turned down due to Britain's steady refusal of China's proposal to install a consul in Hong Kong. Then Wilson suggested that if China will reconsider this proposal, Britain would be willing to open talks on the Hong Kong consul issue. Fearful of being enticed into a trade, our office gave him no definite answer. I assume Ambassador Wilson has since conveyed this message to the British Foreign Office. Therefore, when you next propose the installation of a Hong Kong consul, they may accept it in order to achieve their goal.

However, resolution of the Kashgar issue should not be delayed as this recent proposal by Britain may curtail the power of Russia, our neighbor to the west. If Britain wants her share of the profits, as you've indicated in your letter, she will certainly help us to achieve this goal.

According to Western custom, the establishment of a consulate requires a permit, so there is no reason for us to fear the British proposal. However, if we issue a permit to Russia, Britain may demand the same privilege. I have no assurance that this case can be resolved. If Britain is willing to pay taxes, however, they should be allowed to do so. They had made such a proposal to us at an earlier date, because they have had grand designs on Xinjiang Province for a long time.

As of yet, the British ambassador has not mentioned anything about this case to us. I'll let you know as soon as he makes such a proposal.

It appears that this case would be better negotiated at this office as it is more convenient to do so. Your Excellency's effort in this case is extremely admirable; nevertheless, any proposal should first be submitted to this office for approval. After a round of discussion among our office staff, it will then be submitted to the Imperial Court for a decree.

14TH OF THE FIFTH MONTH

Since the Catholic missionaries began their work in China, ninety priests have been killed. The recent case in Wuhu was fortunate as none of the priests were harmed. There are twenty-five Catholic churches in China, and the controlling power of these establishments is divided equally among twenty-nine priests.

17TH OF THE FIFTH MONTH

Every two to four years, our embassy tends to give a party, and my predecessor, Ambassador Liu, held such a social function four years ago. I've lived in Europe for a year and half now and have been invited to various tea parties held either by the government ministries or by the private gentry. I feel obligated to return such favors. A couple of months ago I sent out invitations to all the dignitaries for a tea party at the embassy today from 10:00 A.M. to 1:00 P.M.

Guests arrived at the embassy in droves, and by noon the total number in attendance reached as high as five or six hundred. Among those invited were ambassadors from various countries and their aides as well as the gentry of London society.

The whole affair was appropriately managed by Margary, who provided the embassy with the most magnificent decorations. The flowers were fresh and beautiful; the fruit was juicy and abundant. It was widely reported that this lavish arrangement surpassed all the other parties given by embassies in London.

18TH OF THE FIFTH MONTH

According to a Paris paper, a law was decreed by the Chinese emperor for the protection of all foreigners and their missionaries. The criminals who led the uprising along the Yangzi River were punished accordingly. Other cases in the past will also be processed and resolved in the near future. The decree has since been posted on the walls of all the cities in China.

29TH OF THE FIFTH MONTH

A recent confidential telegram from the International Office conveyed news of the following uprisings involving missionaries:

> For several months now, problems involving missionaries have been occurring on a regular basis. There have been seven recent cases in different places. In Wuxue, a minister and a layman, both British, were killed. The other six cases involved Catholic churches. The degree of damage differs from place to place. According to rumor, a doctor of the Wuhu church took in a sick street urchin and treated him. Subsequently, the child's father accused the doctor of kidnapping, and the magistrate took the doctor into custody and kept him in jail overnight. The doctor was released after the priest of the church posted bail for him. The release of the doctor roused the anger of local unlawful citizens, who incited a riot and burned down all the churches in town. After this riot, the citizens of other cities joined in the insurrection, which brought on several riots up and down the river.
>
> Two leaders and ten accomplices were arrested in addition to ten rioters. Two were found guilty in court and will be duly sentenced. Nine men were arrested in Danyang and six were detained in Wuxi, but no rulings have been made as yet.
>
> Our office is preparing a memorial for the protection of foreigners and shall submit it to the emperor accordingly. We hope to keep everything quiet and have been discussing settlements with the churches in all these cases.
>
> England, France and Germany have banded together and lodged a strong protest at this office, accusing us of procrastination in handling these cases. We explained to them that all the criminal element has fled town, and we have since

circulated bulletins for their arrest. We are truly doing our best to resolve these cases and have already removed all six magistrates from the cities that were involved in the riots. All the other officials involved were also punished with heavy sentences. However, we cannot arrest innocent people as criminals and must carry out sentencing according to the law. We cannot close these cases before we have investigated the real cause of these riots. Angry protest will not bring about speedy action.

All the above statements are expected to be channeled through the British Foreign Office so that these countries will not be misled by one-sided stories that may damage our friendship with them. Please forward a similar message to Ambassador Xu and ask him to proceed according to these instructions.

After I received this telegram, I cabled the Chinese embassy in Russia and then sent out the same message to the counsellor in France by letter. I went personally to the British Foreign Office and talked to Grey. He recorded every word I said and suggested that all lost properties should be compensated for. He expressed his wish that China will give out heavy sentences to all the criminals involved in these cases as quickly as the legal system allows.

1ST OF THE SIXTH MONTH

The International Office sent news of the Kuishi garrison on the Burma border:

> Captain Zhang of Tengyue informed us by telegram that an Englishman was killed by several natives. He immediately launched an investigation. Later, he learned that the Englishman had lost his horses and gone to look for the animals with his native servants. They camped by the mountains near a native village. The natives sneaked into the camp at night and killed some thirty foreigners. The survivors of the massacre burned down all the native compounds in the village, each compound consisting of five to eight families.

Also, news from Pu'er village indicates as follows:

> Captain Qu encountered two foreign military officers leading a battalion of some sixty soldiers on his way to Menghai garrison. According to the foreign officers, they were ordered by their superiors in Burma to survey the border and will return to Burma shortly.

The letter further stated that some fifty to sixty foreigners arrived recently from Menglong on their way to Nine Dragon River, and I was instructed to notify the British Foreign Office that they should let China know if they intend to send in their troops.

2ND OF THE SIXTH MONTH

Reports from the Tengyue headquarters gave a full account of the burning of the native compounds by the British soldiers. All these facts, which were collected from native chiefs in Luoxiao, stated that after the burning of the three native compounds, which were fifty to sixty miles from Matang, the British soldiers camped by the mountain northwest of the town. Later, they moved the camp to Luoxiao, which is some fifty miles from Tiebiguan and forty miles from Matang.

4TH OF THE SIXTH MONTH

The king of Germany arrived in London a few days ago. Today the ambassadors from various countries came to pay their respects to His Majesty the King at noon in Buckingham Palace. The king made an effort to speak a few words to each ambassador. When my turn came, His Majesty inquired whether I have received any recent news from China and asked after the health of both the empress and the emperor. I answered that they are fine. His Majesty then spoke about Xu [Jingcheng], the Chinese ambassador to his country, and how delighted he was, as this is Xu's second term in Germany. Afterwards, His Majesty asked me to convey greetings in my next letter to China wishing both the Empress Dowager and the emperor good health. Then His Majesty nodded his head and I retreated.

At five o'clock that same afternoon, I went to a tea party given by the crown prince. The queen of England and both the queen and king of Germany were present.

10TH OF THE SIXTH MONTH

A letter of the 8th of this month from the International Office stated that a few years ago Australia laid down laws restricting Chinese immigration into their country. Since this action subsequently caused hardship for all the Chinese merchants and laborers on that continent, several discussions with the British ambassador were held in the Seventh month of the 14th year of the Guangxu Emperor [1888]. Six regulations were drawn up for Ambassador Wilson to forward to his government. However, several years have since passed and there is still no news from the British ambassador. It has been assumed that this list of regulations may never have been reviewed.

11TH OF THE SIXTH MONTH

The minister of the French Foreign Office said that he had received from the Shanghai consul the following telegram:

> In the south of the Yangzi River, various secret societies have risen, one after another, and their members are the culprits who frequently harass foreigners.

Their actions may endanger the reputation of China on an international level, and for the protection of their own people all nations have since united together and sent out some twenty ships to China to maneuver along the river.

12TH OF THE SIXTH MONTH

The International Office instructed me by letter to negotiate with the French Foreign Office regarding the head tax levied on the Chinese in Saigon. It was my understanding that my predecessor had engaged in several negotiations that dealt merely with the Chinese residents in the center and north of Vietnam. The letter further instructed me that this time negotiations should be more conclusive and include all three parts of Vietnam.

Consequently, I wrote to the counsellor in France and instructed him to prepare notes for further negotiation.

13TH OF THE SIXTH MONTH

A telegram from the International Office brought the following news:

> In addition to the seven missionary cases, a thirty-one-room house in Rugao was ransacked, although no one was hurt. In Nanchang only one of the priests' dormitories was demolished. The officials in every province are now on alert, and everything appears relatively peaceful. We hope you will convey to the French Foreign Office the news that the two rioters have been duly executed. The British consul has accused local officials of negligence and continues to raise complaints. Therefore, it's hard for this office to resolve these cases.

20TH OF THE SIXTH MONTH

I attended a tea party given by Lord Salisbury at his country estate. I arrived there by train and proceeded by motorcar to the house, which was the palace of Queen Elizabeth some 300 years ago. Later, the house was given to the ancestors of the Marquis. The house retains the architecture of that ancient period; the men and women in the portraits wear a different style of attire. In my opinion, the ancient costume resembles Chinese clothing.

The garden party was held in honor of the prince of Italy, and ambassadors from various countries and the gentry were guests.

14TH OF THE SEVENTH MONTH

This afternoon I went to Cambridge with my staff in order to return the call of Westheimer, the former British ambassador to China. We went by motorcar and arrived there in one hour and ten minutes. Westheimer is seventy-four years old but walks briskly and led us everywhere himself. There is a large Chinese library filled with books he bought some forty years ago in China. It's a remarkable collection as it even contains rare copies of ancient books in their first edition. Evidently, he purchased them before the Taiping Rebellion, because after those long years of unrest in China, no one could buy such a collection at any price.[30]

20TH OF THE SEVENTH MONTH

For the forthcoming wedding of our emperor, the queen of England put in a special order for a pure silver clock at a watchmaker's. The clock is five feet high and is studded with precious stones.

1ST OF THE EIGHTH MONTH

I received confirmation from the British Foreign Office regarding the installation of a consulate in Hong Kong and the reassignment of the consul of Singapore to the new post of consul general. I had submitted the memorial in the First month of this year and understand that it has since been forwarded to the International Office. Apparently, someone there has tried to halt the procedure because I have yet to receive an answer from them. Now the British Foreign Office has also displayed a certain measure of reluctance and claims that they will issue a permit for one year only. They contend that if the Hong Kong consul doesn't interfere with British policy or go against the will of the Chinese people on the island, the permit will be renewed on a permanent basis. But apparently the culprit in the International Office has tried to put a stop to it in spite of Britain's favorable response because of the belief that such restrictions will cause adverse effects on China's future foreign policy. Subsequently, I sent a series of telegrams home to fight for my cause but received no response. Now, the consul of Singapore, Zuo Binglong, is retiring on account of his parents' poor health, and he is the man whom Britain agreed to have as the Hong Kong consul. To resolve this problem I cabled the International Office and requested a delay on the Hong Kong appointment until the position of consul general in Singapore is filled. I also requested an official statement so that the British Foreign Office here can prepare to issue the permit. I stated clearly that this issue deals exclusively with the problems of the South Sea Islands and therefore it will not intrude into other territories. Furthermore, this will set a good example to the world

---

30. The Taiping Rebellion (1851–64) ravaged much of southern China, especially the areas along the central and coastal Yangzi River, which had long been centers of learning. Many important private libraries were destroyed in the course of the rebellion; hence Hsieh's remark that a collection like that owned by Westheimer could no longer be purchased.

that Britain is giving China treatment equal to that she grants other countries. We must therefore accept this offer from the British Foreign Office.

Shortly afterward, I received an answer from the International Office by
telegram, indicating that the position of consul general of Singapore has been
filled by promoting Huang Zunxian to that position and that discussion on
the Hong Kong consul case should be postponed temporarily. It further stated
that I should wait for an answer before I submit another memorial.

6TH OF THE EIGHTH MONTH

The Pamir plateau is located in the north of Afghanistan over high mountain ranges, and therefore Britain has difficulty defending that area against
Russia. Earlier, Britain had expressed her interest in returning the territory
to China if China will draw a clear boundary to prevent further Russian aggression. The British Foreign Office recently sent a detailed account in total
secrecy and asked Margary to hand it to me personally. It contended that
when Aide Ma of the Chinese embassy was present at the Foreign Office he
was shown a report from a certain Captain Youngblood, who went on an in-
vestigative tour of Pamir by traveling through Kashgar. He claims that
Britain has every intention of clearing this matter with China after receiving
a full report from the Indian government. The main reason of the tour was to
visit the natives of that region and to draw a clear boundary between
Afghanistan and China. According to the captain's view the boundary is
clearly drawn. However, the British Foreign Office would like to seek approval from China first. If China gives her consent, they will inform the
Indian government to go ahead with the plan.

7TH OF THE EIGHTH MONTH

I received a telegram from the International Office regarding the Xinjiang
frontier. According to a recent report, it appears that the British army is
launching an attack on Kanjuti and that the chief there is appealing for help.
I was instructed to make inquiries at the Foreign Office to find out what
arrangements can be made to resolve this conflict. I sent Aide Ma for this
particular mission. Sandison of the Foreign Office stated that the reason behind the conflict was simple: It appears that the Muslim king of Kashmir intends to build a new road and mount a cannon there. Britain has not the
slightest desire to invade Kanjuti. I sent this message by cable to the
International Office.

8TH OF THE EIGHTH MONTH

The Foreign Office of France received a telegram from a French missionary in China stating that their churches and several merchants' houses were burned to the ground in Nanchang and that a Belgian priest and two Italian nuns were seriously wounded. France contends that Belgium and Italy may jointly lodge a protest if they intend to make a special case of this incident; otherwise, they may join England and France in their attempt to resolve all these missionary cases.

After serious consideration I concluded that the French are making another attempt to establish their exclusive right to protect the Catholic churches, as these two particular cases are totally not France's concern in the first place. I plan to deal with both the ambassadors of Belgium and Italy directly, and thus eliminate the influence of France.

9TH OF THE EIGHTH MONTH

Today I conceived a plan to resolve these missionary cases at their sources. I wrote a report addressing both the total amount of money that the church has demanded as compensation and the full investigation that has led to mass arrests of the bandits of the secret societies. Subsequently, I instructed my aide to translate it into English.

10TH OF THE EIGHTH MONTH

During the Fourth and Fifth months of this year, several missionary cases broke open in various provinces along the Yangzi River. The International Office has sent a memorial requesting severe punishments so that all the governors may take swift action to provide security for the foreigners in their respective provinces.

12TH OF THE EIGHTH MONTH

Yesterday I received a telegram from the International Office regarding the latest news from the governor of Hubei Province:

> A letter with the signatures of both the British consul and the captain of the ship was delivered to this office. The letter stated that they received direct orders from their government to cooperate with local officials in an effort to protect the lives of all foreigners residing in the troubled spots of China. They claimed that they will not hesitate to use force when a mob gathers around a foreign compound. Consequently, the governor answered that it is the duty of local officials to protect the lives of foreigners and to put down the insurrections. If

foreign battleships were allowed to shoot over the shore indiscriminately, many innocent lives might be lost. This may lead to more uprisings.

We, therefore, implore you to forward this message to their Foreign Office and ask them to inform their ship captains to stay away from the Chinese coast.

I sent Margary to the Foreign Office with this message. The Foreign Office replied that the proposed policy was the idea of their navy ministry. After several trips they finally relented and subsequently requested their navy ministry to cable the ship captains and instruct them to employ extreme caution during the current crisis.

The Foreign Office later confided to us that according to Ambassador Wilson, all the ambassadors are clearly perturbed that news of the insurrections didn't appear in the Beijing newspaper by decree of His Majesty the Emperor and are disappointed that the International Office claims that it is out of their jurisdiction to launch a full-scale investigation into the case of the anonymous wall posters. The Foreign Office reported that the ambassadors from France, Germany and Italy are making frequent inquiries at their office for further news from China—especially the French ambassador, who devotes all his time to contacting the British Foreign Office and has attempted several times to persuade Britain to reject an early settlement of the Wuhu missionary case.

13TH OF THE EIGHTH MONTH

Yesterday I received a letter of confirmation from the International Office, enclosed with the imperial decree signed in vermilion ink, naming me as a candidate on the nomination list for the minister's position in the International Office.

18TH OF THE EIGHTH MONTH

A telegram from the International Office stated:

> The two convicted leaders of Wuxue have been executed. The other eight men were publicly lashed and subsequently exiled. The British ambassador appeared to be satisfied; however, as for the compensation, which totals 65,000 yuan, he merely acknowledged our letter and requested that the money be set aside until after he receives a final decision from the British Foreign Office. He further claimed that he has to discuss the case with all the other nations before he can give us a final answer. The compensation for the other three missionary cases are 66,000 yuan of silver for Jinkui, 1,400 yuan of silver for Yanghu and 8,400 yuan for Tanyang. The missionaries in these cases have agreed in writing to these conditions. The other four cases call for 4,000 taels of silver for Rugao, 500 taels for Fengli, 9,000 yuan for Jiang'in and 7,000 yuan for Wuxi; these

have all been settled and closed but do not have the signatures of the local missionaries. In Fuwu the two convicted rioters were executed, and the arrests of
their accomplices are underway. A total of 111,000 yuan of silver has been set
aside for the final settlement, and the missionaries' demand for the two vacant
lots adjacent to the church is under court review. Local authorities, who have
been accused of failing to respond to requests for help, are being investigated by
the Office of the South Sea. Furthermore, twenty-one more convicted rioters
will be lashed and sent into exile. All these measures are significant evidence to
prove that we are taking every step to settle the missionary cases as soon as possible. Nonetheless, all the ambassadors remain unconvinced and intimidate us
by sending unfavorable reports back to their own foreign ministries. Please convey this message to the foreign offices of both England and France and simultaneously cable our Ambassador Xu in Germany so that he may inform the
German Foreign Office. We urgently expect further formal statements from
these countries.

19TH OF THE EIGHTH MONTH

Yesterday I cabled the International Office confirming that telegrams have
been sent to the Foreign Offices of both England and France and enclosed a
complaint from the French Foreign Office and a full report for further investigation:

> The French Foreign Office has been tart in their reply and has accused
> China of gross negligence in failing to comply with their urgent request. They
> claim that they are prepared to sever diplomatic relations with China and will
> persuade other nations to follow suit. The general consensus is to draw up a
> protest warning China that unless severe measures are taken to prosecute these
> rioters, China shall face an ominous future with all nations. Further investiga-
> tion has revealed that all the foreign powers are saying that they are prepared to
> bring in additional ships to each seaport in anticipation of the next missionary
> incident as an excuse to invade China. The British Foreign Office insists that
> they must display their naval power since the foreigners in every seaport depend
> on them for protection. Therefore, if we lose this right to protect our own coun-
> try, similar measures may arise in the future. The authorities in each province
> must be ready to use all their available power to protect the foreigners. Guards
> should be posted outside every church, and gunboats must be sent out to patrol
> all the major seaports. Investigations should be launched to seek the arrest of the
> anonymous wall poster writers, and the emperor's decree should be posted
> throughout every province without omitting a single word of the document. Any
> magistrate who is slow to convict these rioters should be penalized, and police
> officials should be made aware that they must assume the duty of protecting the
> foreigners. A response is urgently requested so that I may provide an immediate
> answer to the British Foreign Office.

Afterward, I sent a telegram directly to Imperial Commissioner Li to report that several ambassadors have severed relations with the International

Office and to implore him to make contact with them. I stressed the strong alliance that has united these nations and emphasized that it is no longer a question of a single nation against us. Such adverse action may lead to serious consequences, and therefore extreme caution must be taken in this present affair.

20TH OF THE EIGHTH MONTH

All the churches in Hubei Province are the property of three Franciscan orders. Two of the orders came from Italy; the third is from Belgium and Holland. The church in Nanchang belongs to the third order.

23RD OF THE EIGHTH MONTH

In the early summer General Zhang Xun of Jilin Province[31] informed the International Office that in Haicanwei Bay, 20,000 overseas Chinese are being mistreated by the Russians. He suggested that the establishment of a consulate is urgently needed there so that protection can be provided for our people abroad.

3RD OF THE NINTH MONTH

Information in a secret cable received from the International Office indicated:

> The governments of every nation have taken the telegrams that their ambassadors sent home seriously. They have virtually destroyed all the good will that we have developed with these nations through the years. All seaports are presently under close watch and are well protected. How could they still clamor that their citizens are living in constant fear from day to day? No matter how unpredictable the situation was here, we have never neglected our duty to protect the foreigners. In fact, we have recently instructed both the North Sea and South Sea offices by cable to dispatch more ships for patrol duty.
>
> This year missionary cases have steadily increased. Our initial suspicion was that the secret society people were the villains. However, on the 10th of this month the customs officers in Shanghai discovered thirty-five cases of contraband rifles shipped in from Hong Kong to Chungking. An Englishman by the name of Mason was charged with this crime; later, in his luggage, five pounds of dynamite were found. Incidentally, Mason was the assistant inspector of the tax revenue division of the customs office at Chungking. He was subsequently sent to Shanghai under guard. According to his confession, an Englishman by the name of Esmode is the purchasing agent for the Chungking secret society. The leader of his group is another Englishman, who with six other foreigners was

---

31. Jilin Province is one of the three provinces in Manchuria. (Trans.)

currently residing in Hongkou.[32] This office has since notified the British ambassador, who subsequently authorized the consulate constable to make an arrest in cooperation with local Chinese authorities.

It appears that not all the missionary cases have been completely resolved and that new evidence has suggested foreign involvement with the secret society bandits in their insurrection plans. This significant change is conceivably turning the tide against us. Therefore, I advise you that a comprehensive report must be submitted to the Imperial Court of Britain revealing that these unfortunate missionary cases are not the unlawful doings of the secret society bandits alone but a conspiracy between the bandits and the British citizens in China. This is clearly established by solid evidence. Please beseech the British Imperial Court to cable further instructions directly to the British ambassador so that we may settle these missionary cases according to international law.

Your previous request by telegram contained three major points: 1) severe punishments for the rioters, 2) demotion of local officials and 3) compensation for church property. All three requests have been carried out. We will proceed immediately to cable French ambassador Lemy for a peaceful solution in order to block the threat of war. As far as this recent case involving foreign accomplices is concerned, we would like you to inform all the nations who have signed nonaggression agreements with us. This instruction should be forwarded by cable to Ambassador Xu for Germany and Russia.

12TH OF THE NINTH MONTH

Yuan Shuangqiu Chin wrote to me regarding the installation of a British official in Kashgar. The letter stated:

> Sun Laishan, the minister of state, once mentioned this particular case to me. He said as far as he understood, you, Ambassador Hsieh, had assured us that no possible adversity could occur in the future from this action. However, Vice Minister Xu Xiaoyun protested strongly against this move. He contended that there are too many small Chinese Muslim tribes, which the British may entice into their fold by using Kashgar as a base. This will invariably arouse Russia's suspicion. Consequently the minister of state confided in me that although he initially was in total agreement with you, Ambassador Hsieh, the vice minister held firm to his own idea, and therefore he sought my advice on this particular case. My answer was that you, Ambassador Hsieh, appear to have a better interpretation than that of the vice minister. All the territories in the west have been conceded to Russia, who may take a shortcut through the newly occupied area of the two tribes and sneak into Tibet. If a British official was installed in Kashgar, Russia may suspect a secret agreement between China and Britain. Consequently, Russia may seek our favor and stay away from Tibet. I surmise that due to the vice minister's strong objection, Minister of State Sun may be unable to reach a compromise in this particular case.

---

32. Hongkou is a suburb of Shanghai. (Trans.)

26TH OF THE NINTH MONTH

For a second time the International Office has informed me of the memorial that was submitted regarding the establishment of a consulate in Hong Kong. It was summarized as follows:

> A recent agreement suggested the temporary establishment of a Hong Kong consulate for one year. In our opinion, this doesn't sound like a firm commitment. A memorial was thus submitted to His Majesty the Emperor requesting a decree granting Hsieh Fucheng full power to conduct a complete investigation. We are eager to know whether the Imperial Court of England is sincere in its commitment; otherwise, we should inform them of our displeasure.
>
> Furthermore, Ambassador Hsieh may take all the time he needs to discover solutions to such problems as he continues his negotiation with the British Foreign Office. Henceforth all phases of negotiation shall be at his discretion, and we are expecting a decree for the final decision. To our knowledge, our memorial has since been approved in vermilion ink.

27TH OF THE NINTH MONTH

I received a letter from our ambassador to Russia. According to the Russian Foreign Office, the Russian soldiers seen wandering in Pamir have since returned to their camp. An official report from the Russian embassy stated that on a given date a Russian nobleman did indeed travel through Kashgar to India on official business. It's known that a British chargé d'affaires accompanied the nobleman on this trip. The British officer, who has since returned home, confirmed the report that the Russian soldiers had indeed gone back to their camp. He's known to be trustworthy.

29TH OF THE NINTH MONTH

According to a Shanghai newspaper, the British magistrate sentenced the Englishman by the name of Mason to nine months' hard labor for the illegal transportation and sale of firearms to a secret society.

10TH OF THE TENTH MONTH

With the embassy staff, I conducted a ceremony in the courtyard to wish the Empress Dowager a happy birthday and then sent greetings to Her Majesty by telegram.

12TH OF THE TENTH MONTH

According to the local newspaper, all the Western ambassadors in China have signed a petition appealing to the International Office for a speedy settlement of all missionary cases. The official reply, which accused the ambassadors of unnecessary interference in China's domestic affairs, came days later.

Infuriated, the ambassadors called two consecutive meetings and drew up a stronger protest with ten signatures, including that of the ambassador from Japan. The International Office subsequently cabled all the provinces involved in these missionary cases and told them to make adequate compensation payments to all the churches. After receiving answers from the provincial officials, the International Office issued an official reply, which was again deemed to be unsatisfactory. After several more meetings the ambassadors drew up yet another protest, which proved to be more severe than the earlier ones.

20TH OF THE TENTH MONTH

Ambassador Xu wrote to me regarding the Pamir case. He stated that the Russian Foreign Office contends that the border of the Pamir area is clearly defined. However, they suggested that if Britain, China and Russia wish to resolve their differences in the future, the three nations should assemble their representatives there to draw a clearer boundary.

Consequently Xu forward this information to the International Office. In his opinion, the area, which consists of several Muslim cities, would be too vast to control if we gained more territory than we have now. We should consider ourselves fortunate because presently we are still able to defend our territory against our aggressive neighbor. If we extend our boundary beyond the Congling Mountains, we may lack sufficient strength to control the area. However, Pamir is centrally located among three nations, and both our neighbors are clamoring for more territory. Therefore China cannot exclude herself from the meeting and allow Britain and Russia to have their ways.

Li Chunzhai informed me by letter that the establishment of a Hong Kong consulate may not come through. He further stated that the Honorable Xu Xiaoyun, the strongest opponent, fears that Britain may use the consulate as an excuse to place a British official at Kashgar. Li stressed that the court ministers prefer delaying tactics as the best strategy and abhor policy changes in light of progress; therefore, envoys abroad are absolutely powerless under such frustrating circumstances.

24TH OF THE TENTH MONTH

I took three members of my staff and left London in a motorcar. It was a very foggy day, but when we reached Dover, it turned out to be nice and sunny. We took the ferry across the Channel, and since we sailed against the wind, a majority of the people in the boat became sick.

1ST OF THE ELEVENTH MONTH

The Chinese news bureau of the London *Times* reported that two riots broke out in China: one in Jinzhou in Liaoning Province[33] and the other at Dakou, north of Kaiping. Troops were sent from Shanhaiguan to Jinzhou and from Tietsien to Dakou. Three hundred thousand Chinese converts were killed as well as a Belgian priest.

4TH OF THE ELEVENTH MONTH

In the early morning a telegram arrived from the International Office stating:

> During the night of the 17th of last month riots broke out in Chaoyang, Jianchang and several other towns led by two religious sects known as the "Elixir of Gold" sect and the "Ultimate Truth" sect. A Mongolian prince was killed, and residents were robbed and killed. One Catholic church was burned to the ground, and one Chinese priest and several converts lost their lives. An Imperial decree has been swiftly issued to the Imperial Commissioner of the Northern Ports instructing him to alert the general of the Eastern Three Provinces [Manchuria] so that he may put down the riots with his troops. By the 24th of this month the government forces had clearly won after several rounds of battle, and fresh troops from other provinces have joined forces with the local regiment. Apparently, there will be no more problem putting down the insurrection; however, it's difficult to protect the churches located in this isolated area. Furthermore, the French ambassador flatly refused to hand over the locations of the churches to local authorities, so it will be extremely difficult to protect these churches when their locations are virtually unknown. Since the insurrection broke out so swiftly, it left us no choice but to seek reinforcements from other provinces. Well-trained troops are now stationed outside all the churches in the area, and local authorities are on constant alert to protect the church people. Please convey this message to the foreign ministries of both England and France and then cable this instruction to Ambassador Xu.

6TH OF THE ELEVENTH MONTH

There has been further news regarding the Russia soldiers maneuvering at the Chinese-Russia border. This news was initially brought to our attention by the British ambassador, and I subsequently sent a cable to our ambassador in Russia. The return cable flatly denied any truth to this report.

---

33. Liaoning Province is one of the provinces in Manchuria. (Trans.)

In the early days of the Eighth month the British ambassador brought us information confirming that a Russian lieutenant general had toured and hunted at Pamir with the grand design of occupation in mind. The ambassador further stressed that if this particular piece of land does belong to China, then China should protect her rights. Consequently, a cable was sent directly to the Shiquan garrison in Xinjiang, which immediately dispatched a staff sergeant with a battalion of soldiers to investigate and to watch for further developments. We sent another telegram to Ambassador Xu, who was instructed to make inquires at the Russian Foreign Office. His return cable confirmed our suspicions: there has apparently been a cover-up by the Russians. However, we received additional news from Xinjiang that in the Sixth month of this year, the Russian governor of Tadzhik led a troop of 300 through Chinese territory en route to Pamir. They camped in one of the nearby towns and plastered posters in Russian on the walls claiming that the town is now in the hands of the Russians.

All these incidents are due to the undefined border at Kalun, and ominous disaster may loom on the horizon. Yesterday we cabled Xu again instructing him to make another inquiry at the Russian Foreign Office and to request an immediate withdrawal of the troops from our territory. Later, we received the good news that the Russian soldiers at Tadzhik had been called back. They further agreed to convey our protest to a higher authority so that there will be no violation of our territory; the wooden fence their soldiers erected may be torn down at our convenience.

Consequently, we received another message from the Shiquan garrison informing us of a letter that was sent by a Captain Zhang to his deputy, Wei. The letter stated that the Russian troops had withdrawn completely from the frontier and that everything had returned to normal again. It further contended that the Tadzhik governor didn't really enter Chinese territory but merely reached the border between the two countries.

7TH OF THE ELEVENTH MONTH

Of all the missionary cases, the Wuhu case appears to be the hardest to resolve. On the 21st of the Seventh month, the surveillance commissioner of Anhui Province informed this embassy by telegram that the two French priests of Wuhu had recently submitted a petition to his court. They asserted that two pieces of property, one adjacent to their church and the other adjacent to their consulate, should be included in the compensation deal our government has offered. The Imperial Commissioner ordered the lower court to handle this affair as a separate case in order not to jeopardize the present missionary case, which was expected to be concluded soon. Justice Nie conferred with the two priests and reached the conclusion that a wall will be erected around the church and that a guard shall be posted there to avoid future incidents. At that time the French ambassador, Lemy, was still in Shanghai after his arrival from France in the Eighth month of this year. The two priests cabled Lemy with the final result, and the ambassador's instruction was that this case should be settled between the French consul general and Justice Nie. Later, according to Nie's telegram, a permit was granted to erect the wall and to post a guard. However, the two priests insisted that the two pieces of property should be donated to them as a cemetery ground, with the condition that no building should be constructed there in the future and that only trees may be planted. Thus the surveillance commissioner of Anhui Province has claimed that without the signatures of the two priests, the Wuhu case cannot be closed. Therefore, the indemnity of 11,000 yuan he received from the government is still in his possession.

As for the Danyang case, the governor of Jiangsu Province reported that 8,400 taels of silver would be paid out in three separate installments beginning on the 9th of the Seventh month for the burning of the Catholic church and other lost property. Regarding other cases, the governor reported that 4,000 taels of silver would be paid out for the case in Rugao, with 500 taels for the case in Fengli. To speed up the trials, Magistrate Mu personally paid 300 taels of the court costs.

Furthermore, letters of apology will be sent to all the churches through their respective consulates.

As for the unsettled cases, the governor reported that the case of Yanghu will be closed by the 11th of the Seventh month and that 1,491 yuan must be paid out by the 23rd of the following month. The payment in the case of the Jinkui was finally reduced to 66,000 yuan of silver by adding a piece of property west of the church, which will be included in one contract. However, after prolonged negotiations over both cases in Jiang'in and Wuxi, they have been settled for the sum of 9,000 and 7,000 yuan respectively, although we are still waiting for final approval. These are a few details regarding the compensation fund that the Office of the Southern Ports has distributed to the cities and towns under its jurisdiction.

As for the rioters, penalties have been measured out accordingly, and twenty-one arrests were made in Suzhou. After an initial interrogation, the culprits were found to be simple and ignorant people. Two were sentenced to exile, five to caning and fourteen to pillory. However, a bandit of the secret society by the name of Cao was also arrested in the group. Subsequent interrogation led to solid evidence of conspiracy, and severe penalties will be measured out for the alleged bandit. At the same time, the pursuit of escaped conspirators will be reactivated. The magistrate of Danyang has been removed from his post, as well as the magistrates of Wuxi, Jiang'in, Yanghu and Jinkui. The magistrate of Ruguo was placed on probation. These are a few details regarding the demotions of the local officials of the Office of the Southern Ports.

8TH OF THE ELEVENTH MONTH

The missionary case of Wuxue of Hubei Province opened in the local court with the presence of the foreign clergy, who had been sent there by their own consul in the province. The two convicts, Guo and Dai, who had earlier been sentenced to death by hanging, were now charged with additional murders. This time they were sentenced to beheading after the hanging. Other rioters would accordingly be given heavy sentences so as to appease the foreign consuls.

Just as peace finally seemed to be restored, another incident suddenly erupted in Nanchang of Jiangsu Province. In a telegram from the governor of Jiangsu, it was revealed that a Yao family had lost a child who was later found in the nursery of a Catholic convent. Also found in the church were sixty-five men and women. Before long several fires broke out at both the church and the residences of the foreigners. The local authorities immediately provided protection to the priests and the nuns by putting them on a boat. A French priest was struck by a stone but was not badly hurt. According to the Catholic nuns, the child was brought to the church by a man named Wu, and they gave the man 2,000 coins for his trouble. A warrant is now out for the arrest of this man. Since the incident, both Britain and France have dispatched warships to patrol the coast of Jiangsu. The governor of Jiangsu was alarmed and cabled for our own warships in order to prepare for defense. Consequently, two warships were dispatched, one to Shanghai and the other to Hubei Province.

9TH OF THE ELEVENTH MONTH

A telegram from Shanghai stated that the government troops and the rebel forces were engaging in a fierce battle outside of the Chaoyang city gates. The total number of government troops was 4,500 and the rebel force numbered 3,000. The battle raged for two hours. Finally, the government troops used cannon power to break the enemy line, and subsequently the rebels went down in total defeat. The rebels fought even while retreating, and therefore their casualties reached a record high of 1,100. On the government side, Commander Ye sustained a light wound during the battle, but his soldiers exhibited rare courage by chasing the rebels up to the mountains.

10TH OF THE ELEVENTH MONTH

The British consul claimed that the Mason case of arms smuggling couldn't go on trial without the evidence of a witness. The International Office called a meeting with the minister of the Office of the Southern Ports. They concluded that since the crimes were committed at both Shanghai and Chungking customs offices, the tax commissioners and the foreign clerks in both of those offices could easily be called to testify as witnesses. Tax Commissioner Pei recorded Mason's confession on the 14th of the Eighth month and again on the 26th of the same month. Consequently, a summarized version of the interrogation was forwarded to the International Office. It revealed a large number of foreign followers in the secret society and disclosed several secret storage places for arsenals in the Chungking area. Mason implicated a local clerk, Chen Xingsi, a military officer, Yi, who was the caretaker of the fortification on Jiao Mountain, and the names of six interpreters. The Shanghai customs office translated the uprising plan and implicated a Chinese ship steward in Fujian Province and another in Chungking. However, the other two accomplices, Yi and Chen, were not even mentioned in the translation, and therefore further investigation is required. It appears that the British are making excuses to avoid further court proceedings.

Initially, Hart, the commissioner of the Chinese Customs Office, was prepared to send his own officers to complete the investigation. Later, he refused to interfere when he heard that the Shanghai Customs Office had made an arrest. By then, the British consul had received a telegram from their Foreign Office informing him that their government solicitor would be handling the prosecution.

In the early days of the Ninth month, the French ambassador and Hart both came to the International Office and brought the following alarming news:

> The secret society bandits are plotting to occupy the shipyard at Luoxingta in Fujian Province, and several foreign residents at Zizhulin in Tianjin had to leave their homes in haste during the middle of the night when they were suddenly awakened by mysterious loud noises.
>
> More contraband, including 500 rifles, was discovered by the German tax commissioner on the steamer Pine River during its entry. Since the culprit couldn't be located, he fined the captain 500 taels of gold. The governor of Guangdong Province was instructed to notify the viceroy of Hong Kong that from now on all ships and passengers must be thoroughly searched before entry.

11TH OF THE ELEVENTH MONTH

A letter from Imperial Commissioner Li reached our embassy in which he stated that the reason behind this sudden eruption of missionary cases was as follows:

When the missionaries of foreign countries initially made their entry into China, they instantly created hostility among our local communities. If a magistrate issued an arrest warrant or imposed a fine on a troublemaker, it immediately infuriated the townspeople, who would rise up in protest and accuse the magistrate of favoritism. The more arrests that were made, the more defiance that was aroused in the local communities. However, if the magistrate released the troublemakers, all the ambassadors and consuls would immediately rush over to the International Office and lodge protests. Invariably all the blame falls on the local authorities for failing to provide proper protection to the foreign missionaries.

Rumors are presently spreading like wildfire throughout all the provinces. They claim that the church people extract the eyes and hearts of the Chinese people by using occult power and that they force children and women to perform lewd sex acts and commit a variety of unlawful practices. The local authorities have neither the means to collect evidence so as to convey the true feelings of our people to the foreign powers nor the eloquence to persuade our people that there is not a shred of truth to these rumors. Consequently, the local authorities have no alternative but to harden their hearts and to punish their own people. But such measures can be implemented only on a temporary basis as they will not resolve future problems. Furthermore, local officials must wrestle with their own consciences when they torture captured rioters according to the strict orders of their superiors. The treaty may allow the missionaries to preach their religion to our people, but the hostility between the missionaries and our own people can never be resolved.

In the fourth year of the Tongzhi Emperor [1865], a French bishop discussed at length with Wen Nei, then assistant magistrate of Sichuan Province, a plan to set up a special office to deal with the missionary problems and to draft a list of regulations to prevent future misunderstandings. This plan has since been forward to the International Office by the general of Chengdu. The Catholic hierarchy appears to be genuinely concerned about the hostility between our people and their missionaries and is anxious to prevent misunderstandings in the future. Since the recent eruption of the missionary incidents, two bishops, under the advice of the tax commissioners in both Shanghai and Tianjin, are preparing to divide China into six regions, each of which will be under the control of a bishop. If there's a problem in the future, the local authority can have direct access through the right channels. Now, the French are in the habit of sending in their gunboats whenever a missionary incident erupts. By removing the French from the Catholic church and dealing directly with the Pope, it will be a much easier task for all concerned.

Our office has forwarded this plan by letter to the International Office in China. If this plan can be implemented, it will keep future missionary cases under a certain measure of control. However, the Pope controls Catholic churches only: the Protestant faith, which Britain, Germany and America follow, will not be included.

13TH OF THE ELEVENTH MONTH

A telegram from Rangoon stated that trouble is brewing in the Chinese-controlled territory. The British have erected an army camp along the Nanbang River, and the natives there are alarmed. A letter requesting the removal of the camp has been sent to the British officials, who steadfastly claim that they were following the order of the viceroy of India and cannot tear down the camp without his permission. They also contend that they have the consent of the Chinese government to build the camp to protect the local Chinese merchants.

16TH OF THE ELEVENTH MONTH

The Wuhu missionary case was finally resolved through negotiations between the Shanghai prefect and the French consul general. The earlier demands of the French priests for the piece of property have been eliminated, but more money was added to the original compensation. On the 18th of the Ninth month, a formal agreement was duly signed.

17TH OF THE ELEVENTH MONTH

A missionary in Nanking by the name of Wilson, his two friends and two Chinese companions went down to Ningbo with the intention of distributing church brochures there. As they walked past Butterfly Gorge, they noticed that natives who had been digging a pool eight feet underground had discovered a gravestone with an inscription in ancient script. Wilson took several pictures of the headstone with his camera and had them printed after they returned home. A Nanking scholar deciphered the ancient characters, which identified the site as the tomb of the king of Yue, one of the feudal states of the Zhou dynasty [c. 1100–249 B.C.].

A date was designated by His Majesty the Emperor for an audience with the three ambassadors of Austria, France and Russia at Chengguang Hall. The ambassadors of both France and Russia had earlier requested to be presented at the Great Hall. On the day of the presentation, the French ambassador excused himself by claiming to be sick. The Russian ambassador belligerently challenged that an audience at the smaller hall degraded the status of his country and thereby submitted his credentials only. The presentation was thus canceled at the last minute.

According to a French newspaper, French ambassador Lemy was presented to the Chinese emperor at the Resting Hall on the 15th of the Ninth month. The Resting Hall is not usually a place to receive tribute from envoys, and this should therefore be considered an honor extended to a foreign nation.

The secret societies are in the habit of naming their organizations with the names of famous mountains or rivers. When a new member joins the society, he is given a piece of cloth and a ticket that supposedly provides protection to the holder during his travels. He is also given the assurance that his family will be well protected if there is a riot nearby. Thus the ignorant masses are enticed into the fold of the secret society and become pawns in their criminal activities.

The recent decree of the emperor stated clearly that all local authorities must be on constant alert and should conduct a detailed investigation if such a need arises. If they have the opportunity to locate the leaders of a secret society, they should hand out severe punishment after the arrest of the criminal. If a man mistakenly brings home secret society tickets, he should not be punished as long as he turns in these tickets immediately to the local authorities. If a former member of a secret society willingly supplies the local authorities with a list of secret society members, he should be pardoned and allowed to start his life anew.

18TH OF THE ELEVENTH MONTH

Imperial Commissioner Li informed me by letter that according to the translation of the new map, the territory occupied by the tribes in Pamir is neither within the border of China nor inside the border of Russia.

20TH OF THE ELEVENTH MONTH

News from China indicated that the audience for the Austria ambassador was scheduled on the 25th of the Ninth month at the Western Garden, which is located inside of Chengguang Hall. This place, which has never been used to receive even our own ministers, represented a compromise between the ambassadors and the Imperial Court. At nine o'clock in the morning, the Austrian ambassador entered the three doors of the Western Garden before being received by the officials from the International Office. Then the ambassador was ushered through the glass door and stayed for twenty minutes in the antechamber. His Majesty the Emperor arrived and sat on the throne before the ambassador was brought in with his interpreter. They came through the Zhaojing Gate at the east of the hall bowing as they made their entrance. They bowed again as they reached the dragon pillars. Then they stopped and stood there and read their credentials aloud in their own language. The ambassador then walked alone toward the steps beneath the throne with his credentials in hand. Prince Qing [Yonglin] came down from the left side of the throne and accepted them for the emperor. He placed the document on the table with the yellow silk tablecloth. The ambassador made another bow and His Majesty the Emperor answered with a nod. The ambassador then retreated to the place between the pillars and stood there. His Majesty began to speak and express his appreciation. After another bow the ambassador retreated with his interpreter.

21ST OF THE ELEVENTH MONTH

Several leaders of a secret society were arrested along the coast of Anhui Province and were subsequently put to death.

25TH OF THE ELEVENTH MONTH

"Turkey" is similar to the sound of "Tujue," the name of an ancient nomadic tribe in the north of China. According to an European archeological dig in Turkey, a stone slab bearing both Chinese characters of the Tang dynasty [618–907 A.D.] and a foreign language alongside the Chinese was discovered. After examining the *Tang History*, I discovered that these foreign characters appear to be the language of the ancient Tujue tribe. It is recorded that the ancient tribe arose during the Former Han dynasty [206 B.C.–A.D. 8]. The tribe might have thereafter evolved into a powerful kingdom and developed their own written language by the time of the Tang dynasty.

29TH OF THE ELEVENTH MONTH

Russia's "Siberia" is a direct phonetic transliteration of the ancient tribe Xianbei, which was once located in northern China during the Han dynasty [206 B.C.–A.D. 220]. A powerful nation, the Xianbei exerted considerable strength and remained a potential enemy to China for several centuries before its downfall in the Tang dynasty [618–907]. Consequently, the tribe slowly moved to the northern frontier and was never heard from again.

Later, under the constant threat of the Mongols, the tribe migrated into the wilderness of Siberia and survived. During the Ming dynasty [1368–1644], the Russians chased all the Mongols out of their country, moved eastward and took over the territory of the Xianbei tribe. There is today in Siberia the remains of a city wall built by the ancient Xianbei tribe.

2ND OF THE TWELFTH MONTH

Today is New Year's Day according to the Western calendar. All the ambassadors congregated at the palace of France and offered greetings to the French president. We stood in line and watched the entry of the president, closely followed by the ministers of his cabinet. Each of the ministers acknowledged our presence with a nod. The president stood in the midst of the group, and the Vatican ambassador acted as our representative and read aloud the New Year's greetings.

The president answered with his own speech. He then walked toward us, shook our hands and exchanged a few words with us. Subsequently, there were rounds of hand shaking among the ministers and the ambassadors. Afterwards, all the ambassadors nodded their heads to the president and left.

19TH OF THE TWELFTH MONTH

A wedding date has been set for the grandson of the British queen for the 26th of January. Since the prince is in direct line to the throne, all nations intend to sent their first-ranking ambassador to attend the wedding ceremony. Consequently, I cabled the International Office with the news. On the 12th of this month I received an answer, which instructed me to go to the British Foreign Office and to offer congratulations to the prince. I was further instructed to represent China at the wedding.

Later, the prince died unexpectedly. Again, I sent a telegram home to the International Office. The answer came on the 18th of this month and instructed me to offer condolences at the British Foreign Office.

24TH OF THE TWELFTH MONTH

Margary wrote to me regarding the recent telegram from the International Office about the border dispute between Yunnan Province and Burma. He had gone to the British Foreign Office himself and made further inquiry. He also expressed our desire to know whether the Foreign Office had cabled the viceroy of India asking him to restrict further aggression. The British Foreign Office replied that the British soldiers have never entered Chinese territory, and since the International Office of China did not give the exact location where the British soldiers are stationed, the Ministry of Indian Affairs has been unable to send out the telegram as requested.

Part III

Eighteenth Year of the Guangxu Emperor (1892)

1ST OF THE FIRST MONTH

It was a beautiful day in Paris. I took a carriage ride through the great forest and spent several hours sightseeing.

6TH OF THE FIRST MONTH

Wang, captain of Yunnan garrison, informed me by letter that since Britain's occupation of Burma, our defense line between Tengyue and Longling along the southwestern Yunnan frontier is no longer feasible. Historically speaking, Xinjie, in Burma, was once the territory of the Manmu tribe, and during the reign of the Qianlong Emperor [1736–96], a governor's seal, which is still preserved in a strongbox at Tengyue, was awarded to their former chief. There are nine routes that can be taken from Tengyue to Burma. Each of these routes must pass through Xinjie.

The former ambassador to Britain, Marquis Zeng, had lodged a protest at the British Foreign Office during his term of office demanding the return of Xinjie. In my opinion, it's an excellent idea; however, I doubt if Britain will ever return the territory, which is located at a strategic position on the upper stream of the River of Golden Sand [Jinsha Jiang]. At present there is a British garrison stationed at the western pass into the Yeren Mountains. The excuse the British Foreign Office gave us is that it's their duty to protect the caravans of their merchants.[34]

Several discussions have been held at the International Office, which has concluded that there's no sure way to defend the mountain. However, if we could get Bhamo back, we might be able to use the city as the defense line. As far as the Salween River is concerned, we still control the river valley by the stream in the east, but the stream in the south, where both Tengyue and Longling are located, has been lost to Britain. Lately, British officials were seen at the southern river valley surveying the area.

11TH OF THE FIRST MONTH

According to the theory of Buddhism, the earth is composed of four basic elements: earth, water, wind and fire. By contrast, Western scholars believe the four basic elements to be earth, water, air and fire. Wind is equivalent to air, however, so the basic principles of the East and the West are similar. However, Hong Fan, an ancient Chinese scholar, claimed that there were five elements instead of the four by listing metal and wood in place of wind.

---

34. The Yeren, or Barbarian, Mountains lie in the area along the Burma-Yunnan border, which the Chinese consider their Tengchong (formerly Tengyue) Prefecture. Some cartographers, however, still describe this region as a "disputed area."

But metal and wood are both elements that originate in earth, and therefore do not belong with the categories of earth, water and fire. In my view, Hong Fan's theory is based on the daily needs of human beings. It's a practical theory, although it should not be regarded as a substantive theory of the basic elements of the universe.

14TH OF THE FIRST MONTH

The Ultimate Truth sect, a new religious cult in China, initially became popular in the region of Manchuria. The congregation is usually led by one leader, who calls the annual meetings. The major rule of the cult is abstinence from drinking, smoking and bright-colored clothing. Participants are advised to keep their beliefs discreet. It's a known fact that a husband of this sect will not reveal his faith to his own wife and a father will not disclose his belief to his own son.

The White Lotus sect, once the most popular cult in China, is once again being revived. This cult was notorious for inciting the Hongru uprising at the end of the Ming dynasty [1368–1644] and more recently, during the present dynasty, the Sichuan Religious Bandits' Rebellion.

Other less well-known sects are the Rice Ball sect, the Fresh Fruit sect and the Great Quilt sect. Before the day of scripture recitation the congregation of the Rice Ball sect gathers together and prepares a giant rice ball. During the breaks in their recitation they share a meal by biting into the rice ball. The minister of the Fresh Fruit sect takes up a collection throughout the village before the scripture recitation day to purchase a large amount of fruit, because the congregation is not allowed to eat cooked food during that period. The meeting generally lasts until evening, and the congregation munches fruit during the break. The leader of the Great Quilt cult tours each village twice a year seeking contributions to sew a great quilt. Subsequently, he gathers his congregation in one large room and begins quilt making. The quilt is eventually as long as the room. When the quilt is finished, the date for the recitation of the Amituofo Prayer[35] is set, when the congregation lies under the giant quilt and recites the Amituofo Prayer repeatedly throughout the night. The leader of this sect claims that he is merely teaching his followers to observe the major rules of vegetarianism, but in fact the sect also offers confessional services and horoscope readings, although they tend to keep these activities discreet.

---

35. The Amituofo (or Amida/Amitabha) Prayer is the central practice of the Pure Land or Amidist sect of Buddhism. The promise of Amidism offers ordinary men and women access to rebirth in the Pure Land (or Western Paradise); a believer is required to have faith in the Buddha Amituofo, expressed by invoking the Buddha's name (Amituofo) as prayer.

At first, only the peasants were followers, and they invited the leaders into their homes to conduct confessional services during funerals and prayer services when there was illness in the family. But as these sects increase in popularity, its members are beginning to accuse the Buddhist monks and Taoist priests of being negligent in their performance of these services and are making attempts to take over. Now, some sects have even won over the gentry. In this way the Great Quilt sect has spread its faith into every corner.

15TH OF THE FIRST MONTH

The International Office informed me by letter that the Ultimate Truth sect of both Jehol and Chaoyang has gained an overwhelming following in Beijing, Tianjin and Yingkou. They have established a new home base at Tianjin. The major rule of the cult is abstinence from opium and liquor; moreover, followers receive a tea jelly that is claimed to cure addictions to either substance in seven days if one smokes it. The annual sale of the tea jelly is at a record high. Additional drugs are known to be added to the tea jelly, along with morning dew, which they claim can enhance the potency of the medication. The manufacturing process was initially being done in the prairies of Mongolia. However, a growing hostility began to develop between the cult members and their Mongolian landlords when the cult failed to meet their rental payments.

Also in the Mongolian frontier was a Catholic church at Thirty Clans in Jianzhou. The Chinese Catholic priest, Lin Daoyuan, was well known for his arrogance. Since the arrival of the new religion, the two congregations have been feuding constantly and were at each other's throats for some time. Then came a year of poor harvests, which brought forth bands of horse thieves. The cult members, repeatedly intimidated by both the Mongols and the Catholic converts and goaded on by their own leaders, finally started a riot. During the turmoil the Mongolian Prince Aohan was killed and his mansion burned to the ground. The Catholic church was also destroyed and Lin Daoyuan was mutilated and decapitated. Hundreds of Catholic families were killed in separate incidents and their homes were torched. In Pingquanzhou, a priest from another Catholic church escaped early in the day and thus survived. Several other Catholic churches inside the walled city, fearful of subsequent reprisals, cabled the Office of the Northern Ports for protection.

16TH OF THE FIRST MONTH

Someone has suggested that with China's rich resources, more schools are needed to train students to strengthen China as a nation. Then we will be able to retrieve the profits that foreign merchants have taken from our country. It is an excellent idea; otherwise, we will never be able to halt this steady flow of aggression.

17TH OF THE FIRST MONTH

Throughout the centuries in China, we have believed that the heart controls both human intelligence and memory. During the reign of the Qianlong Emperor [1736–1796], Minister Qi, who had possessed an excellent memory, could not function as a normal person after he sustained a brain injury. This is solid evidence that the brain controls memory.

In the medical books of the West, it clearly states that the importance of the brain is to generate the functions of both human intelligence and memory. Therefore, whenever I encounter a Western scholar, I seek additional evidence.

They claim that the intelligence of a creature depends on the size of its brain. Therefore, even though a bull is larger than a monkey, the monkey is smarter than the bull because the monkey has a larger brain. They further believe that brain death is the total annihilation of a human life.

Therefore, the concept of deity and spirit in China and the belief of the soul in the West are both totally groundless. I inquired further as to whether there is any truth behind the concept of heaven and hell as described by Jesus Christ. They were left speechless.

18TH OF THE FIRST MONTH

A telegram issued by the International Office arrived here yesterday:

> Based on the direct report of the Kanjuti chief, the governor of Xinjiang Territory informed us that Britain had invaded his territory last month and that battles are still raging throughout the area. The conflict apparently rose from road construction that the British initiated in the Kanjuti territory.
>
> A second telegram from Xinjiang reported another conflict between the British soldiers and the Nage'er tribesmen. The Kanjuti tribe, which consists of 500 people, including women and children, has since taken refuge at Tadunbashika.
>
> According to your telegram of last year, the British Foreign Office claimed that their soldiers were merely mounting a cannon within the territory of Kanjuti and assured us that they had not the slightest intention of invading the territory of the tribe. Please make contact again with their Foreign Office and find out the reason behind this sudden clash. We are urgently waiting for your reply.

For some time now I have been contemplating a visit to the British Foreign Office regarding the following two critical issues: the British invasion of the Burmese frontier and the arms-smuggling case of the Englishman, Mason. After receiving today's telegram, I felt the urgency of settling these two pressing problems with Britain. This morning I left Paris with my interpreter and military attaché and sailed for London. It was a stormy day. While crossing the Channel I vomited and felt extremely exhausted after the ordeal. Both Paris and London received some snow today, and the epidemic wave should soon be tapering off.

19TH OF THE FIRST MONTH

In the afternoon, I went to the British Foreign Office with Margary and had a meeting with Lord Salisbury, who serves as both prime minister and foreign minister. Also present were his assistant Sandison and the deputy minister of Indian affairs.

During the meeting, Lord Salisbury stated that the British government has no intention of infringing on China's rights concerning the territory of the Kanjuti tribe, but it must built new roads to defend against Russian invasions. He further stressed that it was wrong for the Kanjuti chief to interfere with British road construction. I continued the discussion with Salisbury and tried every means to convince him that it's wrong for the British soldiers to built roads in Kanjuti tribe territory without the chief's permission.

Finally, Lord Salisbury confided in me that the viceroy of India is in the process of replacing the chief of Kanjuti with the chief's own son, but the success or failure of the attempt has not yet been established. He promised me that he would cable the viceroy of India on my behalf before he gave me an answer.

The negotiation then came to the issue of the Burma-Yunnan border dispute. Lord Salisbury contended that as soon as the change in administration is completed in the British government in the fall, he would be glad to continue the discussion with me about the proper dividing line. I stressed that the wandering British soldiers at the Yunnan border is the prime concern of the natives and that a full-scale war might flare up before the boundary is clearly drawn. Lord Salisbury gave me his word that he would cable the British administrator in Burma to take extraordinary care in order to avoid such a conflict.

As for the case of Mason, Sandison said that he was unable to add additional penalties and made no attempt to pursue the case any further. Therefore, I decided to wait for the outcome of the report on that case before raising any further complaints. I consequently cabled a report on the negotiation of the Kanjuti case to the International Office in China.

20TH OF THE FIRST MONTH

Xinjiang shares a border with Russia and with the lands of several Muslim tribes. However, only the Kanjuti tribe sent an annual tribute of gold to China. The tribute consists of two taels of gold; China gives the chief two bolts of silk after the completion of his mission.

In the fourteenth year of the Guangxu Emperor [1888], the chief of the Kanjuti tribe reported that his neighboring tribe, which is under the protection of Britain, entered his territory and attempted to take over his caravan route. However, the British ambassador has told a different version, which was recorded in an earlier entry in this journal.

In the seventeenth year of the Guangxu Emperor [1891], the governor of Xinjiang reported in a letter that Britain had moved the garrison closer to the Kanjuti tribe, within a distance of forty miles. They brought in the cannon and made preparations to repair an old fortress.

In my opinion, the British are apparently preparing to open a southwestern route through Xinjiang in order to divide Russia's power. It's also possible that they may annex Kanjuti along the way.

21ST OF THE FIRST MONTH

The Westerners believe that the earth is but a star, a conclusion that they reached after several thousand years of research and calculation by their brightest scholars. This is a total contradiction to ancient Chinese beliefs. I am not sure, however, whether this theory is true or false. Shakyamuni Buddha, during a congregation with his disciples, has stated that during the brief time of his sermon, infinite numbers of worlds are created or destroyed. What Buddha referred to as the world is invariably the earth system.

22ND OF THE FIRST MONTH

The name of Kanjuti has been recorded in three separate books over the years but with different names (according to the phonetic sounds of each foreign language). The tribe is of Muslim faith and consists of 8,000 men.

24TH OF THE FIRST MONTH

In the north of Burma, the Yeren Mountains run to the east of the Irrawaddy River and border Yunnan Province. If Britain and China can reach an agreement by dividing the mountains into equal shares, it would be an excellent idea. However, if the Irrawaddy River is used as the natural boundary, China will lose 200 miles from north to south and 70 miles from east to west. Furthermore, the origin of the river is hard to determine, and the river frequently changes its course.

A telegram of the 22nd of this month from the International Office stated:

> The governor of Xinjiang cabled this office regarding the recent British invasion of both the Kanjuti and the Nage'er tribes. The two tribes have combined their forces in an attempt to drive the British troops off their land after both tribes were ordered by the British to work on the road construction. But the tribes were soon defeated by the British forces, which subsequently took over their territory. The chief of Kanjuti was taken prisoner by the British when he was on his way to seek help from the Russians.
>
> In our opinion, the Kanjuti tribe has been paying tribute to China for centuries, and we should provide them with protection. Even though the chief was in the wrong, the British should at least have contacted us before launching an attack on the tribe and removing the chief. Last year, for example, Russian soldiers were seen in Pamir. This office cabled our ambassador in Russia and lodged a protest at the Russian Foreign Office. Russia immediately responded by withdrawing her troops from the Chinese border and ordered the governor of their border province to restrain her troop's activities within her own territory. Now the British have taken over the territory of the Kanjuti tribe and are presently well on their way to Pamir. The Russians may not keep their silence very long and may soon demand their share of the territory.
>
> We hope Your Excellency will immediately lodge a strong protest at the British Foreign Office to inform them that if Britain takes over the land of the Kanjuti tribe, Russia will invariably occupy Pamir. We cannot even find the appropriate words with which to protest. Do advise them to cable the viceroy of India and instruct him to withdraw his troops before Russia lodges a protest.

I went to see Lord Salisbury at the British Foreign Office this afternoon and negotiated with him for several hours. As soon as I returned to the embassy, I immediately sent a cable to the International Office:

> It appears that the British Foreign Office is under the impression that China has given up the undertaking of Pamir and that they are merely offering a helping hand. When I assured them that we'll be posting signs at the border, repairing the cannon and dispatching border patrols, they were visibly satisfied. However, they cannot give us a definite answer until they cable the viceroy of India and receive an answer from him. Furthermore, they claimed that we receive merely a small amount of annual tribute from the Kanjuti tribe, and therefore we don't have the right to exercise controlling power over the tribe's territory. In short, they implied that the Kanjuti tribe is legally not our protectorate. I firmly protested such claims and they kept silent.

25TH OF THE FIRST MONTH

Pamir, located in Central Asia at a height of 13,000 feet, is the highest plateau in the whole world. It extends eastward to the Tienshan and southward to both the Himalayas and Nyenchen Tanglha. The average height of the mountain passes in this area ranges from 4,000 to 5,000 feet, and the highest peak reaches 25,000 feet above sea level. Scattered under these passes are the several valleys that make up the area known as Pamir. At the western foothills of the western mountain slope stands the desert of Turkestan [the Kyzyl Kum]. The weather there is extreme; in the summer there are frequent hailstorms and in the winter, heavy snowfalls. Close to the desert is Kohat, the well-known sheep trading center where herders congregate every summer. An abundance of different species of birds and animals, including water buffalo, roam freely in the desert. Several rivers flow across the area, the two largest of which are Jhelum, with a length of 120 miles, and Ravi, with a length of 100 miles.

26TH OF THE FIRST MONTH

I considered the ancient Chinese theory of the nine levels of heaven and came to the conclusion that heaven may not be limited to even billions of levels. This idea may sound absurd, but in the ancient classic *The Doctrine of the Mean* [*Zhongyong*], such an idea was suggested long before my time. The book explores the thickness of the earth, the height of the mountains and the flexibility of the water. However, it draws no conclusions about heaven but reflects in the following words: "This abundance of brilliance reaches to infinity. The sun, the moon and the stars depend upon such brilliance for their own survival, and all living things on earth take cover under heaven for protection." Heaven is therefore boundless, and my theory is but a footnote to infinity.

In an earlier entry, I recorded that the stars in the vast space of the cosmos rise and fall at will without any obstacles and that they have not crashed into each other since the beginning of time. This statement may serve as a footnote to another quotation in the *Doctrine*: "There is no conflict among the parallels of Tao." From these passages, one can discover the objective perceptions of the ancient sages and the deepest insight in every word and sentence of their lectures. Such messages undoubtedly should be spread to every corner of the world.

I read the *Doctrine* further to the chapter "Good will prevails in China." It states as follows: "Wherever ships and carriages can embark, human beings can exist, heaven can shield, earth can bear, sun and moon can shine upon, snow and dew can accumulate; all beings of flesh and blood tend to lose their hearts to their loved ones. This is the Tao of heaven."

I am totally convinced that the sages of future generations will one day take control of the five continents on this earth. Moreover, I have no doubt that Confucianism will inherit the earth, because the principle of its doctrine is mutual love.

I have been abroad for two years now and have found new meaning in "Zi Zhang Inquires about Proper Behavior," a chapter in the Confucian *Analects* [*Lunyu*]: "'Loyalty, trust, sincerity and respect can be found even among the barbarians.' This is truly the basic principle of the tangible, indestructible Tao. Alas! the words of sages are invariably prophetic."

Pamir is situated between China's Kashgar and Russia's Turkestan. With a plateau in the east and mountainous terrain in the west, it extends from 36.45 degrees to 39.45 degrees north of the Tropic of Cancer.

There are 20,000 households in the 70,000 square miles in the eastern part of Pamir and 50,000 households in the 80,000 square miles in the west. In the north, there are several small tribes where the Lesser Pamir stands. As early as the period of the Tang dynasty [618–907], when the Buddhist master Xuanzang crossed Pamir on his journey to India, history has recorded the existence of tribes such as the Rushan, the Khorog, the Kashgar and the Bakanas. These independent tribes were enveloped by the three large nations of Afghanistan, China and Russia. Afghanistan took control of the Rushan and Khorog tribes, China of the Kashgar tribe and Russia of the Bakanas tribe. With the exception of Mount Ala and the highest plateau, which are presently occupied by Russia, China has territorial rights to the rest of Pamir.

27TH OF THE FIRST MONTH

Someone jokingly asked my opinion of future travel to the moon based on the Western theory that the moon is the planet nearest to the earth. It appears to me that the recent rapid advance of Western technology depended totally on the natural power of water, fire, wind and electricity, yet amid the vast void of the universe, there is no such power available. The only power that exists in space is the light emitted from the sun and the stars, which may prove to be too weak for the practical application of such technology.

Furthermore, a Westerner once devised a way to be lifted up in a hot-air balloon. However, when the balloon reached a height of forty-four miles above the earth, the man started to bleed through his nose and passed out. This proves that human beings cannot survive one second without air, and the fact is that there is no air in space. Even though the distance from the earth to the moon is comparatively small, there are still about 609,000 miles [*sic*] between the two planets. How can we human beings survive this long distance to reach the moon? Therefore, although it's possible that we may locate a giant planet above earth in the future, I am not sure that we will be able to trade with people on the moon.

5TH OF THE SECOND MONTH

As far as one can trace back into the history of China, there were fourteen legendary sages in addition to the seventeen historical heroes who may be considered near sagehood. In the West, however, the most prevalent religion is Christianity, and Jesus is revered as the one and only sage. Before the birth of Christ, there was the religion of Buddhism, which remains popular in Asia. After the death of Christ, there rose the Muslim religion, which commands followers on Africa, Asia and Europe. As far as territory is concerned, Christianity must be regarded as the most popular religion in the world, Islam the second and Buddhism the third. However, each of the founders of the three major religions was born on the continent of Asia. It appears to me that the Europeans may possess impressive physical strength, but they lack extensive spiritual power.

6TH OF THE SECOND MONTH

On the third day of this month I received a telegram from the International Office. It stressed that the chief of the Kanjuti tribe should be pardoned as abduction is certainly not the proper punishment for his past misconduct. If it becomes necessary to establish his son as the chief, Britain should call a meeting with a Chinese representative of Xinjiang to reach a decision. I immediately instructed Margary to relay this message to the British Foreign Office. After hearing the request, the British Foreign Office flatly refused any further negotiations. They claimed that during the fourteenth year of the Guangxu Emperor [1888], the British ambassador clearly settled the Kanjuti affair at the International Office, who accepted the change. They further contended that in the past, China has never interfered with the internal affairs of the Kanjuti tribe, so this sudden change of policy will cause unnecessary problems.

Later, I heard from other private sources that the viceroy of India is perfectly willing to withdraw his troops from Kanjuti territory if the chief will allow his son to take over his position. Since I received no further notice from the British Foreign Office, I decided to make a direct inquiry to resolve this problem. They issued a vague statement saying that they were unable to give us a final decision until further negotiations had taken place. They are evidently being evasive, so today I went to the British Foreign Office to resolve this difficult issue with Lord Salisbury personally. When I asked about the cable expected from the viceroy of India, the Marquis pretended at first that he had not heard any news from India. Consequently, I sat in his office for five hours repeatedly discussing and explaining this affair, and he finally relented. He promised me that he will cable the viceroy of India and stressed that during the ceremony marking the change of power in the Kanjuti tribe, a Chinese representative will be present among the British officials.

7TH OF THE SECOND MONTH

Yuan Shuangqiu stated in his letter that the Russian ambassador had recently notified the Imperial Court that he would like to present his credentials in the Ceremonial Hall of the palace, following the example set by the first Russian ambassador to enter China, during the fifth year of the Yongzheng Emperor [1727]. Ambassador Lemy of France had also made such a request at an earlier date when he was to be presented to the emperor at Chengguang Hall. A letter of regret was sent by the French ambassador at the last minute to excuse him from the presentation on account of his sudden illness. Consequently, the Russian ambassador followed suit. We have written to our ambassador in Russia and instructed him to make an inquiry at the Russian Foreign Office.

8TH OF THE SECOND MONTH

I left the Chinese embassy in London for Dover at 11:00 this morning by motorcar with my interpreter and a military attaché. It was a beautiful day, and we had a peaceful voyage. We reached Calais at 2:00 and arrived at the Chinese embassy in Paris by motorcar at 7:30 in the evening.

9TH OF THE SECOND MONTH

I cabled the International Office regarding the Kanjuti affair as follows:

After several rounds of negotiations with the officials of the British Foreign Office, I discovered that they have no intention of involving us in the said affair and insist on keeping to our earlier agreement. After my persistent, strong protest they relented and promised to discuss the matter with the viceroy of India. However, they warned me that the outcome may take longer than we expect. As a precaution, any request that the British ambassador presents to the International Office in the future should be firmly rejected. Further, both the Burmese border issue and the Mason case should be forwarded to the embassy so that I can deal with them directly.

13TH OF THE SECOND MONTH

At the invitation of the French president, I attended the palace ball in the evening with three members of my staff. We watched the dancing and returned to the embassy by midnight.

15TH OF THE SECOND MONTH

During the reign of the Daoguang Emperor [1821–1851], peasants in China heard that it was easy to make money in Cuba. One after another, they began to sail to that country. By the twelfth year of the Tongzhi Emperor [1873], it was estimated that there were 143,000 Chinese immigrants in Cuba. However, in the sixth year of the Guangxu Emperor [1880], the Cubans suddenly tightened their control over Chinese immigration. Chinese immigrants began to suffer under the extreme cruelty of Cuban officials and forwarded this information home, which had the effect of halting the flow of immigrants from China to Cuba. Although the Cuban penal system for Chinese immigrants has relaxed somewhat in recent years, there are still only 40,000 Chinese immigrants left on the island. One out of a hundred Chinese in Cuba may succeed in becoming a merchant, but the rest remain indentured servants.

17TH OF THE SECOND MONTH

I have earlier recorded in this diary the difference between Chinese and Western custom with regard to addressing a person by his or her given name and family name. Now I discover still more differences between these two cultures. According to the Chinese custom, if we address a person by his or her given name, this is disrespectful. By contrast, by Western custom, we pay a person respect by addressing him or her by the given name. The common people tend to be called by their family names, and their given names remain unknown to others. It appears that only titled persons are allowed to be addressed by their given names together with their family names. The most respected people in society tend to be addressed by given name only. For example, the present queen of England is addressed as Queen Victoria. Perhaps this is not a nickname Her Majesty received during childhood; it may be a name between a given name and a nickname.

Their custom of calling their offspring or their birds and animals by their own given name is a sincere expression of their affection and respect for their loved ones. Hence, if a Westerner names his or her child with his or her own name, the child will be regarded as a cherished son or daughter. The English people even give their yacht or carriage, dog or horse, factory or store and mountain or river their own given names. The law of the land makes no attempt to stop these actions, which are regarded as an expression of affection and respect for those objects about which they care deeply. This is an obvious difference from the etiquette handed down through the centuries by the people of the Zhou dynasty [c. 1100–249 B.C.], who firmly believed that one must avoid addressing one's elders or superiors by their given names. Even though Western customs seem closer to those of the people of the Shang dynasty [c. 1600–1100 B.C.], who tended to honor the principles of human character, this practice nevertheless appears to me a trifle outrageous.

19TH OF THE SECOND MONTH

The Writing Preservation Society [Xizihui] in China was organized by a group of scholars many centuries ago. Its purpose is to display reverence to the ancient sages who developed the written language and so to restrict people from tainting or mutilating books and papers with written words. Over the years the society has fostered the belief that one who dares to violate such prohibitions will be duly punished on earth and by the deities in heaven. There is no such tradition in Europe. I have seen people reading the newspaper in a carriage, and they discard the pages as soon as they finish reading them, allowing them to fall into the gutter. They wipe utensils with newspaper and even use it as toilet paper. Yet they are not afraid that God will punish them for their sin.

4TH OF THE THIRD MONTH

This afternoon I visited the House of Commons in the French Parliament and sat in the balcony, where seating has been provided for the ambassadors of various countries. It was a short session as few bills were introduced today. A man of fifty sitting at the left was pointed out to me as the famous orator Clemenceau, who successfully unseated the former president of France during the period of the Sino-French War [1883–1885]. He is a firm believer in peaceful negotiation and has in the past overridden the power of seven presidents for his cause. However, today he remained silent.

5TH OF THE THIRD MONTH

I went touring around the hills east and west of Paris with my aides. It was an hour's drive from the embassy by motorcar.

6TH OF THE THIRD MONTH

I went on a tour of the Eiffel Tower with my aide and paid two francs for each floor we visited. We rode to the top floor by elevator and took in a full view of the whole city.

8TH OF THE THIRD MONTH

A banquet was prepared at the embassy for the secretary of the French Foreign Office and included all those serving at various departments under him. Also among the guest list were several former officials who had been previously stationed in China. However, the only guest who was regretfully absent during the gathering happened to be the guest of honor, the secretary of the French Foreign Office.

9TH OF THE THIRD MONTH

The Hulu kingdom of the Kawa people is located in the southeast of Yongchang Prefecture in Yunnan Province. China maintained no direct contact with this small kingdom throughout the centuries until the early reign of the Qianlong Emperor [1736–1796]. At that time a Chinese merchant, Wu Shangxian, persuaded Bangzhu, the tribal chief, to go into business with him by building a silver mine known as Maolong. It was a successful operation and the volume of production expanded to several hundred thousand. In the vicinity, another silver mine at Polong was occupied by Gong Liyan, a descendant of Prince Gui of the former Ming dynasty. With their steady silver production both mines soon became a real threat to Burma.

The Chinese merchant then advised the tribal chief of Hulu to travel to the capital of China on a tributary mission and to ask for the title of "King of Hulu" from the Chinese emperor. Unfortunately, the chief failed in his mission and left in distress. While crossing the border of Yunnan Province, he was arrested by the local authorities and later died of starvation in jail. Consequently, all his employees were let go and the mine left deserted.

Meanwhile, Burma's military force had broken into the Polong mine, brought Gong Liyan to Yongchang Prefecture and had him killed. Later, the chief of the nearby tribe Mu also surrendered to the Burmese military. After successfully eliminating these two tribes, Burma began to conquer all the tribes between China and Burma along the Yunnan border, thus posing a direct threat to China.

22ND OF THE THIRD MONTH

Russia recently built a shipyard at Hunchun in addition to several new fortifications. Repair work has also been done along both harbors. Battleships have been seen patrolling the ocean with several gunboats following behind; the defense lines are clearly being drawn. Inside the city the construction of the railway is also being stepped up.

Russian battleships may be divided into three levels. They have a total of thirty-six first-rate battleships. Twenty-eight have been dispatched to guard the Baltic Sea and eight have gone to the Black Sea. The total number of their second-rate battleships is forty-eight. Thirty-eight of these went to the Baltic Sea and ten to the Black Sea. The total number of their third-rate battleships is eighty-eight. Forty-nine have been sent to the Baltic Sea and twenty-nine to the Black Sea. Of the remaining ships, seven are in the Caspian Sea and five [*sic*] are at Hunchun.

24TH OF THE THIRD MONTH

With my family and staff I boarded the train in Paris in the morning. We reached Dover at 5:40 in the afternoon. Then we traveled to London by motorcar and arrived at the embassy by carriage at 9:00 in the evening.

28TH OF THE THIRD MONTH

The systems of government of all the nations on the five continents of this earth are either monarchies or democracies. In a democratic country, government policy tends to follow public opinion for the benefit of the nation, a result that varies with the feelings of people. The leader of such a state is not allowed to abuse the people with absolute power or to gratify his or her own personal desires. Since the ministers and generals of such a nation may be in power today and lose their positions tomorrow, they do not dare suppress the people. This system coincides with the philosophy of Mencius,[36] who advocated the importance of the people and firmly believed that the people should override the power of their kings. However, there are certain obvious disadvantages to this system, such as the conflicts between opposing parties, which at times infringes on the welfare of the state. The leaders, uncertain of their sustaining power, are unwilling to take on heavy responsibilities. Thus, without the leadership of a central power, the will of the people alone may lead the nation into chaos.

---

36. The sage of the Warring States Period (the latter part of the Zhou dynasty [453–221 B.C.]), Mencius is the primary successor to Confucius. (Trans.)

In a monarchy, the sovereign has absolute power and can establish the best policies in accordance with national interest. Such a state will eventually prosper with a wise king. The disadvantage of this system, however, lies with the unbalanced power between the ruler and the people. Some of these states tend to enslave their people without giving them security and happiness. Russia is a good example of such a state. Furthermore, without the general consensus of public opinion, one absolute ruler cannot control the affairs of the entire nation, which will therefore likely fall in the long run. Consequently, there are advantages and disadvantages to both systems. Which, then, should be considered the best system? My answer is: If the right person is placed in the proper position, either system will function well, and if the wrong person is given the responsibility of governing, either of these two systems will end in disaster.

30TH OF THE THIRD MONTH

Korean officials were sent to investigate and assess the strategic potential of Cheju Island, which has a narrow strait that channels into a harbor wide enough to accommodate twenty battleships. Furthermore, it is along the route that the Russians must use to send their fleets from south to north.

1ST OF THE FOURTH MONTH

Before the time of the legendary Yao [21st century B.C.][37] a democratic system was prevalent in China. His successor, Shun [21st century B.C.],[38] gathered a group of his followers at his homestead during the first year of his reign. A village was established in the following year, and in the third year, a city took shape under his leadership. Thus "City Lord" became Shun's title.

At that time, it was an established rule that the people had the right to elect a man of integrity as their lord, and among the lords, the most virtuous would be selected as the Son of Heaven [king]. This is the primary model of the democratic system in the early centuries of China. Many centuries later, Qin Shi Huang[39] introduced totalitarianism into China after he successfully defeated the other six states and established the first empire. The first two dynasties of Qin and Han maintained this pattern, and thus the monarchy became the one and only government system in China.

---

37. Yao was the first of the two ancient legendary sage-kings. (Trans.)

38. Shun was the second sage-king and the son-in-law of Yao. (Trans.)

39. Qin Shi Huang was the first emperor of China (221 B.C.). (Trans.)

2ND OF THE FOURTH MONTH

A Swedish engineer who is also a long-time resident of London came to pay me a visit at the embassy today. Since he was once in charge of the railroad construction between Kaiping and Shanhaiguan, I asked about the current cost of railroad construction. His answer was that it tended to differ from country to country as the costs of material, labor and land all have to be taken into consideration. Since labor costs in China are low, the cost of a mile of railroad track may be as low as £6,000.

4TH OF THE FOURTH MONTH

According to a new theory of an Englishman, with the steady improvement in warfare on the European continent, Britain may soon have no problem controlling her colonies. He suggested another good idea: to build a railroad through Canada as a rapid transit to the East.

5TH OF THE FOURTH MONTH

For years, the French have repeatedly made devious plans to occupy Cambodia. Now they have succeeded in driving the crown prince of Cambodia out of his own country to Siam and have subsequently taken over Cambodia. The Cambodian people are outraged by such a flagrant invasion of their country, but they are totally helpless under such superior power.

9TH OF THE FOURTH MONTH

In the afternoon I attended a garden party at St. James Palace hosted by the queen's second son.

Later that night, a telegram arrived from the International Office in China. It stated that on the plateau of Pamir, all three nations — Britain, China and Russia — should exercise a measure of restraint and not invade each other's territories. Recently, Russia proposed that all three nations should share the administrative responsibility of the area, which sounds plausible enough. Also, the governor of Yunnan Province recently conducted a survey at the Burma-China border and expects the border dispute to be resolved in the nearest future.

Another matter the cable mentioned is the French ambassador's persistent demand on behalf of French merchants for their share of profits in the construction of a railroad bridge. It subsequently stated as follows:

> Since the project is under the jurisdiction of the Office of the Northern Ports, who awarded the building contract to the French, this request should be

met. Nevertheless, according to an earlier record, during the building of the
Tangshan railroad, a contract for the building materials was awarded to the
English merchants. Understandably, building materials should be kept to a standard size, and according to the 1885 treaty, France is not allowed to monopolize
the profits on the railroad. However, Ambassador Lemy repeatedly came to this
office demanding to know the total amount of the profits. So far no agreement
has been reached. This could be the primary cause of his grievance, which subsequently triggered the "Swedish Girl Affair." Lemy contended that according
to the early treaty between China and France, France is recognized as the protector of Sweden. This office did a thorough search of all early documents and
found not a trace of evidence for his claim. He was thus rebuffed accordingly.

Later, we received a cable from Your Excellency stating that if there are no
diplomatic relations between two countries, a third friendly nation is allowed to
step in as the protector. Consequently, this office cabled Guangdong Province,
instructing the local authorities to accept French representation in this case.
Obviously, Lemy uses every opportunity to abuse his power in all international
incidents. Therefore, we wish you would find a way to inform the French
Foreign Office so that we may preserve the present good relationship between
our two countries.

10TH OF THE FOURTH MONTH

A letter from Zhang Qiaoye indicated that both the Russian and French
ambassadors have made requests to be presented to His Majesty the
Emperor at a larger ceremonial hall instead of the hall designated at an earlier date. By citing the tradition initiated during the reign of the Yongzheng
Emperor [1723–1736], the Russian ambassador proposed an audience at the
Hall of Great Peace [Taihedian], but was subsequently turned down. The
Russian ambassador then promptly submitted another proposal in writing
and was directed to be presented at Chengguang Hall. Later, when our
ambassador arrived at Russia, another place was selected for him to be presented to the czar. This is obviously a direct rebuff. Therefore, the
International Office has been consistently changing dates due to these unexpected problems.

The French ambassador, however, was ill and had forwarded his portfolio
to the International Office after he felt he was unable to keep the appointment. The International Office has since submitted another memorial so that
the date for presentation may be rescheduled. Simultaneously, a cable was
sent to Ambassador Xu in Russia instructing him to make a direct inquiry at
the Russian Foreign Office. A cable was also sent to their ambassador in
Beijing with the instruction that he should be presented when all the other
envoys of various nations are presented during the lunar New Year celebration.

Since the German ambassador has been selected as the leader of the international diplomatic corps, he arranged to take over the peacemaking role.

After studying the copy of the notice from the International Office to the Russian envoy, he concluded that, according to Western practice, a sovereign may grant an audience to a subject at any designated place, and the same procedure may apply to an audience with a foreign envoy. However, the envoy has the right to request the place where he will be presented. If the emperor insists on receiving the envoy at another place, it may appear to be a deliberate insult. We will fight for our right.

After scrutinizing the official documents in their translated version, the International Office discovered an error. The original copy states that in the future, all envoys will be received at Chengguang Hall. But in the translated version the word "future" was translated as the word "permanently." Evidently, this is the cause of this long dispute.

11TH OF THE FOURTH MONTH

According to the biographies of Yunnan native chiefs in the *Ming History,* Manmu was once a part of Tengyue that was later conceded to the Mu people. When Mangtiduan rose from Dongwu and conquered Burma, Sizhe, the native chief of Manmu, became his subject. Later, the chief surrendered to Chinese forces, but soon was under Burma's control again.

In the present regime, during the thirty-first year of the Qianlong Emperor [1766], a Chinese army under the leadership of Lieutenant General Zhao Hongbang captured Xinjie in Manmu but was later defeated. Thus began the Burma crisis.

13TH OF THE FOURTH MONTH

The arrest of secret society leader Gao Dehua last year in Anhui Province yielded a vast amount of information. It appears that there are several dozen agents scattered throughout the cities of Anhui Province. Their two largest branches are these at Shashi and Anqing. Both branches were preparing for revolt on the 15th of the Tenth month. Several agents had already been sent out to procure boats at every port for the uprising. Conceivably, they were just biding time, waiting for a shipment of guns to be brought in by the foreigner, Mason. If Mason's contraband operation had been successful, the result could have been devastating.

15TH OF THE FOURTH MONTH

At midnight, there's merely a thin crescent of moon left visible in the sky, which remains stationary for three solid hours. I recorded this phenomenon so it may be compared with the heavenly formation in China that same night.

16TH OF THE FOURTH MONTH

With Margary and several others, I attended the first party of the season at St. James Palace. This evening the third son of the queen acted as the official host for the occasion.

18TH OF THE FOURTH MONTH

Ambassador Xu to Russia wrote to me regarding the garrisons stationed at Pamir:

> The Russian Foreign Office has claimed that even though their ambassador informed them that the soldiers in Pamir had been recalled, a number of garrisons are still left in place there. They contended that where these garrisons are allowed to remain in Pamir, there will be soldiers, which cannot be regarded as a complete withdrawal. They appear to be not completely satisfied with the retreat.
>
> Initially, the International Office assumed that since Pamir is not within Chinese territory, our first priority should be to defend our own frontier, as it's not feasible to interfere in a conflict between the two powerful nations of Russia and Britain. I am not exactly clear when China began to set up the garrisons that are now stationed on over half the territory in Pamir. As far as I know, the most distant garrison is known as Samarkand and is presently stationed at Yashil Pamir by the shore of Lake Issyk, a location that the English newspapers claim can be clearly defined by a stele inscribed with Chinese characters. According to the historical record, the stele was placed there to commemorate the successful campaign of the Qianlong Emperor, whose mighty army had chased the retreating enemy troops of Russia over the said border. Later, China neglected to take care of that stretch of land, and it was assumed that China had given up that piece of territory. Consequently, Russia refuses to recognize our territorial rights in Pamir. Nevertheless, their Foreign Office now contends that Pamir is legally the territory of three nations and that the boundary should be clearly drawn.

20TH OF THE FOURTH MONTH

During the Han dynasty [206 B.C.–A.D. 220], due to an abundance of gold, one tael of gold was only worth three taels of silver. In the Ming dynasty [1368–1644], the ratio was initially four to one and then rose to five to one in later years. At the end of the Ming dynasty, however, when the eunuch minister was in power and shamelessly solicited gold goblets from each high official of the government, the ratio soared from ten to one to thirteen to one south of the Yangzi River. In the early years of the present dynasty, the price of gold was put under firm control at six taels of silver. Over the years gold prices have steadily climbed, reaching twenty-two taels of silver in the sixteenth year of the Guangxu Emperor [1890]. This year the value of precious metal jumped to an all-time record high of twenty-six taels, which equals thirty-six foreign silver dollars.

I attended a party at Buckingham Palace at noon today. This time the wives of all the ambassadors were also included in the guest list. The queen, mourning the death of her grandson, was absent. The third princess and the fourth princess took their mother's place and acted as hostesses. The second prince was also absent today.

22ND OF THE FOURTH MONTH

I attended another party at Buckingham Place. The third, fourth and fifth princesses hosted the party. The second and third prince were also present. The total numbers of guests there today was fifty, which was half the number of guests at the two previous parties.

23RD OF THE FOURTH MONTH

According to a telegram of the 16th of this month from Tianjin, an extra 800 electric lines in the north will be put into use by connecting the lines to those in Irkutsk in Russia. Negotiations with the Russians on this matter have almost been completed.

24TH OF THE FOURTH MONTH

According to news received from officials of the Far Eastern Company in London, Russian officials have left Shanghai. Presumably, the contract in London between Russia and our country mentioned earlier has been signed and sealed. As far as the Tianjin negotiations are concerned, we are presently waiting for the nod from Moscow. Once the lines are connected to Irkutsk, the price of electricity will remain in the two-yuan range so that the profits of the company will be thoroughly protected.

29TH OF THE FOURTH MONTH

I attended a dinner party at 22 Arlington Street, the townhouse of Lord Salisbury, to celebrate the birthday of the queen. After dinner we were invited to a tea party at the Foreign Office.

6TH OF THE FIFTH MONTH

A professional engineer claims that the speed of the motorcar has reached its limit and that higher speeds may jeopardize the operation of the vehicle. The highest speed at present is ninety miles per hour, with an average speed of sixty to seventy miles per hour.

7TH OF THE FIFTH MONTH

The newly appointed ambassador to China, O'Connor, came to pay me a visit. Some six years ago he was the British ambassador to China and lived in Beijing for two years. Later, he was transferred to Bulgaria, and Wall took over his position in China. Now Wall has been transferred to Rumania after receiving mounting criticism from British merchants. Thus O'Connor was again appointed as the British ambassador to China. According to O'Connor, he will set sail for China in the fall. The man gives the impression of being an honest person, but he is shrewd by nature. Nevertheless, he's agreeable and will be cooperative in our future negotiations.

In the evening I attended a tea party at the British Foreign Office where the king of Bulgaria was the honored guest. Officially, the king claimed to be on a tour; in fact, he's soliciting advice from the British prime minister, Marquis Salisbury, who was instrumental in establishing Bulgaria as an autonomous state. Both the Russian and French ambassadors were absent from the party because both countries have recently become close allies, and France tends to take the Russian side against the British.

8TH OF THE FIFTH MONTH

The British Anti-Opium Society insists that the government should set a quota on India's opium harvest, claiming that India should not be allowed to harvest opium with China as their sole consumer in mind. Last year's yield of opium in India decreased by 3,000 boxes, and the total export figures was 4,000 boxes, which is less than the figures of two years ago. But China's opium import figures, in fact, have risen to 6,000 boxes, which is higher than the figures a year ago. The question has been raised as to where the surplus of opium is coming from. Some speculation suggests that India may be sending opium through the South Sea Islands to China. Another possibility is that the South Sea Islands may be harvesting their own opium and sending their cargo directly to China.

As I understand, the opium demand in China has quadrupled the production figures of India. However, even though China's imports have increased since last year, the total amount of accounts payable this year has decreased. Evidently, the price of foreign imports of opium has dropped.

11TH OF THE FIFTH MONTH

Last winter, the secretary of the British Foreign Office made a speech in Parliament regarding the anti-opium smoking issue. He stated that Britain would not waste the life of a single soldier or one single bullet to defend the import of opium into China.

16TH OF THE FIFTH MONTH

A telegram arrived today from the International Office in China with the following message:

> The International Office flatly rejected Russia's demand for a total withdrawal of our troops from the frontier. However, in our opinion, the Pamir case is still in hot dispute between Britain and Russia. It may strengthen Britain's position that we are now in direct conflict with Russia.
>
> We expect that Your Excellency will subsequently deliver this message to our ambassador in Russia so that he may seek more information by contacting the British embassy there. A former staff person at our Russian embassy, Qing Aitang, was in the habit of submitting secret messages on Russian troop movements to the British embassy there. Since the British distrust the Russians, they appreciated such an effort on our part and tend to reward us accordingly.
>
> The territory of Pamir may still be in dispute, but it's truly our territory according to our old map of the Western region. In the Fourth month, we sent an illustrated map with a letter to the Russian ambassador as new evidence for further negotiations. We urge Your Excellency to request a copy of the map from our ambassador in Russia. It may clear up the doubt that Pamir is indeed our territory and demonstrate that other foreign powers have no right to violate our territorial right there. During future negotiations with the British Foreign Office, Your Excellency should mention this new piece of evidence. If this dispute is not settled promptly, troubles may multiply in the future. Now, with the help of Britain, the problem may be resolved. Do brief our ambassador in Russia of your future plans to negotiate with the British Foreign Office as soon as possible.
>
> The Yunnan frontier dispute is far from being settled, as France flatly refuses to negotiate with us. Do you perceive any breakthrough in this case?

17TH OF THE FIFTH MONTH

Years ago I had a serious discussion with my friend Cao Jingchu on the philosophy of Buddhism. I pointed out the problem of their reverence for life regarding the animal kingdom, suggesting that if the slaughter of animals is halted, the survival of future generations of human beings on this earth may be threatened. Cao gave me the following answer: "Life begins with energy, yet energy is exhaustible. For this reason, there are limitations set on the reproduction of the birds in the sky, the animals on the mountain and the fish in the river. The reason why one fails to see the limitations on reproduction is due to our relentless slaughter of such living beings for our food supply. Once the slaughter is halted, the birth of these beings will naturally decline. And if birth is completely eliminated, slaughter will follow suit." He left me speechless.

Now, in my discussions with Western scholars, I have commented that if all the wilderness on this earth is developed into cities and towns, we human beings may one day find ourselves without an inch of land to live on. They replied that when all the land is occupied by people, we human beings will automatically stop reproducing. Their rebuttal sounds similar to the answer Cao once gave me. Therefore, I record both these theories as a testimony for future generations.

18TH OF THE FIFTH MONTH

The appearance of the dragon is clearly reported in the history of China, yet Westerners refute its existence. The Westerners require solid proof as evidence before they will believe in the existence of such a creature.

19TH OF THE FIFTH MONTH

I was unable to attend the previous reception at the court of St. James, which was hosted by His Highness, the second son of the queen of England. This afternoon there was another reception held at the same place by Her Highness, the third daughter of the queen. I attended the function with Margary and Zhang Sixun. Four receptions have been held this year, this one being the last one of the season; therefore, the number of guests was merely four or five hundred.

21ST OF THE FIFTH MONTH

Today I received a telegram from the International Office. It stated:

> According to a report from Cavalry Captain Zhang, the Afghanistan chieftain arrived at Samarkand with several other chiefs from his neighboring tribes. He claimed that because the territory from Samarkand to the foothills of the mountains is not within the region of China, the Afghans and their allies have the right to station their troops in Samarkand. They also insisted that their territories are not within the boundaries of the British colonies. Their attitudes were totally belligerent, and therefore Zhang withdrew his troops to our own area.
>
> Samarkand has long been the primary cause of Russia's heated dispute with our government. If we allow Afghanistan to take over Samarkand, Russia will never leave us alone. Further, Samarkand is actually within the territory of China, even though it has long been under the protection of the Russians. The British should be made aware of such information.
>
> According to the news from our ambassador to Russia, the Russian Foreign Office has claimed that due to an agreement between Britain and Russia, Afghans are not allowed to travel across their own border. Russia also assures us that the Afghans are forbidden to trespass into our territory.
>
> Now the Russians have clearly violated this agreement. Please inform the British Foreign Office of this intrusion, seek out the motives behind this trespassing and report to this office immediately.

Our embassy held a banquet at the Grand Hotel this evening. Among the guests were the secretary of the Foreign Ministry, the deputy secretary of the Foreign Ministry, the secretary of Indian affairs, the former British ambassador to China, the newly appointed British ambassador to China and the former ambassador to Chile. In addition, the British Foreign Office brought in the House Speaker, the chairman of the House Committee, the Japanese ambassador and the Prussian ambassador.

22ND OF THE FIFTH MONTH

Ambassador Xu in Russia informed me by letter:

> A month ago, the Russian ambassador to China appeared at our International Office and demanded the total withdrawal of our garrison at the outskirts of Kashgar. The International Office flatly rejected this proposal and contended that as long as the boundary among the three nations is not clearly drawn, there is no possible reason for discussing such a move. This message was subsequently conveyed to the Russian Foreign Office, which insisted that a total withdrawal must occur before the boundary line is finalized. They claimed that since Pamir may not be within the territory of China, China may have violated the territorial rights of other nations by placing garrisons there. The International Office has consistently refused to comply, as we fear that a total withdrawal may lead to further Russian aggression. Such is the true cause behind the present dispute between Russia and our country. In fact, of all the garrisons we have stationed in the Western frontier, Samarkand is located furthest from our territory. The city stands at the northern shore of Lake Issyk, where the Qianlong Emperor erected a monument to commemorate his victory. Since it is situated close to Russia's Ferghana territory, Russia is anxious to claim it as their own.
>
> Last year two British officers toured the area. The Russians immediately sent out their patrol and chased the British officers away. I'm counting my blessings that this recent turn of event has so far not developed into a real crisis.
>
> This spring the Afghans paid us several visits and laid a claim on Samarkand. The International Office contended that the British were instrumental in this unexpected aggression in that country. However, in my opinion, the Afghans are terrified of the Russian threat as it is too close to home for them. They may act as if they are in serious dispute with us, but, in fact, they share the same fear that we have of the Russians. The best policy now is to reason with them and to convince them that they should confer with the Russians directly to redefine the boundary between their two countries. Thus we may succeed in creating another enemy for the Russians.

24TH OF THE FIFTH MONTH

A telegram from the International Office to Ambassador Xu in Russia on the 23rd of the Fourth month stated:

The Russian ambassador has made a request at this office for a total with-drawal of our garrison in Bukhara, which is located west of Kashgar, after he received a direct order from his government. Obviously, Russia has stepped out of bounds, and it's impossible for us to accept such a proposal. Please convey this message to the Russian Foreign Office.

At an earlier date, the Russian ambassador had asked us to withdraw our garrisons from Alichur and Lake Yashil, which we have done. As for the other garrisons, the Russians claim that they are not within the territory of Pamir, whereas we insist they are. However, we are absolutely unwilling to withdraw any of our troops from these garrisons without further negotiations. We expect our present differences to be resolved when additional evidence is brought forth. However, this doesn't necessarily mean that once our garrison is stationed in a place that we will claim the territory as our own.

Furthermore, according to our map of the Western regions, both Alichur and Yashil were beyond our boundaries. We have since informed Intendant Tao, the administrator of Pamir, of this fact. It is possible that all the other gar-risons may be located beyond our boundaries, but we absolutely will not retreat any further.

A recent telegram from Intendant Tao revealed that on the 14th of the Second month, a brigade of Russian cavalry 300 strong under the command of a Russian general arrived at the Russian territory of Karakul.

The chieftain of Andizhan, who had earlier left with his men for Samarkand, is presently watching the troop movements of the Russian army. According to his report, both Britain and Russia are using the river as the natural boundary. Samarkand is a disputed area, and both Britain and Russia are interested in tak-ing it over. We ask you to contact Intendant Tao directly by telegram and advise him not to be too obstinate. Then inform him about the old boundary line according to the map of the Western regions.

On the 2nd of the Fifth month, another telegram from the International Office stated:

First they requested us to withdraw the garrison at Yashil, which we have done, and now they demand that we withdraw all the garrisons along the fron-tier. We absolutely cannot accept such a proposal, as all these garrisons have been stationed there for more than ten years. We can neither accept the fact that all these territories are within the boundary of Pamir, nor will we agree that they are not.

According to the recent telegram from Intendant Tao, in the Third month of this year, Afghanistan sent three messages to him accusing us of invading their territory of Yashil and insisting that we withdraw our troops. Undoubtedly, Britain was instrumental in provoking this incident, because in order for the British army to attack Kashgar, they must go through Pamir; therefore, we mustn't withdraw our garrisons there. The strategy to defend our position against Britain can not be as simple as that against Russia. We must undertake negotia-tions and draw clear borderlines as soon as possible. There is no way we can leave Britain out of the negotiations that we undertake with Russia. Please inform the Russian Foreign Office calmly; use the strategy of divide and conquer.

25TH OF THE FIFTH MONTH

A telegram from the International Office revealed Russia's attempting to occupy the Murghab [Aksu-daria] River. It stated:

> This ominous news was brought forth during a visit by the Russian ambassador after our steadfast refusal of their demand for the total withdrawal of our garrisons from the western frontier. After several rounds of intensive negotiations, the Russian ambassador finally relented and agreed to send a cable back home to stop such a move. We subsequently told him the news of Afghanistan's recent invasion and occupation of the Chinese territory. He appeared unconcerned. He was cool to the idea of a neutral zone as he claimed his country is only interested in defining the boundary. The fact of the matter is that if Afghanistan withdraws its occupational force, Russia may subsequently take over the land, and Britain will again lodge a protest. This case can only be resolved by means of a neutral zone, so please discuss this further with the British Foreign Office. The result of any negotiation should be forwarded by telegram to Ambassador Xu in Russia so that he may continue his efforts to negotiate with the Russians.
>
> Furthermore, the authorities in Kashgar should also be informed that they must not create an incident if they find Russian soldiers in their territory, because the Russians have promised that they will not give us further trouble.
>
> In addition, funds for the installation of telegraph facilities at the frontier have recently been allocated.

26TH OF THE FIFTH MONTH

According to an editorial in today's newspaper, Russia has recently focused all her efforts on developing her Asian territory, and Britain, being at the far side of the ocean, was totally unaware of such aggression. Russia has since acquired nearly 20,000 square miles of territory in Mongolia and 10,000 additional square miles in the vicinity of Afghanistan. These territories are virtually frozen wastelands; nevertheless, land is the prized possession of every nation.

The newspaper further urged that China and Afghanistan should make haste in redefining their boundaries with Russia.

27TH OF THE FIFTH MONTH

Austria launched a train powered not by coal but by electricity. Its top speed is 124 miles per hour. The trial run will begin in Vienna, and all the other European countries and America may follow suit.

28TH OF THE FIFTH MONTH

A former attaché of the French embassy went on a tour of Hunchun and came back with the information that the Russians now have a railroad around the Caspian Sea that can bring their troops to the northern front of India in a matter of a few days. The Russians are presently stepping up their military buildup around the harbor.

29TH OF THE FIFTH MONTH

The queen of England invited the ambassadors of every country to a concert at Buckingham Place at ten o'clock today. I went there with two of my staff. The queen was absent from the concert, mourning the recent death of Her Majesty's grandson. The crown prince and his family were also absent.

4TH OF THE SIXTH MONTH

A letter from the International Office stated:

> During the middle of the Third month, the Russian ambassador came to this office and pressed for the total withdrawal of our garrisons in Pamir. We subsequently cabled Intendant Tao and instructed him to withdraw the additional troops we recently placed there and to keep the regular number of soldiers at the garrisons. There are eight garrisons in the city of Kashgar. The Samarkand garrison, installed fifteen years ago, is a new addition. Even though it is located in the territory of Pamir, a stele placed there in the twenty-fourth year of the Qianlong Emperor [1759] to commemorate His Majesty's successful campaign gives solid evidence that the city is situated within our territory. In the tenth year of the Tongzhi Emperor [1871], Britain held a conference with Russia on the Pamir issue and agreed that the Kulyab River should be the natural boundary for Afghanistan, but later Britain regretted such a hasty decision.

12TH OF THE SIXTH MONTH

Kashgar was once the old city of the Muslim chieftain Poluonidu and covered the area of some sixteen towns. In the twenty-third year of the Qianlong Emperor [1758], General Zhao Hui chased Huo Jizhan west [sic] to Yarkand. Poluonidu led his troops to Yarkand and joined forces with Huo there. The city was under siege for several months but refused to surrender. General Zhao Hui subsequently retreated to Aksu [Yangi-hissar], and later, with additional troops, launched another attack. Both Huo and Poluonidu were defeated and fled through Kashgar. So when our troops reached the city, the Muslim people surrendered, and thus the territory was added to the empire.

17TH OF THE SIXTH MONTH

The wealth of Russia cannot compare with that of Germany because the majority of the territory in Russia lies in waste due to an extremely cold climate. The land in Germany is fertile because the Germans know how to make agricultural improvements. Furthermore, German people are industrious and do not leave their land uncultivated.

The wealth of France, however, exceeds that of Germany, because France possesses the richest soil in the whole of Europe. Furthermore, the French people are highly skilled workers, and their finished products are the best in the world. Their most popular product at present is grape wine, which brings in a large amount of money from other nations.

However, the wealth of England is comparatively higher than that of France. Their skills in production may not be as good as those in France, but their natural resources from coal mines are extremely profitable. Furthermore, they are shrewd traders and know how to make better business deals than the French. Hence, they are able to absorb all the wealth of the world and channel it into their own country.

Nevertheless, America is in a better position than England, because its territory is as large and rich as that of China. However, they know how to take better care of their land than we Chinese. Furthermore, there is no need for them to seek wealth outside their own territory as their natural resources are superior to those in other countries. Since more than half of their territory has not yet been cultivated, the progress they will make in the future is incalculable.

As far as power is concerned, France is behind Germany, Germany behind England and England behind Russia. The power that America possesses, in my opinion, should be placed between Germany and France.

18TH OF THE SIXTH MONTH

Half a month ago I went with Wang Xingshan and took a trip on an electric train underneath the Thames to the south shore. This is the only such train in London, as the electric train is still a rarity and in the initial stages of construction.

20TH OF THE SIXTH MONTH

Before I came abroad, I thought that all the ambassadors of Western nations were in the habit of threatening Chinese officials into submission and creating problems whenever they could. At that time, I believed that all Westerners were belligerent because they were brought up in an uncivilized culture. Since my arrival to Europe I have had numerous occasions to meet various officials from the Foreign Offices and have discovered that they also have a set of systems and regulations to follow. During negotiations they appear to be reasonably polite and observe the value of friendship to a certain extent. They neither threaten me with the superior power of their own country nor flaunt the knowledge of their advanced Western technology. Such is not the case for England and France alone but for all the other Western nations as well. Furthermore, it is not just the attitude of the officials in the Foreign Offices, but all the officials in every level of their government who behave in the same manner. For example, the former British ambassador to China, Westmore, is well known in Beijing as an ignorant, violent man. But in my association with him, I have found the man congenial, sincere and willing to help all he can whenever I have a problem. Furthermore, his great intellectual capacity and brilliant ideas would be regarded as above average even in China. But if he were given the chance to return to China, there would be no guarantee that he would not continue to give us trouble.

The threats that foreign nations pose to China did not begin today but started during the reign of the Daoguang Emperor [1821–1851]. During those years of intermittent war and peace, China lost every battle in its attempt to drive the foreign invaders off its land. Ever since then, foreign powers tend to look upon China with the utmost contempt. In the succeeding years of the Xianfeng Emperor [1851–1862] we were compelled to accept the humiliating terms of unfair treaties after disastrous defeats, which subsequently brought forth further humiliation from the foreign powers. Later, special governmental offices were installed to deal with foreign affairs. But our officials, unfamiliar with foreign culture, tended to mistrust the foreigners and procrastinated whenever an international incident occurred. Unfortunately, these characteristics are not comprehensible to the foreign mind. When a firm stand should have been taken against foreign aggression, our officials argued with them on the most trifling points of the issue. When gentle persuasion was required, they retreated without any further negotiation. Consequently, the officials of the early years failed totally and miserably in their undertaking of foreign affairs. Such blunders frustrated even the most mild-mannered foreign envoys and left them no choice but to resort to threats in order to accomplish their mission. Therefore, the honest ones learned to be skillful in their protests and the gentle ones sought threats as their only means. This trend has become a tradition that cannot be changed overnight and probably will remain intact for a long time. Alas, when can we find a minister who has a knowledge of foreign culture who can be kept permanently in the International Office so that he may correct such detrimental habits of our own officials?

22ND OF THE SIXTH MONTH

The failure of the Chinese tea trade is completely due to the fault of our own merchants, who had mixed the tea refuse in with the exported tea of the best quality to gain greater profit. When the British merchants discovered this, they hired Chinese tea planters and sent them to teach the Indians how to plant and harvest their tea in the Chinese way. Since then, China has lost all its profits from tea. However, on account of the climate and soil, Indian tea cannot surpass Chinese tea in quality, and the British and American gentry remain in favor of Chinese tea. An English physician even emphasized the benefits of drinking Chinese tea in a London newspaper. Consequently, Western merchants continue to make their tea purchases in China every year. Therefore, if the tea merchants in China clean up their act, they will have a good chance to win back their best customers.

27TH OF THE SIXTH MONTH

There are three major reasons for the failure of Chinese trade. First of all, to gain more business, Chinese merchants tend to reduce the prices of their products. In the end, they cannot keep up the quality of their operations. Second, to maintain their profit margin, they cut the costs of their production by using inferior materials, such as mixing tea with shredded willow leaves. Third, with the recent advance of telegrams, bad news travels fast.

28TH OF THE SIXTH MONTH

The former British ambassador, Westmore, has since become my good friend. He has frequently expressed his love for China, as he cannot erase the fond memory of the exquisite Chinese scenery from his mind. Yet he knows in his heart that at the advanced age of seventy-four, he shall never see China again. He often talks to me about the various Chinese officials, past and present, whom he has dealt with at the International Office. He contended that Prince Gong [Yixin] possesses an unusual intelligence that has virtually saved China from disaster. He also expressed his admiration of the prince's impressive appearance and claimed that he has seldom met such a distinguished-looking man. He regards Grand Secretary Wenxiang as a statesman who was totally devoted to his work and his country. As a capable assistant to the prince, Wenxiang fulfilled his duty as expected, although he could at times be obstinate. But that was in the early days, and Wenxiang had absolutely no training in foreign affairs. He could have been a more skillful foreign affairs expert if he were working in today's world. Westmore respected Minister Dong Xun as a scholar but criticized his ability as an administrator. When I pressed him for Dong's true weak point, he replied that Dong was too timorous. I then asked his opinion of Royal Attendant Guo Songdao. Westmore considered Guo to be a greater scholar than Dong and a harder worker. But he contended that Guo was totally unaware of human relations and therefore had trouble getting along in Chinese society. Westmore then claimed that Minister Wang was an extremely intelligent man and that Ministers Mao and Tan were both good and honest men. Consequently, he smiled knowingly and said, "Hengqi, Chonglun, Jinglian and Chonghou were mere functionaries posted at the International Office, and none of them are worth the time or effort to discuss." When I mentioned Grand Secretary Shen Guifen, he suddenly got very red in the face and said, "I really don't understand how a man like Shen could be placed in the International Office! I just can't understand that man." And then in a loud voice he exclaimed repeatedly, "I just don't understand that man! I just don't understand that man!"

I know Minister Shen to be a man meticulous in his undertakings and one of the most efficient administrators in government service. However, he is unsuitably placed in the International Office because he is too suspicious and indecisive by nature. These two characteristics are not compatible with foreign habits; therefore, he and Westmore almost reached a breaking point during their negotiations over the Yunnan-Burma Affair.

29TH OF THE SIXTH MONTH

In the ancient classic *The Spring and Autumn Annals*,[40] a lord of the feudal state Qi was criticized for both his failure to provide for the welfare of his people as well as his consistent exploration of faraway lands. The criticism clearly focused on his inability to be a capable leader, and historians during that period contended that he should not be regarded as a benevolent ruler of the people even though he was the hegemon of the five major feudal states of the late Zhou period. Nevertheless, at the time, historians did not criticize his efforts in exploration. Only in later centuries, when pseudointellectuals misinterpreted the true meaning of such criticism, did anyone claim that his failure was specifically caused by his relentless exploration. In time, these very words of criticism became the basis of essays for the civil service examinations. Consequently, when those successful candidates became government officials, they implemented this idea as government policy. Such a policy may be regarded as a good policy during peacetime, but the present chaotic times

---

40. A history of the Latter Zhou (11th century B.C.–220 B.C.). (Trans.)

clearly reflect its weakness. Understandably, the foreign powers see such an error in China's policy, and have therefore consistently invaded our territory along the frontier because they know we will not be persistent in fighting for our rights during those confrontations. As a result we have lost the Liuqiu Islands, Indochina and Burma. On the northern frontier, we lost several thousand miles north of Heilongjiang Province; in the western frontier Russia devoured the majority of the Muslim tribes and Britain snatched up the rest. Now we are in the precarious situation of losing Korea as well.

All these losses are due to our government's policy, which discourages the exploration of foreign territories. Now we are not even allowed to install consulates in Hong Kong, Saigon and Kuala Lumpur, which several hundred thousand Chinese call home. And in both Old Gold Mountain [San Francisco] in the United States and New Gold Mountain [Sydney] in Australia, our people have made a good living throughout the years but are now being driven out of their homes and losing everything they own. All this humiliation our people suffer is caused by our government policy. Our merchant ships are not allowed to sail past Singapore to the West, and our battleships are also denied such rights. Our envoys to foreign nations are unaware of our national interests, and when they negotiate, they make no effort to correct past errors for the good of our future. Our ministers at the frontier are totally ignorant of our territorial rights, and their only concern is to avoid further confrontation.

All these problems have come from the misinterpretation of ancient history, which has caused great sorrow and loss to both our people and our country.

2ND OF THE INTERCALARY SIXTH MONTH

The first Western man to enter China was not a merchant but a missionary priest. As I understand, all priests become learned men in their own countries before they make the trip to China. Therefore, they all strive to learn the language so they can preach their religion to the Chinese. The Chinese word for father is *Ye* and for resurrection is *Su*. Since the leading saint of the Christian religion was resurrected from death, they use two similar sounding characters to represent the name of Jesus in the Chinese language: *Yesu*, which means "the father who is resurrected."

4TH OF THE INTERCALARY SIXTH MONTH

European nations may frequently change the ministers in their Foreign Offices, yet they seldom remove the deputy ministers or their assistants. Most of them have stayed in the same office for many years, and some of

them have spent a lifetime there. Therefore, these officials in the Western
Foreign Offices are familiar with their business and seldom make mistakes.

There are very few high-ranking officials in our International Office who
are experienced in foreign affairs. Many of them work there in name only,
and some of them just come and go as they please. No one is actually taking
care of daily official duties. Some high-ranking ministers, such as Li
Gaoyang and Yan Chaoyi, took pride in their ignorance of foreign affairs and
never showed up once in the office all year. Therefore, some of the lower-
ranking officials who have been in office for over ten years have no knowledge of foreign affairs. Those who do learn the basic principles generally
expect to be promoted to high-ranking outside positions. If they fail to seek
such promotion, their colleagues tend to look upon them with disdain.
Therefore, the few efficient officials who do learn the procedures of foreign
affairs are promoted out of the office. Once they have been promoted several
times, they can never come back to the International Office. Under such circumstances, no minor official undergoes the proper training in foreign
affairs.

In my opinion, if we expect China to be self-reliant, we must train our officials in the proper knowledge of foreign affairs. To provide for such training,
we must start from the International Office. To place the International Office
in proper standing, we must prolong the terms of the minor officials.

6TH OF THE INTERCALARY SIXTH MONTH

In the West, the three basic principles of good government are to provide
the people with security, food and education. Reformers in China have
offered twenty-one new guidelines to ensure the means of livelihood for her
people, as follows:

1. Manufacture machinery to promote a high rate of production.
2. Build railroads to reduce costs of transportation.
3. Establish post offices and newspaper offices to improve communication.
4. Negotiate trade agreements with other countries to promote international
   commerce.
5. Increase the number of consulates to protect merchants who travel abroad.
6. Connect telegraph wires to those of other countries to speed up
   communication.
7. Provide government subsidies to help merchants.
8. Install a commerce department to promote better business.
9. Establish museums to initiate research projects.
10. Appoint a president and vice president to the Chamber of Commerce.
11. Establish vocational schools for the training of skilled laborers.

12. Adjust the Custom Office tariffs in order to control prices.
13. Open wilderness areas to promote agriculture.
14. Invest in mining industries to increase the wealth of the people.
15. Print paper currency to stabilize the monetary system.
16. Provide lectures in chemistry to improve the knowledge of natural sciences.
17. Select the right men to do daily routine work at government offices.
18. Adjust the regulations governing waterways to speed up transportation.
19. Keep accurate and up-to-date ledger books to avoid delays in payment.
20. Establish a banking system to increase the national wealth.
21. Seek new technology to strengthen the power and wealth of the nation.

10TH OF THE INTERCALARY SIXTH MONTH

In 1880, there were 21,745 overseas Chinese living in San Francisco. In 1890, the total number rose to 25,870. Despite the increase in cruel and unfair treatment that they have endured at the hands of U.S. immigration during the past decade, the Chinese population in San Francisco has risen by 4,000.

Has the birth rate of the Chinese population there increased or have more Chinese moved to San Francisco?

16TH OF THE INTERCALARY SIXTH MONTH

According to the director of an English observatory, many dark spots appeared on the sun this year; some stretch to 100,000 miles in length and 60,000 miles in width. This phenomenon is believed to be the cause of this year's poor business and recent damaging rainstorms.

20TH OF THE INTERCALARY SIXTH MONTH

I had a conference with the British Foreign Office on installing a new chief for the Kanjuti tribe. During the conference, the Pamir affair was discussed.

22ND OF THE INTERCALARY SIXTH MONTH

Before the Russians dispatched their troops to Pamir, their Foreign Office alerted the British ambassador in Russia that they were sending some of their soldiers on a patrol mission in an area where a few Chinese troops were still stationed. They assured the British that they had not the slightest intention of occupying the land. The initial conflict on Pamir began when an Afghanistan tribe stole a sheep from a herd of the Buhui tribe for a sacrifice. This action subsequently brought the Chinese troops into Pamir. The

Russians expected their presence to curtail further aggression in Afghanistan and simultaneously drive the Chinese soldiers off Pamir, and therefore they also sent in their troops.

On the 12th of this month a telegram reached London reporting that three divisions of the Russian army had entered Pamir from three different directions. At that time in Samarkand, there were 100 soldiers in the Afghanistan garrison. When they heard about the Russian invasion, they immediately brought in 300 more men during the night. Thirty Russian soldiers arrived at Samarkand but were unaware of the reinforcements at the Afghanistan garrison. Five Russian soldiers were killed immediately and twenty-five were captured. Russia asked for the return of their soldiers, but this request was rejected by Afghanistan.

A second telegram of the 19th reported that Russia and Afghanistan were engaging in a fierce battle on Pamir, and the victory or defeat for either side was yet unknown. The report further stated that the Russian army had entered the Chinese side of the Pamir and driven off the Chinese troops stationed near Karakul. All the newspapers in London are in an uproar, and the British Foreign Office has admitted that the Russians didn't keep their word as they had promised previously. The newspaper editorials strongly suggest that China should immediately lodge a protest before their share of land in Pamir is taken away by Russia.

25TH OF THE INTERCALARY SIXTH MONTH

In recent years, Chinese people have tended to follow the trends in the West, as they are fascinated by the convenience of the newly invented Western products. In my opinion, there are many things in China that far exceed those in the West.

For instance, Chinese cooking is the best in the world, whereas there are merely two ways of cooking in the West: frying and boiling. Therefore, food in China is better than that in the West.

Clothing in China is generally made of silk, soft and colorful, whereas men in the West wear black woolen suits all year long. Even though their women do dress better, they only put on fancy attire for parties. Therefore, clothing in China is better than that in the West.

Chinese build their houses on the ground level and spread out. In every section there is a courtyard, where exquisite pavilions and fancy railings of intricate designs are displayed. Westerners construct their houses upward several storeys high, but there is no single courtyard inside the house. Therefore, houses in China are better-looking than those in the West.

Food, clothing and housing are essential to daily life, yet none in the West is better than that in China. Therefore, wise men in China: You must not be overwhelmed by Western trends and consider everything in the West to be better than that in China.

27TH OF THE INTERCALARY SIXTH MONTH

If China intends to participate in the world of international commerce, we Chinese must learn the skills of new Western technology. There are only two ways to reach that goal: natural science as the essence and technology as the means. If we acquire the essence of natural science, we will be able to learn new ways of doing calculations and to draw blueprints of the machinery. Even if we only scratch the surface of their scientific knowledge, we will at least learn a few basic skills of their new technology.

Hence, we must establish many institutes of higher learning and recruit students with superior intelligence for such scientific study. At the same time, we should also install more vocational schools. With the aid of the machinery, we can accomplish ten days' labor with one day's work, and substitute one man's energy for a hundred men's strength.

With these accomplishments, we will be able to speed up production at a minimum cost. With the reduction of costs, we will be able to make more sales abroad.

Furthermore, there are eight more ways to promote our business ventures abroad:

1. Install a Department of Commerce in our government system.
2. Set up new regulations to help the establishment of business corporations.
3. Encourage individual inventions of new technology.
4. Penalize merchants who sell counterfeit merchandise abroad.
5. Follow the trends of the West to increase our volume of sales.
6. Set up annual exhibitions to attract foreign buyers.
7. Amend the rules and regulations of customs offices to further our national interest.
8. Add additional shipping routes.

13TH OF THE SEVENTH MONTH

People in London are in the habit of taking a vacation at the seaside in the early summer, spending two to three months there. This summer I followed this tradition and rented a house at Brighton. At four o'clock this afternoon I took my family and Interpreter Wang, boarded the train at Victoria Station and arrived at Brighton two hours later.

14TH OF THE SEVENTH MONTH

I toured the city of Brighton with Interpreter Wang in a carriage and stopped at the old pier. It cost two pence to be admitted to an open-air concert where the seating capacity could be extended to fit several hundred people. Across from the river there is a new pier, and between these two piers there is another one under construction.

15TH OF THE SEVENTH MONTH

I went to the new pier with Wang to enjoy the cool breeze. The new pier is made of wood planks, and I feel more secure walking on it. We also visited the aquarium by the seashore, which exhibits a large assortment of unique sea creatures. It appears to me that this aquarium possesses more specimens from the sea than the one in London.

16TH OF THE SEVENTH MONTH

I walked to a small garden with Wang and then went to Princeton Park by carriage. We took a tour through the villages and caught a bird's-eye view of the countryside from the hilltop. We then visited St. Augustus Well. It is said that by drinking the water from the ancient well, one will enjoy good health throughout the year. A glass of water costs three pence. Wang drank half a cup and complained it was bitter. I didn't dare drink the water.

17TH OF THE SEVENTH MONTH

Tomorrow is the day set for the conference at the British Foreign Office on the issue of the Yunnan-Burma border dispute. A representative from the Indian Affairs Office will also be present at the meeting. I've sent Ma Qingchen twice already, but his negotiations have produced no concrete result. Therefore I sent for Ma by telegram and instructed him to protest with persistent reasoning until they agreed to set the borderline at the foot of the Yeren Mountains or at least by the Irrawaddy River. This would give the tribal chiefs along the river some measure of peace.

A second item on the agenda should be the river itself, which should be regarded as a neutral zone for all the parties concerned. The third item should be the establishment of a Chinese customs office at the north shore of Xinjie. And the last item should be our territorial right in Laos. Presently, 70 percent of Laos has already been drawn into Siam. Since Laos is a close neighbor of Vietnam on the opposite side, France may give us some problems in the future, so it's best for us to define a clear borderline with them right now.

18TH OF THE SEVENTH MONTH

I went for a carriage ride with Wang along the coast to Worthing. We went uphill over the countryside and passed through a newly harvested wheat field. The scenery was delightful!

On our way there we stopped by an orphanage for a visit. The director of the institution was most gracious and took us on a tour of the facility. There were 300 orphans; male and female live in separate dormitories. The facility includes a school, a work place, a bathhouse, a kitchen, a chapel and a dairy of twenty-five cows. We arrived at their lunch hour, and as a rule they do exercises on the school grounds after lunch. Consequently, we had the opportunity to observe the children in action. Their own music band played while all the children did their exercises. The children were agile in their movements and kept their steps uniform. The age of the children in the band was around ten, but they played remarkably well. Later, a choir of the seven-year-olds stood up and sang in the most serious manner. I was quite impressed by their performance.

All the teachers there are women, and all of them treat the children with affection. As I understand it, the children are each taught a skill so that they can make a living when they grow up and must leave the orphanage. This kind of welfare for the children is what our saintly ancient kings strived to provide for their people during the time of their reign. I didn't realize that it has finally been carried out in this foreign land.

19TH OF THE SEVENTH MONTH

The Lao tribe, after which Laos was initially named, resided at the south-western frontier. There were many branches, each of which evolved into a different tribe. The tribal name first appears in the section "Native Chiefs" in the *Ming History,* but it is actually a branch tribe only. In the latter part of the Ming dynasty [1368–1644], Laos began to be known as the kingdom of Nanzhang, and during the reign of the Emperor Yongzheng [1723–1736], their chieftain began to offer tribute to China.

20TH OF THE SEVENTH MONTH

I went back to London with my family and staff by train.

25TH OF THE SEVENTH MONTH

As far as national wealth is concerned, China cannot compare with the European countries. But unlike them, our national debt is relatively low.

Twenty years ago China was totally free of debt. In the early years of the Guangxu Emperor, France launched an attack on our east coast after her successful colonization of Vietnam. All the coastal provinces were ordered by decree to build up their defenses. Lacking the proper funding, both Fujian and Guangdong provinces borrowed money from foreign merchants. The International Office at that time also took out a foreign loan for the purchase of additional cannons and spare parts for shipbuilding, which came to the substantial sum of 200,000 taels of gold. Payment of the loan, including the interest, was arranged on a yearly basis, and now the amount has been reduced to less than 100,000 taels of gold.

27TH OF THE SEVENTH MONTH

The ancient classic *The Spring and Autumn Annals* records that a rock dropped from the sky as a comet and was seen passing by in the feudal state of Song.

Later, the same kind of phenomenon was recorded in the *Han History*.

There is a black rock several feet long exhibited in the London Museum that is believed to be the fallen rock of a comet. To my knowledge, a shooting star is not actually a piece of rock but the debris from a falling star. All the celestial bodies were initially evolved from a whirling dust of energy, and our own earth is but one of the stars.

Furthermore, according to *The Spring and Autumn Annals*, in the fourth year of Duke Zhuang in the feudal state of Lu, shooting stars showered through the night sky like a rainstorm. However, there was no appearance of a comet. Perhaps the night sky was too bright for the naked eye to perceive the comet. In all possibility, a nearby star might have been exploding and spewing debris everywhere, including that falling on the earth.

28TH OF THE SEVENTH MONTH

A telegram from the International Office stated:

> Ambassador Wilson of Britain has informed us that according to the British Foreign Office, Your Excellency has terminated negotiations over the Yunnan-Burma boundary dispute by order of this office. However, he contended that Britain remains interested in continuing this negotiation. Our reaction to his statement was that we have never given such authorization, but perhaps Your Excellency might have suggested another date for negotiations as your early rounds of negotiations didn't run as smoothly as expected.
>
> Ambassador Wilson also strongly protested that Xinjie is not within Chinese territory and brought a Chinese map as evidence. The map was drawn during the reign of the Qianlong Emperor [1736–1796], and Xinjie didn't come

under our protection until the reign of the Jiaqing Emperor [1796–1821]. Please make a note of this fact, which may be used in your future negotiations with the British Foreign Office.

My return cable went as following:

> I have made several requests for a complete withdrawal of British forces from Xinjie, and now their Foreign Office is making up stories that I terminated the negotiations. Apparently, they are desperate, and we must firmly refuse to accept their terms. After the withdrawal I am positive peace will prevail among the chieftains of the various tribes along the border. Please ask Ambassador Wilson why, if this area is not within the boundary of China, Britain is taking the trouble to defend the territory. Britain cannot refute the fact that the area was previously under China's protection. Furthermore, a cable from Kanjuti reaffirmed the fact that Xinjie is within the territory of the Yeren Mountains. If British forces leave Xinjie, they will be retreating west of the Irrawaddy River, which may be defined as the natural boundary for all parties concerned. Even though Britain has colonized Burma, according to the old treaty, several thousand miles of territory around the Yeren Mountains are not included within the territory of Burma. When the time comes to redefine the boundary, this territory should be equally divided between our two countries. This summer I discussed this plan with Lord Salisbury and he was in complete agreement with me. If we fight for our right to keep the river as the natural boundary, Britain will probably accept this suggestion, because the territory around the Yeren Mountains west of the river is twice the size of the other half.

1ST OF THE EIGHTH MONTH

In the seventeenth year of the Guangxu Emperor [1891], according to the report of the Foreign Customs Office in China, the total production of herbal medicine from all provinces reached 330,000 *dan*.[41] Only 1 to 6 percent of the medicine was kept by China. The planting and harvesting of opium poppy seeds has greatly improved in China over the years. It will compete successfully with Indian production in the future, and although it's not the initial desire of the Chinese peasants to go into the production of opium, it's the only way they can make any money.

2ND OF THE EIGHTH MONTH

The dispute over the territory around the Yeren Mountains region of the Yunnan-Burma border, in my opinion, can be easily resolved if we will accept the Irrawaddy River as the natural boundary. Earlier, the British

---

41. A *dan* or "picul" was a standard measure of volume, subdivided into ten *dou* ("bushels"); and a *dou* in turn subdivided into ten *sheng* ("pints").

Foreign Office requested by letter that I put this suggestion in writing. I have since complied in a detailed plan sent on the 26th of the Seventh month. So far I have not received an answer. Today I sent Ma Qingchen to pay Sandison a visit at his office and let him know that as soon as British forces withdraw from the area, we will accept the river as the boundary.

I further contended that since we are determined to include this territory within our boundaries, Britain has no excuse to refuse our proposed terms, provided we follow three major objectives: friendship, reasoning and perseverance. It's simply a waste of time to negotiate further or to put it in writing, because in the end Britain has to agree to our terms, and I don't see why she can't accept our terms now. This action would maintain the British tradition of upholding justice and nurturing good friendship. Furthermore, the area around the Yeren Mountains east of the river consists of merely one-fourth of the disputed territory. Britain can have the other three-fourths; China only needs the one-fourth. We are ready and willing to let Britain have the lion's share of the bargain.

I further contended that China previously invested no effort in territory exploration and therefore neglected the area along the frontier. Now she realizes that profits may be made in these areas, and for the sake of saving face, she cannot easily give up her territorial rights. If China can retain her strength, neither Russia nor France can worm its way into these territories. As a result, China can protect the commercial interests of Britain, which is undeniably an advantage for Britain's future enterprises. If Britain sets a good example by allowing China a small share of the land, then Russia will invariably withdraw her forces from Pamir. Consequently, Britain's desires will be fulfilled if Pamir becomes Chinese territory. I implored Sandison to calculate the advantages of this great plan, which, I assured him, will outweigh the minor loss he anticipates.

Sandison's reply was that in a few days' time he should receive the answer to my request from the Indian Affairs Office. He shook hands with Ma and they parted.

9TH OF THE EIGHTH MONTH

Ambassador Xu in Russia contacted me by letter regarding the joint request for Russia's total withdrawal of her troops in Pamir. He contended that the British ambassador in Russia had informed him that according to a recent cable from the British Foreign Office, Britain cannot lodge a joint protest with China because the Russian forces have not penetrated the border of Afghanistan. He further stated that the Russian troops are in the process of retreating to their own territory on account of the approaching severe winter months. And according to a recent cable from the International Office, the Afghan troops have retreated to Samarkand.

Yesterday, I received a cable from the International Office stating that the Russian forces had been withdrawn from Pamir. I checked all the newspapers today. One paper stated that China had already retreated from the Russian side before the arrival of the Russian general at Pamir. Another paper said that forty-four Russian soldiers had entered Tashkurghan but were driven out by the Chinese garrison there. There is also a rumor raging in Germany that Russia is mobilizing an army of 12,000 in order to enter Pamir next spring.

Khokand was once the territory of the largest Muslim tribe. Russia has periodically invaded the place since the tenth year of the Xianfeng Emperor [1860] and finally occupied the entire territory in the ninth year of the Tongzhi Emperor [1871].

10TH OF THE EIGHTH MONTH

According to international law, when two nations are engaging in warfare, other nations are not allowed to sell firearms to either of the two warring parties. During the war with France in 1885, the French navy intercepted shipments of orders that several of our provinces had previously placed with the munitions plants of England. Later, these shipments of firearms were sent directly to Hong Kong, then rerouted to mainland China.

11TH OF THE EIGHTH MONTH

According to the *Survey of the Yun River and the San River,* the Salween River flows from the east to the west of Mengyan. The Dazhou River and the Binlang River run along the land in the north. Both rivers come from the northwest and combine into one when they reach Mengyan; from there it is known as the Taying River. However, according to Wang Zhenzhu's *Survey of the Binlang River,* the Binlang River meets the Taying River at Tengyue, and the natives there call the combined stream the Haipa River.

12TH OF THE EIGHTH MONTH

According to a report from Moscow in the *Times,* the Russian general did return to Pamir on the 14th of September. His army consisted of two cavalry brigades and two infantry battalions. It will be absolutely impossible for the general to camp his army there in the winter, because earlier, another general and his army almost froze to death on Pamir.

16TH OF THE EIGHTH MONTH

According to a further report in the *Times*, the total number in the Russian general's army is 700. He may lead his forces back to Pamir next spring.

21ST OF THE EIGHTH MONTH

I received a cable from the International Office confirming that my name has been placed by decree on the nomination list for Royal Censor.

1ST OF THE TENTH MONTH

The total of annual import taxes collected on all the foreign merchandise entering the customs offices under the jurisdiction of the Office of the Northern Ports is 324,000 taels of silver. The cargo is transported by water via the West River or by land through Qinzhou to Guangxi Province.

4TH OF THE TENTH MONTH

The total of annual tariffs on imports collected at Longzhou is only 26,000 taels of silver. The reason for such a small amount of revenue is due to the lack of better transportation. As soon as the northern railroad is completed, business will improve.

6TH OF THE TENTH MONTH

Ancient people in China recorded the occurrence of events with knots along a rope. In later centuries, the sages substituted written words for the knots. Our ancient history claims that Emperor Shi created written characters and Cang Xie composed sentences with these words. According to a Buddhist scripture, the initial inventors of written words were three brothers. Fan, the oldest, wrote from right to left; Qu Lu, the second, from left to right and the youngest one, Cang Xie, from top to bottom. The Confucian scholars adopted the smooth style of Cang Xie. Mozi, a contemporary of Confucius but with a different philosophy, composed his writing in the style of Qu Lu, which was eventually brought to the West. All the writing in India follows the style of Fan as does that of the Mongolians and the Muslims.

7TH OF THE TENTH MONTH

A letter from the International Office revealed that according to a recent cable from Ambassador Xu, the Russian general has truly left Pamir and that presently they are getting ready to define the new border.

In the tenth year of the Guangxu Emperor [1884], negotiations were held at Kashgar on the boundary issue. It was concluded that the boundaries of both countries should begin at the foot of the Yeren Mountains, with Russia's line going to the southwest and China's line straight southward. The territory to the west of the mountain should be included within the Russian border, whereas that to the east should belong to China. Border disputes are hard to resolve, and since this present dispute started at an earlier date, we should insist that the borderline go straight south as agreed upon so as to avoid unexpected treachery. Intendant Tao was asked to send men there to survey the area in order to draw up a map, which will be mailed to the International Office.

Russia has consistently claimed that Pamir is the territory of both Russia and China; therefore, Britain has no business getting involved in this dispute. Furthermore, the envoy of Kashgar has frequently warned us that China mustn't be swayed by Britain's innuendos.

However, in my opinion, it would be better to have Britain's direct involvement in this dispute. At the same time, I'm aware that such a move will offend Russia. Nevertheless, we cannot exclude Britain because the British ambassador had a clandestine meeting with me two years ago about this Pamir affair, and therefore Britain is already involved in this dispute. If the British Foreign Office makes a further inquiry about this dispute, I will have to tell them about the Kashgar negotiations and our own commitment to the earlier agreement. And if Britain is still interested, she must openly express her intentions to Russia, with which China is more than willing to comply.

10TH OF THE TENTH MONTH

Today is the birthday of the Empress Dowager. I led the embassy staff in offering greetings by prostrating before the altar set up in the courtyard.

14TH OF THE TENTH MONTH

According to the *Strand News*, the boundary between Yunnan Province and Burma is hard to define. China's claim to the land east of the Irrawaddy River is not plausible. The story contends that according to a survey by Indian officials, there have been very few Chinese tradesmen traveling through that area over the years, and only four years ago did a few Chinese settlements begin to appear there.

17TH OF THE TENTH MONTH

The leader of the London anti-opium society lodged a protest at the Office of Indian Affairs against the legalization of opium in that country and the subsequent sales of the substance to China. The Minister of Indian Affairs claimed that China is producing more opium in her own country than India ever exported to China. He further stated that if restrictions were placed upon opium harvesting, then the Indian farmers will produce marijuana to make up the loss, which is more detrimental to human health than opium.

22ND OF THE TENTH MONTH

Minister of War Wang wrote to me with the following message:

> It will be hard to draw a clear borderline between Yunnan Province and Burma because the territory in dispute has constantly changed hands since the late Ming dynasty [1600–1644]. During the reign of the Qianlong Emperor [1736–1796], there was a period of peace along the Yunnan frontier. It was then that a rough map was drawn. In fact, the disputed area has been the territory neither of China nor of Burma for centuries. The map was likely produced after a series of consultations, and therefore was not based upon historical fact.
>
> Hka, the wilderness in the territory of the Longchuan tribal chief, is located about 170 miles from Longchuan. Your estimate of thirty miles between these two places is definitely wrong.
>
> The Mengmao are one of the tribes in the Tengyue area and are situated east of the Irrawaddy River. The British map you mailed to me indicating the Mengmao on the other side of the river is also incorrect.
>
> In my opinion, Britain's interest lies in the northwest route from Tengyue, which leads directly into Tibet. The route begins in India, passes through Tibet, and then goes directly to Burma. I understand that a new jade mine has recently been discovered near the route. Evidently, Britain is worried that China may obstruct her exploration team, since they must pass through the northwest of our frontier to reach the mine.

26TH OF THE TENTH MONTH

I received a cable from the International Office stating that the British ambassador to China, O'Connor, was received by His Majesty the Emperor on the 25th of this month. A book written by the queen of England was offered by the ambassador as a gift to His Majesty. I was thus authorized by decree to express appreciation on behalf of His Majesty the Emperor. This afternoon I went to the British Foreign Office and personally delivered the message.

28TH OF THE TENTH MONTH

In early history, Burma was but a small kingdom on the other side of the regions of various native tribes at the Yunnan frontier that paid tribute to China regularly until the late Ming dynasty [c. 1600–44]. Burma became powerful during the early reign of the Qianlong Emperor [1736–96] and subsequently occupied all the territories of the native tribes between China and Burma along the western frontier. Consequently, China sent in troops and penetrated deep into Burma. Thus a defeated Burma resumed its place as a tributary to China.

29TH OF THE TENTH MONTH

Each dynasty took a different approach to its Burma campaign. In the Yuan dynasty [1271–1368], Minister Dawu'er built a fleet of ships by the two rivers Axi and Ahe and sailed into Burma. His navy captured two cities in succession and Burma surrendered. The location of these two rivers was not recorded, but they may be situated between the present Chindwin River and Mon River. In the Ming dynasty [1368–1644], the Burma campaign was led by both Deng Zilong and Liu Ting. Deng and his army went into Burma through Yao Pass, while Liu and his forces took a different route through Longchuan. Deng claimed sovereignty as far as Manmu.

In the present dynasty, the Burma campaign was under the leadership of Imperial Scholar Yang Yingju. Five divisions of his army took five different routes to launch an attack and joined with the allied forces of Siam in their final assault.

30TH OF THE TENTH MONTH

After many years of peace, all the strategic points of access to Burma have disappeared. Some of them are now occupied by primitive tribes and a few of them have been infested by wild beasts. Without road repair, these routes have become unpassable. Presently there are only three major routes to Burma, all of which pass through Manyun. They are known as the upper, middle and lower routes; they are frequently used by merchants and require three days' journey. All three routes are relatively safe, judging from the fact that merchants frequently make trips through there.

1ST OF THE ELEVENTH MONTH

Burma is located at the extreme southwest of China. Rich in soil and abundant in harvest, its population has reached over several hundred million. There are ninety-nine tribes whose chiefs have close contacts with China. Since their mines possess the most precious metal and stone and their lakes and rivers are filled to the brim with fish, it's the most prosperous nation in the southwest.

Burma became known to China during the Han dynasty [206 B.C.–A.D. 220]. However, since their language is similar to those in India, any exchange of messages between China and Burma must be translated. Furthermore, unlike tributary countries such as Korea and the Liuqius, who keep records of their contact with China, Burma must keep its records secret, according to the strict rules of its own law. Since the incident of this year, a search through Burma for records has been underway, but so far only documents of twenty-six tribes have turned up. When these records are translated into Chinese, however, the names of many cities, rivers and mountains change in writing and thus have caused a great deal of confusion. Therefore, it is difficult to pin down any location during the negotiations with Britain.

2ND OF THE ELEVENTH MONTH

Yao Wendong, candidate for the post of Yunnan Intendant, informed me by letter that Britain has recently completed building a railway between eastern India and Burma that affords direct access to Burma and Tibet.

5TH OF THE ELEVENTH MONTH

I had written to Yao Wendong before he left his position as the advisor to the Chinese embassy in Germany and asked him to conduct a complete survey of overseas Chinese communities on his way to his new post in Yunnan Province as well as to investigate the disputed area between Yunnan and Burma. Today I received his detailed report on both these issues.[42]

Yao stated that he set sail from Europe in the First month and arrived in Burma by the 22nd of the Third month. On the 4th of the Fourth month he hired a river boat and reached a port west of the Yeren Mountains on the 5th. He continued his journey by bamboo chair and went through rugged mountain terrain. The journey took him about four days, and while in the mountains he caught sight of the red-haired natives there. After he reached the other side of the mountain, he came upon the river valley that extends all the way to the Yunnan frontier.

6TH OF THE ELEVENTH MONTH

Yao's report further stated that the Yunnan frontier is obviously in a precarious position due to Britain's occupation of Burma. Fortunately, due to the towering height of the Yeren Mountains, Yunnan is not in immediate danger. But if we lose the mountains to Britain, their armed forces could march directly into Yunnan Province without any hindrance.

---

42. Yao Wendong (1852-?) published an account of his investigation of Yunnan in 1892, entitled *Yunnan Kanjie choubanji* (A Report on the Yunnan Border and Frontier Issues). Since Hsieh was personally acquainted with Yao, he undoubtedly had a copy of Yao's book in hand.

According to the *Ming History,* the Yeren Mountains were known as the "Southern Teeth," located within the boundaries of Yunnan Province and not part of Mt. Hkakabo Razi.

Yao also contended that Britain's desire to capture Yunnan Province for its strategic position has been a known fact for a long time. Once the British enter Yunnan, they can reach Sichuan Province directly and control the upreaches of the Yangzi River. They can then march into Hunan Province to complete a total occupation of northern China. Therefore, surrender of Yunnan Province to Britain will cost China a fortune, and the loss of the Yeren Mountains will threaten the defense of Yunnan Province. Yao further emphasized that his analysis is based totally upon the theory of the distinguished seventeenth-century scholar of the former Ming dynasty, Gu Yanwu.[43]

7TH OF THE ELEVENTH MONTH

Yao's report continued:

In addition to the western route from Burma to Yunnan, the southern and northern routes are both essential to our defense. The southern route is in the formal territory of the tribal chief Mengken, who was there during the reign of the Qianlong Emperor [1736–1796]. The city of Mengken, which is situated by the Lu River, is a major commercial port in the frontier where all the merchants congregate. In my opinion, both Xinjie and Mengken serve Yunnan as wings of a bird; Xinjie straddles the mountain and gives protection to the west of Yunnan, whereas Mengken leans against the river and defends the south of the province. Such strategic points will likely become the center of future conflict. In the early years, Britain suggested to return to us the territory at the lower stream of the Lu River—which, incidentally, is exactly the same location—but unfortunately we hesitated and didn't accept the offer.

The route at the north of the mountain was once the territory of two native chiefs during the Ming dynasty but is now occupied by primitive people. This area belongs neither to China nor to Burma. There are three routes to China through this area. If this territory falls into Britain's hands, the defense lines around all three provinces at the frontier [Yunnan, Tibet and Xinjiang] will be in jeopardy.

On the mountains there are millions of rubber plants that are a precious commodity to the Westerners. Also in the mountain are two gold mines with rich ores. We should never give that up to help the enemy.

While I was traveling through the mountains, all the native people came out and gave us a hearty welcome. Even the overseer of the rubber plantation sent a message to me acknowledging his loyalty to China, because he is originally Chinese.

---

43. Gu Yanwu (1613–82) was a maternal ancestor of Hsieh Fucheng.

There are sufficient records to certify that both the western and southern routes to Yunnan are in Chinese territory. As for the northern route, which is farthest from Burma, we can send in our troops for immediate occupation, because according to international law, any nation can rightly take over any unoccupied territory.

8TH OF THE ELEVENTH MONTH

Yao included a further secret message:

In the spring of last year, 200 Chinese braves[44] were stationed atop the Yeren Mountains in a place known as Camp Safeguard. They were hired by a Chinese merchants' group to safeguard their trips through the mountains. The braves' leaders, Zhang Tianming and Huang Zhenglin, have both been merce-nary leaders as well as on the nomination list for the post of corporal in the reg-ular army. They are intelligent and brave men who have earned the respect of the Chinese merchants. But because they repeatedly refused to heed the extor-tionate demands of Captain Zhang of Tengyue, Zhang petitioned to have them removed from his army. One consequence of this was that the British forces were thus able to enter Manlong and take over their old campground. Since the loss of Manlong, our troops have been denied entry to the western side of the mountain, and accordingly, we have lost access to the upper, middle and lower routes. Later, Captain Zhang received a message from the British army, which expressed its desire to camp by Hongbang River. Zhang hurriedly moved his camp and retreated. In all, we have lost three of the nine major routes.

At the intersection of the three southern routes known as Mayang, Pen'gan and Handong is the Xipa River. If we send in our troops to camp by the river, we will be able to defend our territory against British forces at that strategic point. The reason why we have no troops stationed there is due to the over-spending of Captain Zhang, who now has no funds with which to recruit more soldiers. Since British officials have proclaimed that the troops of both sides must not invade each others' territories, those tens of thousands of British sol-diers stationed at the southern strategic points of the river have made no attempt to cross the river. Therefore, these three southern routes are the only routes that we still have a chance to occupy and defend.

The northern three routes, Xima, Xidong and Guyong, reach Tengyue by land and the Irrawaddy River by water. There are two pieces of flat land on the mountain top known as Lima and Dadifang. The land is rich but deserted. We can send in our people and build two towns there.

At the foot of the mountain there are two places, Xiage and Yunmao, that shield the openings to the three routes and provide access to the rubber planta-tion. If we station our troops at Yunmao and defend Xiage as well, we can easily contact the forces at Camp Safeguard in Manlong. Then we can not only control

44. "Braves" (*yong*) is the name given to the men who served in local militia throughout much of China in the nineteenth century. In the face of the Taiping Rebellion and the inability of the Qing Imperial armies to suppress local disorder, local leaders in China turned to organizing militia groups for self-defense. "Braves" included both local volunteers and mercenaries.

the mouths of the three routes but also the whole river valley. Furthermore, we will be able to barricade the route to the rubber plantation.

Dadifang was originally the territory of the tribal chief Min, who was driven off by British forces when Captain Zhang failed to answer his call for help. He has since retreated into the mountains, and we have consequently lost the entire mountain. What a pity!

10TH OF THE ELEVENTH MONTH

The origin of the secret society of Brothers and Elders [Gelaohui] can be traced to Sichuan Province. The founders were actually survivors of the Blue Lotus cult, which was in turn once known as the Red Coin Society. The unit leaders are referred to as Hat Buttons. The chief of the staff is the Big Hat Button and the president is the Old Hat in the Hall. These groups are well organized and equipped with a full staff. Each new member receives a long strip of cotton and is encouraged to recruit more members for the society. One who recruits 100 members is installed as the Leader of the Hundred Followers and one who brings in 1,000 men will be the Leader of the Thousand Followers.

Each unit in a different city or province is given the name of a famous mountain, a well-known river or a popular hall such as the Dragon Mountain, the Tiger Mountain, Loyalty Hall or Friendship Hall. In this manner, their power extends throughout the empire and is channeled into all the provinces. Their organizational structure is divided into five units, each of which is represented by one of five colored banners. Those units in Hunan, Hubei and Jiangxi provinces fly a white banner; those in Guangxi, Guangdong, Fujian and Zhejiang provinces fly a black banner; those in Anhui, Jiangsu and Henan provinces fly a blue banner; those in Yunnan, Guizhou, Shaanxi and Gansu provinces a red banner and those in Sichuan Province a yellow banner, using the imperial color yellow as a tribute to their origin.[45]

Presently, there is no trace of their activities in Hebei and Shaanxi provinces; however, people in Shangdong have begun to be tarnished by this cult. And the militia of Hunan Province, which has been in existence for a long time, is filled with the members of this cult.

Foot soldiers who entered the society before their corporal must stand at attention to him in camp during the day, but at the night meetings of the society in the mountains, the corporal must prostrate himself at the foot of his soldiers. Punishments such as flogging are doled out indiscriminately among

---

45. Secret society leaders tended to claim to be the descendants of the former Ming royal family. Since, under Manchu rule, the mere mention of the name Ming could bring mass execution to one's family, my great-grandfather couldn't clearly indicate the true origin of the secret society. (Trans.)

the members during these meetings, and no one dares to protest such an unjustified penalty. Since the surrender of the Taiping rebels, this group has been spreading its doctrine like wildfire throughout the countrysides of all the provinces, and they have subsequently absorbed countless numbers of vagabonds and hooligans into their fold.

Marquis Zeng once suggested that we should implement rigid law enforcement and adopt gentle persuasion at the same time in order to exterminate this vicious cult.

11TH OF THE ELEVENTH MONTH

The combined territories of upper and lower Burma cover 280,000 square miles, which is three times larger than the total territory of the three islands of Great Britain and one-sixth that of India. Burma extends 27 degrees north of the Tropic of Cancer, 10 degrees south of the Tropic of Cancer, 103 degrees to the east of London, and 92 degrees to the west of London.

There are three routes from Manyin to Manmu. The upper one goes straight westward fifty miles to Wulu, passing by Huoyen Mountain, sixty more miles to Longpo and sixty more miles to Manmu. The middle route leads forty miles southwest to Baxuito, sixty more miles to the Hongbang River and fifty more miles to Manmu. The lower route goes southward by the Taiyin River fifty miles to Bangxi, fifty more miles to the Hongbang River and fifty more miles to Manmu. From there, it takes a day's journey by river to reach Xinjie.

13TH OF THE ELEVENTH MONTH

China's trade with the South Sea Islands began during the Han dynasty. It tapered off during the late Ming dynasty when Portuguese invaders occupied the islands.

During the early years of the present dynasty, restrictions on overseas trading were strictly observed, but after the total conquest of Taiwan in the eighteenth year of the Kangxi Emperor [1679], a series of debates was held in the government regarding easing the restrictions. The reason raised at that time was that the profits earned from the import tariff would provide almost enough financial security for the Chinese population. It's a pity that they didn't think far enough. For if the Chinese navy had taken over the South Sea Islands after their conquest of Taiwan, the export tariff would have far exceeded the import revenues they anticipated. Now several European powers have entered these islands in turn and have taken control. There is nothing we can do to bring them back to our fold. What a pity, what a pity!

14TH OF THE ELEVENTH MONTH

Electricity lines in America are the longest in the world, and her school system is also the best. Rich in mining resources and ingenious in new inventions, their industries have turned out the best products in the last fifty years. However, all this progress was accomplished after they began to recruit laborers in China. Without the Chinese work force, I don't think they could have attained such sudden prosperity. It makes one wonder why they now want to deport all the Chinese laborers.

15TH OF THE ELEVENTH MONTH

A letter from Ambassador Xu revealed that the boundary line on Pamir according to Russian assessment is unacceptable to us and that they will not keep their promises. Russia's desire to extend their territory further south does come close to our proposal; therefore, we tentatively ceased negotiations. However, the most pressing problem is that Russia still has more than 200 left stationed by the Murghab River, even after they announced total withdrawal. According to information from the International Office, Russian troops are now stationed at Karakul. In compliance with the agreement on Kashgar, this place should be included within Chinese boundaries. We have repeatedly lodged protests with the Russian Foreign Office demanding further withdrawal of their troops, but they insist that it's a disputed area and therefore haven't even given us an answer. According to the latest information, Russia may send out another mission next spring, and therefore all present negotiations in writing and personal contact may be regarded as a complete waste of time.

1ST OF THE TWELFTH MONTH

In the last few decades, China's economy has deteriorated to its lowest point ever. The average man works day and night yet still cannot support his family. By comparison, the living standard of a hundred years ago is about three to four levels higher than that in the present. When Westerners tour China, they are surprised at the meager standard of living of the Chinese population and the low cost of labor. However, the thrifty nature of our people is another factor. People in the West tend to lead a life of extravagance and each year spend three times the amount of money that a Chinese uses to support himself annually.

4TH OF THE TWELFTH MONTH

On the 26th of last month I sent a cable to the International Office stating:

> Initially, the negotiations over Yunnan-Burma affairs were about to be finished.
> The British Foreign Office had essentially agreed to our point of view, that the Yeren Mountains were a suitable border. But the viceroy of India consistently turned down our proposal. He suddenly launched an attack on the native tribes with his own troops and is closing in on the Yunnan frontier.
> Please lodge a protest with Ambassador O'Connor of Britain and demand to know why the Indian troops refuse to withdraw from Xidong and have instead advanced into Xima. Obviously, the British Foreign Office would have us lodge a strong protest, which, they hope, will reach the office of the Indian viceroy.

On the 28th, I received a response from the International Office asking about the exact location of Xima. I wired back on the 30th, indicating that it is located within the boundaries of Yunnan Province, at the site of an old fortification. I also stated that the viceroy of India is at fault as he had no right to enter our territory until the boundary negotiations between Britain and China were finished.

Today I sent another cable to the International Office stating the following:

> The British officials of the Ministry of Indian Affairs are aggressive and arrogant. They insisted that they cannot continue negotiations until the native tribes are defeated. Their reason for attacking the natives is to provide protection for the caravans of British merchants; but now they even invade our territory. Please inform Ambassador O'Connor that it's wrong to discontinue negotiations. It is also wrong for them to send in troops. If they do not withdraw their armed forces, we will also send in our troops to defend our territory and to protect our own people. The British Foreign Office has hinted broadly that we must protest firmly before they can help us. The security of Yunnan Province is hanging in the balance; we must combine our efforts to achieve our goal. Please wire the governor of Yunnan Province and advise him to put his army on alert and to prepare for an all-out defense.

5TH OF THE TWELFTH MONTH

I wired the International Office again today:

> The real reason for keeping the Yeren Mountains within our boundaries is for the safety of Yunnan Province. The British Foreign Office is willing to settle this matter amicably, but the Ministry of Indian Affairs, which is responsible for several attempts to invade Yunnan over the years, is determined to occupy the province. However, if we stand firm, they will invariably retreat. Then the Foreign Office can take this opportunity to continue negotiations with us without any delay. Once this case is resolved, Ambassador Xu will have a better position from which to negotiate the Pamir case.

6TH OF THE TWELFTH MONTH

I documented the Yunnan-Burma border incident and submitted my report to the International Office.

9TH OF THE TWELFTH MONTH

This afternoon I went to the British Foreign Office with Margary to discuss the Yunnan-Burma boundary incident further.

10TH OF THE TWELFTH MONTH

I sent a cable back to the International Office and informed them that the incident at the Yunnan frontier has reached a crucial point, as India is preparing for further aggression. I also told them about the recent visit I paid to the British Foreign Office and the statement I delivered, contending that due to public outcry, China must send in her troops for the protection of Chinese merchants there in accordance with international law. The British Foreign Office acknowledged my announcement and promised to confer with the Ministry of Indian Affairs in order to resolve this problem. In my cable, I asked the International Office to issue a similar statement to Ambassador O'Connor when he next comes for a visit.

14TH OF THE TWELFTH MONTH

The following is the conversation between [Foreign Secretary] Rosebery and myself on the 9th of this month.

Hsieh: Yesterday I received a letter from Sandison that conveyed a message from the Ministry of Indian Affairs. Presently, the boundary dispute between Yunnan and Burma remains unsettled, but India has totally disregarded international law and sent their troops into the disputed area. I am sure such action didn't meet with the approval of your office.

Rosebery: I'll convey your message to the Ministry of Indian Affairs.

Hsieh: It appears to me that the only interest the Ministry of Indian Affairs has in mind is territorial expansion. They indulge every whim of your military officers and totally disregard the legal procedure of proper negotiations between two countries. In my opinion, they should be placed under the control of your office.

Rosebery: The officials of the Ministry of Indian Affairs are more familiar with the geographical details of the frontier than are we. Therefore, we have to follow their suggestions.

Hsieh: This case involves a boundary issue between two countries, and yet India blatantly intruded into the disputed area with her armed forces, which violated the rights of China as a nation. People in China are outraged by this attack and are clamoring for military action against India to protect our own merchants in accordance with international law.

Rosebery: I definitely will convey this message to the Ministry of Indian Affairs. But the natives there are too belligerent. They attacked the Indian police and had to be punished.

Hsieh: These natives never stepped out of their own boundaries. But when India sent police inside their territory, they had to protect their own interests. Furthermore, that area is presently in dispute, and neither China nor Britain can determine to which side the territory legally belongs. Even if the natives are as guilty as you claim, once the negotiations are completed and boundary lines are clearly drawn, then the legal owner of this territory can eventually launch an investigation and mete out the proper punishments for the natives. This present military action of India tends to cast doubts on the sincerity of Britain in future negotiations and widens the gulf between our two countries. And yet, the Ministry of Indian Affairs contends that the boundary dispute will soon be resolved. I truly don't understand their motive in this case.

Rosebery: I will confer further with the Ministry of Indian Affairs and then inform you of the outcome.

I answered that I will wait for his reply, and we then parted.

15TH OF THE TWELFTH MONTH

Yesterday I received a cable from the International Office that read:

> The governor of Yunnan confirmed that according to the report from the city of Tengyue, there is a Xima[46] located within the area of the Giant Boulder Pass [Jushiguan]. However, there is another native camp known as Xima that was recently burned to the ground by the British troops. It is located several hundred miles outside the gate, which may be the Xima you mentioned in your last dispatch.[47]
>
> Secondly, Ambassador O'Connor claims that according to a recent dispatch from his government, the British patrol was attacked by the natives of Xima. Consequently, the British built a camp there for their own protection. According to our own research, there are two Ximas on the map, and they are both located within the boundaries of Burma.
>
> In your last dispatch you repeatedly mentioned that the British Foreign Office hopes that we lodge a strong protest with their government; this sounded like a mere excuse to us. When we discussed with Ambassador O'Connor the recent dispatch he received from the British Foreign Office, he appeared evasive and acted as if in cohorts with the viceroy of India. Please conduct a thorough investigation into this matter before we make another move. It was suggested to us that we should demand a complete, immediate withdrawal of the British forces and inform the British government that the proper punishment of the natives should be measured out after the boundary is clearly drawn. Submit

---

46. The place mentioned by the governor of Hunan, "Xima," is homonymic with the place Hsieh asked about, "Xima." But the two ways of writing the names are very different in written Chinese.

47. This third "Xima" differs from the previous two.

such a proposal and see what kind of response they give us. We will wait for your answer.

My return dispatch stated:

The Xima I have referred to as located in the wilderness is not included within the territory of Burma. Please reexamine the location. Otherwise, we will have to accept Britain's claim to this territory. The British Foreign Office may be in cohorts with the viceroy of India; if so, we have even more reason to lodge a strong protest. Please make another demand for the total withdrawal of the British troops and inform Ambassador O'Connor that punishment will be duly measured out to the natives once the boundary is clearly drawn. It appears to me that the British government is waiting for a secret message from their ambassador and is gravely concerned about the outcome of this boundary dispute. Please be more suspicious of the ambassador's words.

17TH OF THE TWELFTH MONTH

I received this year's staff promotion list. Both Clerk Wang Wenzao and student Guo Jiaji have been promoted to aide positions at the embassy.

20TH OF THE TWELFTH MONTH

A letter from Minister Xu Xiaoyun stated:

The appointed duration of your present position will expire soon. I will soon prepare a memorial and submit several names for your replacement to His Majesty the Emperor for approval. Your exceedingly unbending capability as ambassador is a well-known fact in the International Office and at all levels of government. Even former British ambassador Wilson frequently mentioned his admiration of your integrity and expressed his regret that you will soon end your stay in England. This proves how much trust the British government has placed in you as the Chinese envoy to her country.

The negotiation of the Yunnan-Burma border is a matter of serious importance. We presently lack the right personnel to handle this problem and therefore depend solely on your ability as our negotiator. Our opponent is a race greedy by nature, and therefore negotiations may be extended indefinitely. Your excellent cordial relationship with Britain during past negotiations has earned more credit for you than for all other envoys. Henceforth, we are obliged to ask you to stay longer until the dispute is resolved.

Furthermore, during our discussion about the coming vacancy when Xu Jihe retires, His Majesty made the remark that you are doing a great job. Accordingly, you may likely surpass all the others on the list for the promotion and be given that position. I hope that you will not mind staying half a year longer and delaying your trip home. As soon as the Yunnan boundary case is resolved, I will immediately submit the name of your replacement to His Majesty the Emperor and shall not compel you to prolong your stay abroad.

The loan incurred by Chen Jitong was repaid in full with the help of the Office of the Northern Ports. It's a foreign loan co-signed by Bo Xing; therefore, we must provide repayment of the loan.

As far as Pamir is concerned, Russian troops are constantly plundering the frontier. Even though they have temporarily retreated, there is no guarantee that they will not return next year. This is the best time for us to negotiate with them in redefining the boundary. This case is not an easy task, as we do not intend to send in our troops to fight for a few pieces of wasteland in the wilderness. However, empty words will not halt military invasion, and we probably will lose more than we will gain in the future. Since Britain offered no help when the Russian troops slaughtered the Afghan soldiers, Afghanistan is now apparently afraid of Russian power.

The salaries of the diplomats, from ambassador to counsellors, have been raised to double the amount of last year's pay. But the wages of the embassy staff remain as those of last year.

23RD OF THE TWELFTH MONTH

The military officers of the European nations are all well-educated men and familiar with such fields as land surveying and engineering. When they lead their troops to war, they know where to camp, where to set up an ambush and where to mount the cannons. Therefore, the success rates of their campaigns are reasonably high, and their social positions are regarded as superior to those of government officials. For this very reason, more young men are willing to enlist in the army than to work in the government. Consequently, they are able to build mighty armies.

24TH OF THE TWELFTH MONTH

According to the ancient text *Zhuangzi*, a giant fish in the North Sea was transformed into a huge bird whose wings spanned the entire sky. This tale is believed to be only a fable. However, in the late Ming dynasty, a feather of a giant eagle was seen by the Imperial Scholar Ling Han in a treasure storage room. He recorded that there was room enough for two persons to sit inside the tip of the feather.

Since my arrival in Europe, I have visited several museums but have failed to see a specimen of such a huge bird.

27TH OF THE TWELFTH MONTH

The International Office conferred with the English ambassador O'Connor and suggested that the Chengguang Hall in the Western Garden be the designated place for his audience with His Majesty the Emperor. It's the same place where the Austrian ambassador had his audience last year.

The time was set for 10:30 in the morning on the 25th of this month. The ambassador arrived with four of his staff and was cordially received by several of our ministers. Twenty minutes later, His Majesty the Emperor came to the hall and mounted the throne. The ambassador entered through the east gate followed by his aides and interpreter. He bowed down and His Majesty acknowledged his presence with a nod. He spoke his tribute to the emperor in English; it was subsequently translated into Chinese. He then submitted his credentials, which were accepted by Prince Kang. He then bowed again and retreated. Afterward, he gave the published diary of his queen to the International Office as a gift to His Majesty the Emperor.

Part IV

Nineteenth Year of the Guangxu Emperor (1893)

1ST OF THE FIRST MONTH

When translations of Western books were first introduced to all the ministries of the Chinese government, critics condemned the project as a sheer waste of time. Now, after less than twenty years, scholars are enthusiastic about newly acquired knowledge such as the revolution of the earth around the sun, the application of both electricity and the steam engine and even basic studies such as photography, the printing press and railway construction. On the annual civil service examinations, mathematics has since been added as one of the major subjects, because it is now regarded as the foundation of all science.

Therefore, it is essential that the names of all the students with high math scores on the annual examination be recorded so that they may be called upon to work on future projects such as the renovation of our cities, the construction of fortifications, the setting up of industrial machinery and the technique of launching torpedoes. Needless to say, all these projects will be vital to our national interest.

4TH OF THE FIRST MONTH

The crown prince of England held a party for gentlemen at St. James Palace this afternoon on behalf of Her Majesty the Queen. I went to the party with several members of my staff to participate in the first major social event of the year.

6TH OF THE FIRST MONTH

I went to two tea parties at six o'clock this afternoon. They were held by the navy ministers, Lord Spenser and Marquis Londonberry, respectively.

7TH OF THE FIRST MONTH

European nations levy taxes on both liquor and tobacco that bring in a substantial amount of revenue to the government. There are four billion inhabitants of China, many of whom enjoy smoking and drinking. Even if three cents were levied on each adult, the results would be staggering.

8TH OF THE FIRST MONTH

A list of international railroads will be published by the Russian Railroad Association.

11TH OF THE FIRST MONTH

Russia is planning to harvest tea on her soil, since a Russian merchant, a long-time resident of China, learned Chinese tea-planting methods. We have lost a sizable profit since India went into the tea business. Now Russia will also take a share of our tea trade.

12TH OF THE FIRST MONTH

The queen of England held a party for gentlemen and their ladies at Buckingham Palace today, and I went to the party with my advisors.

Burma rises from the south near a tributary of the Malay River and extends to the north to the foothills of Mt. Hkakabo Razi, and includes the region of the Yeren Mountains. It extends from the Mekong River in the east to the ocean in the west. It's several hundred miles in width and 1,200 miles in length. The inhabitants of Burma are of Indian, Chinese and Mongolian ancestry.

The first settlers of Burma were people from China who arrived there during the reign of King Jing of the Chou dynasty [c. 544–519 B.C.]. After 600 years, however, they migrated to another place. During the Han dynasty [206B.C.–A.D. 220], Burma was known as the kingdom of Dan. During the reign of the Han Emperor He [89–106], tribute was offered annually by the king of Dan to the Chinese Imperial Court. During the Song dynasty [960–1127], the kingdom of Burma made her first appearance in our official history, and during the Yuan dynasty [1271–1368], several roads were constructed to reach Burma. An Imperial official was posted there but was later removed. During that period, Burma moved her capital to Pugan. In the early Ming dynasty [1368–1644], six Imperial representatives were posted there, and later four more were added to make an even number of ten. All ten officials governed the region with the king of Burma and several other frontier tribes such as the Mengmi and the Mengyang. In the later years of the Ming dynasty, the chief of Mengmi attacked Burma and killed the king. After some twenty years, the crown prince drove the enemy out of his kingdom and consolidated all the regions of Burma into one kingdom. Two Chinese Imperial representatives were casualties of the conflict. The new king of Burma continued his assault on the territories of the remaining tribes and soon succeeded in annexing these tribal areas into Burma. During the tenth year of the Ming emperor Wanli, the Burmese king launched an attack on Chinese-controlled territory with a cavalry of elephants, but he was driven back by the forces of Yunnan's Governor Liu. The Burmese troops were defeated, and both the Mengyang and Manmu tribes subsequently surrendered to the Chinese army.

13TH OF THE FIRST MONTH

I attended a tea party at the home of the vice admiral of the British navy.

14TH OF THE FIRST MONTH

In the twenty-second year of the Ming emperor Wanli [1594], the Yunnan governor created eight gates at Tengyue and placed a garrison there as well. He subsequently built a fort at Mengmao and negotiated an alliance with Siam for the defense of the territory. Burma, under the constant threat of Siam, soon exhausted her national resources and was unable to offer tribute to China. By the end of the Ming dynasty, Burma was once again making frequent assaults on the Chinese frontier.

In the thirty-ninth year of the Kangxi Emperor [1700], the chief of Pegu tribe led the troops of both the Netherlands and Portugal into Awa and captured the king of Burma. Consequently, Burma was annexed to Pegu.

In the nineteenth year of the Qianlong Emperor [1754], the king of Awa was assassinated. The chiefs of various tribes combined their forces together and united Burma into one nation again, which created disturbances along the Chinese border. In the thirty-second year [1767], China launched a major attack on Burma. Burma appealed for peace and Burma remained unscathed. In the thirty-sixth year [1771], Siam was taken over by Burmese forces. Later, Siam rallied around a former minister, Zheng Zhao, and succeeded in putting him on the throne. Zheng not only recovered all the territories Siam lost but also pushed the tribe of Chief Mengyun as far as Mande in the east of Burma. Consequently, China recognized the sovereignty of Siam, and Burma began to offer tributes to China again. In the fifty-second year of the Qianlong Emperor [1787], China sent a special envoy to Burma and recognized the sovereignty of that country. By then, Burma had developed into a prosperous nation and was fully equipped with a strong military force.

In the sixth year of the Daoguang Emperor [1826], Burma launched an attack on India and went down in total defeat.

16TH OF THE FIRST MONTH

After Burma's defeat in India, the British navy entered the waters of Burma and prepared to attack Awa. Fearful of repercussions, Burma sought for peace, paying 3,000,000 taels of silver as an indemnity and conceding the territory along the coast. In the second year of the Xianfeng Emperor [1852], Burma again engaged in warfare with Britain, conceding Pegu during the peace negotiations.

Britain consequently posted an official to control the area, which became known as Rangoon. The British navy then sailed down the Irrawaddy River as far as Bhamo and placed a consul at the capital of Burma. The king of Burma at that time was known to be corrupt and repressive.

In the ninth year of the Guangxu Emperor [1883], France annexed all the territory of Indochina, which subsequently posed a great threat to Britain. In the eleventh year of the Guangxu Emperor [1885], Lord Salisbury launched an attack on Burma. Britain dispatched its armed forces through India and captured the king of Burma in Mandalay. Consequently, Burma became another colony of Britain. A governor of Burma was duly appointed, who now serves under the supervision of the viceroy of India.

18TH OF THE FIRST MONTH

There is no river longer in Burma than the Irrawaddy River, which is also known as the Great Golden Sand River. The river begins to flow from two tributary streams. The eastern one begins in Tibet at twenty-eight degrees north of the Tropic of Cancer, and the western one begins among the Yeren Mountains at twenty-seven degrees and forty points north of the Tropic of Cancer.

19TH OF THE FIRST MONTH

To the east of the Irrawaddy River are the two major rivers of Burma. One is the Bailong River, which begins in the depths of the mountains of the Dan people and after 260 miles combines with several small streams before flowing into the Gulf of Martaban. The other is the Lu River, known as the Salween River in English. The river begins from Mengding in China and flows southward to the territory of the Kalani mountain tribe. Along the river banks of that area is the principle logging center of the lumber merchants. Winding through and combining with several other small rivers, the Salween River passes by the frontier of Siam, and after combining with several more small streams, flows into the Gulf of Martaban.

20TH OF THE FIRST MONTH

A letter from Ambassador Xu reached me today containing the following statement:

> Negotiations over the Pamir boundary case here have since been shelved and Russia flatly refuses to withdraw her troops from Karakul. When the weather warms up, Russia will likely dispatch more troops to patrol the border area. This will surely increase tensions along the frontier. However, the International Office has not formulated any concrete plan regarding this issue.
>
> Last winter, the British ambassador to Russia made an inquiry at the Russian Foreign Office regarding the future date of further negotiations. But

the Russia foreign minister, Gortchakov, has not fully recovered from his illness, and his under secretary gave this reason as an excuse for the delay. He contended that he must discuss this problem with the minister before he can set a negotiation date. Have you made any progress in your negotiations yet?

Last month Yang Zitong was named as ambassador-at-large. Cui Enren had previously submitted a petition to the International Office on behalf of a Chinese merchants' group for funds for the expense of hiring call girls for social functions. The International Office subsequently reprimanded him for this immoral request. This man did everything he could to maintain his official position, so this sudden change of posts may be due to the public outcry over his improper conduct. As I understand it, he frequently involves himself in various unlawful dealings. It's envoys like Cui that disgrace all of us.

22ND OF THE FIRST MONTH

I attended a party at Buckingham Palace party to which ladies were also invited.

Rangoon is the city in the Pegu region where a British prefect is stationed. It is India's third seaport, located at sixteen degrees north of the Tropic of Cancer. At the mouth of its harbor, a myriad of boats are anchored, which indicates a brisk business enterprise operating inside the city compound. A number of Chinese merchants there initially came from Fujian and Guangdong provinces, and their numbers have reached to more than 10,000, in addition to some 20 merchants from Yunnan Province.

There is a place there, known as the Pagoda of Eight Families, where a Ming official was once posted. There is also a historical building, the top of which is entirely covered with gilt bricks, more than 300 feet high. It was erected during the time of King Jian of the Zhou dynasty [c. 580 B.C.] and is constructed on a foundation 166 feet high. The height of the Grand Bell is sixteen feet, with historical details etched on both sides.

Mandalay controls Bhamo in the north and extends to Rangoon in the south. Britain named the city as the capital of Burma soon after its occupation on account of the city's strategic position. It is located twenty-two degrees north of the Tropic of Cancer.

The high mountain located sixty miles north of the city contains ruby mines and is known as Mogu. It is also known to contain a variety of other precious minerals.

24TH OF THE FIRST MONTH

The Dan people established their nation rather early in time and began to pay tribute to China during the Han dynasty. Their territory is located east of the Mekong River and extends west to Burma, south to Siam and north to

China. There are numerous tribes within this territory, but they have failed
to ally with each other. Therefore, over the years, they have toiled as laborers
for Burma. They have been divided into many parts since the British occupation, the number of which incidentally coincides with the original ninety-nine
tribes that Burma claims existed in the territory.

25TH OF THE FIRST MONTH

I attend a party at St. James Palace that was for gentlemen only.

The Yeren Mountains face Tengyue in the east, extend to Xueshan in the
west by the river and reach Bhamo in the south and Tibet in the north.
Located at twenty-four degrees north of the Tropic of Cancer, the mountain
range contains the tributary streams of both the Irrawaddy River and the
Chindwin River. Along the banks of the Chindwin, at the base of the mountains, there are mines rich with amber. About 300 more miles further to the
northwest are the Baituoke Mountains. To the north of the mountains are the
Naya Hills, now under the control of a British official at Asami. To the south
of the mountains is Xueyifushan Peak, 8,266 feet high. This is the extremity
of the Yeren Mountains. To the north of the mountains is Xiaogan Peak, at
the foot of which the Asami River flows. This is the natural boundary of the
Yeren Mountains. Obviously the region on the west bank of the Irrawaddy
River is several times larger than that on the east bank, which corresponds
closely with the Chinese frontier. The east bank rises from the south of
Tianma Pass and continues along three rivers: the Taiping, the Mulei and the
Nantaibo. The native inhabitants of the Yeren Mountains are ferocious creatures with red hair. Chinese merchants must travel in groups and be armed
with swords while making the crossing.

There are nine routes for going across the mountain ranges. South of the
Taiping River, there are three routes, known as Mayang, Pen'gan and Handong.
In the north there are three more routes known as the lower, middle and
upper routes. All six of these routes reach Bhamo. Further north there are
three more routes, known as the Xima, Xidong and Guyong. At the intersection of these three routes, one can cross a river to Menggong. All nine routes
lie under the shadow of Mt. Xueshan, which is located in the west of Yunnan.
This mountain range ends south of the Mulei River, where it joins with the
southern edge of the Yeren Mountains at the exact site of the nine passes.

29TH OF THE FIRST MONTH

I dispatched Margary to the British Foreign Office to discuss the Yeren
Mountains further with Sandison. Regretfully their discussion failed to produce any satisfactory results.

17TH OF THE SECOND MONTH

In a few months time I expect to be returning home. I took out my writing brush and wrote a couplet on a pair of banners, which I intend to send back home immediately to adorn the front gate of my new home. The couplet went as follows:

Exchanging views with relatives and friends, one should avoid talk of lawsuits or money.

Selecting friends by their talents, one should seek out those who are knowledgeable about world affairs.

21ST OF THE SECOND MONTH

In the late afternoon I sent Margary to the British Foreign Office to see Sandison regarding the Yeren Mountains issue.

24TH OF THE SECOND MONTH

On the 4th of April, a drastic change took place in the cabinet of the French government. France had invaded Siam on the 1st of April. Fearful of reprisal, Siam retreated. France's initial intention with this attack was to take over a large island in the Mekong River that is both strategically positioned and commercially valuable. Thereafter, the question of whether France should drive the Siamese troops off the east bank was heatedly debated in the French Parliament, because France intends to divide the country with the river as the natural boundary.

26TH OF THE SECOND MONTH

I went to the British Foreign Office in the afternoon and discussed the Yeren Mountains issue with Lord Rosebery.

4TH OF THE THIRD MONTH

Westerners operate machinery by the power of water and fire. Since early times, China has used a pedal machine to harness the power of water. Presently, in several provinces such as Fujian, Anhui and Sichuan, this practice is still prevalent. Paper manufacturers use pedals to crush bamboo with amazing speed, and farmers obtain flour by grinding grain into powder. There is no difference between using machinery or a grindstone to produce flour. Japan has also used this same method over the centuries. With the exception of metal, which must be melted down by fire, water power is most dependable.

In the interior of China, there are pedal machines installed on hilltops. We should try to acquire new methods to harness the power of water, because it will cost much less than to do so with fire.

6TH OF THE THIRD MONTH

In the thirteenth year of the Guangxu Emperor [1887], the International Office asked several European ambassadors what improvements they would like to see in China's tea export industry. The answers were the same: decrease the tariff. The commissioner of the Maritime Office, Hart, also suggested such a change as he thought it would improve commerce in China in the long run. Yet the following year criticism of such a decrease arose claiming that it would damage Imperial tax revenue. Therefore, the reform was subsequently shelved.

8TH OF THE THIRD MOUTH

An airship society has existed in Germany for a long time. Recently, the Kaiser awarded 50,000 Marks to the society in the hope that they will develop a huge airship.

Both Ximas, the one at the Chinese frontier and the one at the foot of the Yeren Mountains, are located thirty-two miles from the Irrawaddy River.

9TH OF THE THIRD MONTH

This afternoon I attended a Buckingham Palace party for gentlemen.

11TH OF THE THIRD MONTH

This afternoon I went to the British Foreign Office with Advisor Ma and discussed the boundary dispute between Yunnan and Burma with Lord Rosebery.

25TH OF THE THIRD MONTH

Yesterday I attended a party at Buckingham Palace that included lady guests.

This afternoon I went to an opening ceremony conducted by the queen for the newly constructed addition to the British Parliament.

26TH OF THE THIRD MONTH

I dispatched a cable to the International Office with the following message:

The Yunnan affair has been discussed over and over again, but the British Foreign Office repeatedly denies the previous agreement they negotiated with Marquis Zeng. Both the Cheli and Menglian native chiefs once paid regular tribute to Burma, and now these territories are included in the neutral zone. Burmese officials are now scheming to get out of the deal, claiming that it is humiliating to pay tribute according to previous agreements.

Constantly intimidated by the Ministry of Indian Affairs, the British Foreign Office frequently ceases negotiations with me or my staff. They contend that they have reached the point of exhaustion in their endeavor. However, we must closely watch the action of India, which is bent on invading the Yunnan frontier. If we lose these frontiers and fall victim to their conspiracy, other powerful nations may be tempted to take additional territories from us. Please render all the effort you can muster and insist that the Irrawaddy River should be considered the boundary. With a firm stand, they may keep their promise as per the previous agreement.

The British Foreign Office has just sent me a dispatch stating that they have come to an agreement with the viceroy of India, who is willing to surrender the territory southwest of Mengding known as Kegan, which stretches to the left bank of the Lu River. The length of the region is estimated to be 750 miles. Also, the area that is parallel to the territory of the Mengmao native chief on the opposite bank of the river will be surrendered to China; it is approximately 800 square miles. The Hanlong Pass, which had long been lost to Burma, will also be returned to China during the official signing of the treaty. Both the territories in the north and south of Xima in the Yeren Mountains, which are estimated to span over 300 square miles, will also be surrendered to China. We will be given total control of the territories of both the Cheli and Menglian native chiefs, and Burma will be denied the right to interfere in their internal administration. Furthermore, Burma will continue to offer tribute to China next year.

All these territories are located at the frontier, so it will be easy for us to keep control. The retreat of the boundary may follow the Yunnan-Burma map, which would resolve the border dispute. It may differ considerably from the agreement Marquis Zeng previously negotiated, but it appears satisfactory. Even though all these territories are located in the wilderness, we at least have made some progress:

1. We have gained respect from other foreign powers.
2. We have ended the conspiracy of India.
3. We have provided protection to all native chiefs in the Yunnan-Burma frontier.
4. We have avoided territorial loss inside Yunnan Province.

The British are a shrewd race of people who are apt to break their promises whenever they have the opportunity.

With Ambassador O'Connor's persistent intimidation, we should hasten to submit this new agreement to His Majesty the Emperor for final approval before they change their minds again. As soon as we obtain a decree, I will discuss the trade regulations at the frontier before finalizing the agreement with the British Foreign Office. I expect all these procedures to be completed in the next three months. The previous agreement tended to focus on the return of our lost territory. The present negotiation attempts to project the benefits of trade regulations, and so it should be easily accepted.

Since I cannot leave my post until a replacement is appointed, please make haste.

3RD OF THE FOURTH MONTH

The U.S. Supreme Court recently ordered the registration of all Chinese aliens, yet out of 100,000 Chinese in America, only 4,000 were registered. Consequently, 96,000 Chinese must be deported. But since the estimate of the cost of such deportation procedures overwhelmed the U.S. Congress, the legislators are seriously considering rescinding the order. Nevertheless, the president of the United States insists on enforcing the ruling before he will appoint an envoy to China. The United States has only 1,000 citizens living in China and therefore harbors no fear of retaliation.

4TH OF THE FOURTH MONTH

The project of constructing electric lines in cooperation with Russia has been completed. The cost of telegrams by sea or land is identical, to the disappointment of our country, and only Russia has reaped profits from this project. Now all the other ambassadors are displeased, especially the British ambassador, but it's too late now to withdraw from the deal.

11TH OF THE FOURTH MONTH

Ambassador Xu sent me a letter stating:

> There has been a significant development regarding the Pamir affair. In view of our recent efforts to increase our military forces and to build up our defenses, Russia has realized that we are determined to put up a fight. Therefore, the Russian Foreign Office has approached me and asked for a definite location for negotiations. Last month Russia contended that as long as our troops stay within the confines of the garrison, their army will not advance onto Chinese soil.
>
> Qing Aitang finally had the opportunity to see Gortchakov and expressed to him our peace initiative, to which Gortchakov concurred. In my view, we may avoid the crisis we anticipated. However, as far as the boundary dispute is concerned, there are still differences to be ironed out.
>
> Last year Grand Secretariat Hong Jun mistakenly placed Chinese territory outside our boundary lines when he had a map drawn up. It's believed that he followed the British Foreign Office map, which you previously forwarded to the International Office. There were obvious mistakes regarding the area, but the copier claimed he was following the Russian map. This map, therefore, became a much discussed subject among the scholar-officials in the South City.

12TH OF THE FOURTH MONTH

Traditionally, the Chinese believe that each family should keep its lineage intact. It is firmly believed that a childless couple will become hungry ghosts, because they will have no one to visit their graves to offer food to their spirits.

By contrast, Western men tend to stay unmarried even if they are millionaires. It's not unusual to see high-ranking government officials who remain bachelors in their advanced years. Then they tend to marry women who are half their age simply to amuse themselves. Their idea of marriage is obviously not for reproduction as they do not consider it to be important to have children. The reason is apparently due to their faith in Jesus, whose preaching advocates that spirits require no food.

15TH OF THE FOURTH MONTH

Westerners both rich and poor tend to be more health conscious than Chinese people. Those with minor positions generally have meat dishes as their daily meal. After dinner, they partake of fruit, drink coffee and then smoke cigars. Every morning and evening, they drink milk or beef tea, and their daily allowance is invariably three to four silver dollars. Even though their clothing is made of plain black wool, I understand that each suit is rather expensive.

In my opinion, Western people are accustomed to being clean and tidy, are inclined to flaunt their wealth, and firmly believe that diet affects one's health. Hence, even their servants manage to eat meat every seven days so that they may maintain their strength.

Chinese indentured laborers abroad receive merely two to three silver dollars each day; therefore they tend to be thrifty, never eat meat and dress shabbily. The Westerners look upon them with total contempt, because they claim that the Chinese are living like animals, and since the Chinese are no better than animals, why should they treat the Chinese like human beings?

The recent government policy in the United States to deport Chinese laborers may stem from this very observation. If our people take reasonable care of themselves in their eating habits and appearance, they may well be spared such cruel treatment abroad.

20TH OF THE FOURTH MONTH

Yesterday I attended a party given by the British Foreign Office. It was actually a celebration of the queen's birthday.

22ND OF THE FOURTH MONTH

The largest library in London contains a large selection of Chinese classics. Every day, there are 300 people studying in the library. They arrive at the library in the early morning and leave the building late in the evening. Obviously, they have developed a genuine understanding of the sayings of our ancient sages.

5TH OF THE FIFTH MONTH

Next year the Empress Dowager will celebrate her sixtieth birthday. By decree the birthday celebration must be kept within the limits of a budget. There are 5 to 6 hundred million taels of gold in reserve at the Ministry of Finance. But a check of the birthday celebration of the Emperor Qianlong, which was many years ago, revealed that 36 million taels of gold were spent. Therefore, the present reserve is definitely insufficient. The Ministry of Finance has since issued orders to all levels of government that their daily budgets must be kept to the barest minimum.

14TH OF THE FIFTH MONTH

I paid a visit to the new American ambassador to Britain. He is in his seventies and was once the Minister of Foreign Affairs. He is a gentle and kind man and has been a good friend of Zhang Qiaoye for many years.

15TH OF THE FIFTH MONTH

A letter from the International Office indicated:

> Regarding the Pamir affair, Ambassador Xu has petitioned to set up more garrisons at Tashkurghan and several other places nearby. By recent decree, we have ordered the Shenji base of the Office of the Northern Ports to issue more military equipment and the governor of Xinjiang to dispatch more troops into these areas as a defensive measure. In the Second month of this year, Ambassador Xu informed us by cable that Russia has expressed its willingness to negotiate, and we must decide which territory in the west of Mt. Sarakoran we will concede. We have conferred with the Russian ambassador here accordingly and have informed him that we will withdraw from the south of Yashil to Sarikol. The Kashgar agreement must be kept, although the terms may be renegotiated. The Russian ambassador agreed to wire the Russian Foreign Office for approval but has not given us any answer yet.

A letter from Yang Yuchang revealed that the Pamir affair may soon be resolved as the Russian ambassador acted rather ingratiating toward us.

However, although the Russian Foreign Office still insists that we retreat to Sarikol, the British ambassador wants us to stop at Kanwahan; therefore, a final decision may not be easily reached.

18TH OF THE FIFTH MONTH

On the 9th of the First month of this year, my dispatch to the International Office stated:

> Among the nine passes in Tengyue, the Hanlong Pass has long been lost to Burma. Now, after an extensive research of Huang Maocai's *Diary of Travels in Western Lands* [*Xiyou riji*], I have learned that Tianma Pass was also taken by Burma. However, on a map of Yunnan Province, the gate was drawn inside our border. Also, Tongbi Pass is located behind the Hongbang River according to this Yunnan map, but foreign maps clearly indicate that the pass is located to the west of the river. Britain suggested that we use the river as the natural boundary but insisted that Tianma Pass is on the Burmese side. Please cable the governor of Yunnan Province and ask for the exact locations of these two passes. Let us know as soon as possible.

On the 18th of the same month, I received a cable from the International Office:

> The governor of Yunnan Province informed us that Tianma Pass is located in the territory of the Mengmao tribe, which has since been taken over by primitive people; however, it lies within our boundary lines. Tongbi Pass is located at the east of the Hongbang River, which is under the control of the Nanmian tribe. The foreign map is definitely wrong.

On the 27th of the Third month, my dispatch to the International Office stated:

> The British Foreign Office contended that if Hanlong Pass is located at the southeast of the Mengmao tribe's territory, they are willing to return it to us; otherwise, they are unable to give us a firm commitment. Please make a thorough check of the location in order not to be cheated during the official signing of the boundary agreement.

On the 21st of the Fourth month, I sent another dispatch by cable:

> Earlier, the Yunnan governor claimed that Tianma Pass is now occupied by primitive people, but according to the British Foreign Office, it is now in the hands of the Mubang tribe. Please cable the governor of Yunnan Province again and find solid evidence to prove their mistake.

On the 15th of this month, I received another dispatch from the International Office:

> According to the findings of the governor of Yunnan Province, Hanlong Pass is located in the Yuanding Mountains, which sit between the Mengmao and Zhefang tribes. The mountains stretch for eighty miles from the Mengmao tribe; the distance is even shorter from the Zhefang tribe. The pass remained in the hands of Burma for a long time. It was then occupied by primitive people and later taken over by the Zhefang tribe. The map that the governor of Yunnan drew last year indicates the pass slightly too far to the southwest.

On the 17th of this month, I received another dispatch from the International Office:

> According to a recent report from the governor of Yunnan Province, Tianma Pass was originally in the territory of the Mengmao tribe. Later, it was occupied by primitive people. Whether or not it is presently controlled by the Mubang tribe cannot yet be confirmed. Tianma Pass is definitely located in the territory of the Mengmao tribe, and we have an old document to substantiate this fact.

21ST OF THE FIFTH MONTH

Qing Aitang's letter to me revealed that France has summoned the deposed king of Vietnam back to Paris from Algiers. This may be interpreted to mean that France is seriously considering putting him back on the throne. The present young monarch is but a playboy, and the ministers of that country wish to see the return of their former king.

He further reported that the French Foreign Office claimed that according to international law, each nation must seek the approval of the other nation before changing an envoy. China sought such approval from Britain, yet failed to do so with France, and they would like to know the reason for such negligence. Our answer to them was that since France never sought approval from China and Britain did, this is the reason for the difference. Consequently, the French Foreign Office demanded that they must be notified in the future of any such change.

The French Foreign Office also forwarded the following statement:

> We received a telegram yesterday from Vietnam and understand that the Yunnan-Vietnam boundary issue has been resolved. There are only two minor issues that require further discussion. Since Laos also shares a border with Yunnan Province, the boundary line there should also be clearly drawn before problems develop in the future. We have our hands full protecting Vietnam; therefore, we have no desire to occupy more land in distant places.

We made a survey of Laos and found the mountain ranges treacherous and the climate horrid. The land there is definitely not equal to the rich fertile soil along the tributary streams of the Irrawaddy River. Therefore, negotiation of the boundary line there shall not pose any problems.

We have briefed Ambassador Lemy to inform your International Office, but have not yet received an answer.

22ND OF THE FIFTH MONTH

The second grandson of the queen of England, the Duke of York, who is now second in line to the throne, shall be getting married tomorrow. I cabled the International Office on the 20th of the Fourth month requesting permission to send official congratulations to the Duke for the coming happy event. The answer arrived today instructing me to put a message of congratulations in writing and send it to the British Foreign Office on behalf of His Majesty the Emperor.

Today I went to the British Foreign Office and was greeted by Lord Rosebery. He personally took the letter and promised he would offer the message of congratulations to the queen on my behalf.

I heard that the envoys of various countries had sent wedding gifts to the Duke. I have a set of valuable Jingtai blue porcelain pieces in my possession. I chose two tall vases, two flower baskets, two small incense burners and a tall wine kettle as wedding gifts and sent them to the Duke's residence. The Duke expressed his appreciation by letter and claimed that they are the best gifts he has received for his wedding.

The crown prince held a garden party in honor of the queen and the wedding today. As many as 2,000 guests from both the nobility and high-level government offices arrived at the party. I also attended.

23RD OF THE FIFTH MONTH

An earlier cable from the International Office stated:

> Russia, in her attempt to occupy Lesser Pamir, claimed that we have conceded Kanjuti to Britain. We repeatedly explained that the area is under both British and Chinese control, but to no avail. In addition, Russia brought out the fact that Kashgar officials had sent a herd of 300 sheep to the British official who is now posted at Kanjuti.
>
> To prove that Kanjuti is truly under the control of both countries, we propose to place an official there. Such an action will the suspicion of Russia and halt her aggression in Lesser Pamir. Please inform the British Foreign Office that we have no desire to interfere with the authority in Kanjuti. But if Russia takes over Lesser Pamir, this will also harm Britain. Report to us their reaction as soon as possible.

I sent Ma Qingchen to the British Foreign Office several times, but they flatly refused our proposal. Consequently, I submitted a dispatch to the International Office with the following message:

> I negotiated with the British Foreign Office regarding the posting of a Chinese official at Kashgar. Their answer was that Kashgar is under the control of both countries, and Britain has never attempted to overrule our authority there. The natives there may find it hard to adjust to the addition of one more official. Lesser Pamir is internationally known to be the territory of China and therefore, China should take a firm stand.

Yesterday I met Lord Rosebery and informed him about a recent incident. It involved a British official who prohibited Chinese authorities from issuing travel papers to the Kanjuti chief. I emphasized that Britain appears to be interfering with our tributary offerings again. Lord Rosebery contended that traditionally China has never posted an official in Kanjuti; however, he would do everything possible to stop such unpleasant incidents from recurring at Kanjuti in the future.

26TH OF THE FIFTH MONTH

A telegram from Imperial Commissioner Li asked that I find and hire an expert because he intends to develop a textile industry in China. This was subsequently followed by a request for the purchase of 100 fine-weaving machines, which must be able to produce 500 bales of textiles per day.

10TH OF THE SIXTH MONTH

I met with Qing Aitang to find out more details about his discussion with the French Foreign Office regarding France's recent conflict with Siam. He reported their conversation as follows:

> *Minister:* The frequent confrontations between Siam and France were instigated by Britain. In the last few months, it has intensified almost to a breaking point.
> *Qing:* What is France's position on resolving this problem?
> *Minister:* Siam recently invaded the left bank of the Mekong River, which is legally the territory of Vietnam. It is only 100 miles from the military camp of the Siamese army to the capital of Vietnam, and France has the obligation to provide protection for Vietnam. First of all, we have to help Vietnam regain their lost territory and then ensure that the river remains the natural boundary. Second, our merchants in Cambodia lost their businesses when they were thrown out by Siamese officials. We absolutely must ask Siam for an indemnity. Third, French soldiers and Vietnam officials were surreptitiously murdered by Siamese officials during the invasion of Vietnam, and so Siam must pay compen-

sation money to the families of all the victims. Fourth, several days ago, Siam blasted French gunboats with cannonfire while the boats were entering the waterway. As a result, a merchant ship was destroyed in the crossfire, and we are demanding compensation for that. In addition to these four demands, we also request three million francs for the military operations we needed to respond to Siam's aggression. We have since sent the former governor of Saigon to Siam demanding a reply within two days. We expect that Siam will come to the realization that France is serious about these demands. As a matter of fact, France has neither the ambition nor the desire to deprive Siam of her sovereignty. As soon as she agrees to meet our demands, we are willing to negotiate peace with her.

Qing: All the lands on both sides of the river are legally Chinese territories. We would like to know why Your Excellency has now claimed the river as the boundary.

Minister: France has no intention of taking over China's territory. However, China and France must jointly determine the clear dividing line between the tributary and the river. This problem should be easy to resolve. If not for Britain's recent instigation of a conflict between France and Siam, a peaceful solution would have been reached at a much earlier date. Britain has no love for Siam. All it cares about is creating conflict between us so that they may reap a profit. The problems between Vietnam and France were also instigated by Britain. If Britain truly cares about China's interests, then why have they taken advantage of this opportunity and snatched up Burma? Last year Britain took over thousands of miles of fertile land in the north of Siam; therefore, France must annex the left shore of the river to compensate for her loss.

11TH OF THE SIXTH MONTH

According to a French newspaper, France has won several battles against Siam without the loss of a single soldier and has succeeded in occupying several islands.

12TH OF THE SIXTH MONTH

Since Russia failed to conquer westward, she extended her power steadily eastward. At an earlier time, there was a great distance between China and Russia. Then the Russians gradually entered the region of Siberia by the south of the river. During the many Muslim uprisings, they marched further southeast and reached the Korean border. Fortunately, there are towering mountains in the south of Heilongjiang Province that have so far hindered a Russian invasion. But the Russians are now building a railway through the mountains and are determined not to stop. I heard from an English missionary that a Russian official had revealed to him that in twenty years' time, a Russian railway will reach the Chinese border. Their ultimate ambition can be easily discerned.

13TH OF THE SIXTH MONTH

A letter from Ambassador Xu stated:

On the 16th of the Fifth month a cable arrived from the International Office informing me that a brigade of Russian cavalry 800 strong has reached Murghab, according to a recent dispatch from Xinjiang's Governor Xiao. I immediately lodged a protest at the Russian Foreign Office, and they contended that this regiment was merely a replacement for the old troops stationed in the garrison there. I received no further details on this issue. They subsequently lodged a protest against the advance of our troops (our troops at Tashkurghan did make a slight advance during the spring). Soon another cable from the International Office arrived stating that the Xinjiang governor was ordered to stop any further troop movement. The Russian Foreign Office appeared to be satisfied, and I assume by this summer all issues will be resolved.

However, negotiations on the boundary remain a problem. In the Second month of this year, after we gave the envoy in Kashgar the exact location, the Russian Foreign Office contended that we should abide by the Kashgar treaty and that there was no need for further negotiations. The International Office instructed me to seek further negotiations with the Russian Foreign Office. At first they used the illness of their foreign minister as an excuse and maintained that everything would be taken care of as soon as the minister regained his health. Then they refused to negotiate after their protest against our troops' advance. A few days ago, I met with their under secretary, who contended that he cannot begin negotiations until he hears from the governor of Tashkent.

Obviously, they are trying to stall. The International Office has instructed me to be more flexible with the nonessential points. I suppose no concrete plan has yet been formulated. Last fall, the British ambassador to Russia confided in me that the promise he obtained from the Russia Foreign Office removed all the obstacles for me in dealing with the Russians. The reason why Russia ceased its troop advancement this year is obviously due to Britain's help. However, if Britain and Russia reach an agreement and leave China out, Russia may step up its aggression.

16TH OF THE SIXTH MONTH

General Zhang, who had previously placed a large order for machinery, was recently accused of corruption by the Imperial Censor. As the governor of Guangdong Province, he had invested a great deal of government funds in developing industry and mining. He may be guilty for his failure as a business manager, but he neither took bribes from the people nor wasted public money for his own selfish gain.

19TH OF THE SIXTH MONTH

A cable from Bangkok stated that Siam has yielded to all of France's demands. The entire amount of indemnity would be met accordingly, and the territory east of the Mekong River would be conceded to France. In a few days' time Britain and France will begin their negotiations regarding the boundary lines among Siam, Burma, Cambodia and Vietnam.

27TH OF THE SIXTH MONTH

On the 22nd of this month I cabled the International Office:

> Under intimidation, Siam conceded to France all the territory on the left bank of the Mekong River, which borders Yunnan Province. The French Foreign Office has repeatedly urged us to draw a clear boundary there, and we should immediately instruct the governor to conduct a thorough land survey without delay. Do not be misled by the gentle persuasiveness of the French Foreign Office, because at that time France was on the brink of war with Siam. We should follow the example of Britain and request negotiations between the French Foreign Office and our own envoy for a binding agreement before finalizing a treaty on the boundary issue.
>
> If we wait until the Siam problem is completely resolved, the boundary issue may not be as easily resolved as it could be now. Please tell Ambassador Lemy about this proposal first, and I will then send Qing Aitang to try at the French Foreign Office. If he fails to do so, then your office should contact Lemy for further negotiations before it is too late.

Yesterday I received a reply from the International Office:

> As far as Siam is concerned, Lemy claimed peace is their only objective. East of the Mekong is legally in the possession of France; therefore France is not invading the territory of Siam. He suggested that we draw up a map to define the boundary at the latitude of twenty-three degrees. This proposal will grant them the entire region of Cheli; to expose his error, we have cabled the governor of Yunnan Province to request further investigation. Your request for a binding contract is not feasible. France once obtained an agreement from the tribal chiefs of the Cheli region who formerly offered tribute to both Burma and Siam. But later, they broke the agreement. Therefore, such a move may not be a good idea.
>
> Britain's claim that Cheli is our territory is obviously a trick. This boundary issue should not be postponed for another three years. We hope that you will find out the number of tribal chiefs in the Cheli region who are regularly paying tribute to Siam. If you can obtain a map of the exact locations of these tribes, we would appreciate that.

I immediately sent a cable back in return:

> Lemy is trying to hide something, and his further actions should be watched closely. As I understand, there are four cities west of the Mekong and eight cities in the east. What France has in mind is to take over the eight eastern cities. When France printed their map of the region, all eight cities were included in

her territory. Qing Aitang subsequently confronted the French Foreign Office, who admitted its mistake. Britain may be setting a trap by yielding the Cheli region to us, but according to the old map and the map that the governor of Yunnan Province recently sent to me, the eight cities are located in Yunnan. We definitely should not give them up. Siam is still an independent nation, and it's none of France's business to know how many native chiefs are paying tributes to Siam.

Today I dispatched another cable as following:

After considering the matter carefully, it seems that Lemy is rather deceitful. The purpose of negotiating a binding agreement with the French Foreign Office is simply to declare that the twelve cities are not to be put under French control. It may not be an easy task; nevertheless, we should give it a try. Once it is established, it will save us a lot of trouble later on. If France refuses our proposal, then we will know the truth about her treachery. Please contact Lemy and proceed with the negotiation of the boundary issue as soon as possible.

29TH OF THE SIXTH MONTH

In the early years of the Emperor Qianlong [1736–1796], the Amur River in Heilongjiang Province was regarded as the natural boundary between China and Russia. Along the mineral-rich south shore of the river, several garrisons were stationed, and China was in total control of the region. Later, the Russians sneaked into the mouth of the river and took over the harbor. They named the harbor Nicolas, and since then, Russia has extended her power into the south side of the river. Several thousand *li* [300–400 miles] of each shore have been taken over by Russia, who later shared control of the river with China.

30TH OF THE SIXTH MONTH

Through deceit, Russia traded 400 miles of territory in Hunchun with China and built a large trading port at Haicanwei. They recruited Koreans into their army and, together with their own Russians, have increased the number of soldiers to 100,000. Along the river banks they mounted several large cannons and numerous small ones. From the harbor to the Yuanji River, the distance is 90 miles, and from the city of Hunchun to the river it is 300 miles. This is the trade route along which all the merchants pass before entering China. Russia has established a garrison and a customs office thirty miles from the city gate and levies heavy taxes on all the cargo of various merchants.

Since Hunchun borders Korea in the west, Korean natives over the years have sneaked into Chinese territory and established a village there. Now

Russia has taken over the village and levies taxes on these farmers. There are only a few miles to travel from the village to the province of Heilongjiang, and therefore the Russians can easily pass through the area with no problem.

1ST OF THE SEVENTH MONTH

The natives of Heilongjiang are experienced hunters but lack the courage to be good soldiers. Peace has existed too long in the area, and therefore the male population there is not combative. They cannot even be employed to catch marauding bandits—the local authorities must rely on outside cavalry to police their region. Immediate military training will not suffice as there is not enough manpower in the province.

The weather there turns extremely cold as early as the Eighth month of each year. When the river freezes, the natives travel by sled over the ice. These sleds move extremely fast, so there is no transportation problem.

Since China doesn't have her own steamboats, the local gold mines along the river must rely on Russian vessels for transportation, and therefore no Chinese flag flies on the boats. This problem can be solved if we build our own steamboats.

12TH OF THE SEVENTH MONTH

Since the reign of the Tongzhi Emperor [1862–1874], religious riots have occurred fifteen times. But none of these resembles the recent riots, which have risen simultaneously within a radius of several miles.

21ST OF THE SEVENTH MONTH

On the 11th of the Fifth month, in the outskirts of the Great Northern Gate of Guangdong Province, fire broke out in the kitchen of the Wen'an Arsenal. Four storage rooms were totally destroyed, numerous houses in the surrounding villages were burned down and many lives were lost. Even though the storage places were surrounded by a canal with a high wall, it didn't prevent the fire from spreading into the countryside.

28TH OF THE SEVENTH MONTH

I took my family to Brighton for the summer holiday. Interpreter Wang and Military Attaché Wang both came along with us.

2ND OF THE EIGHTH MONTH

This afternoon I went to visit the palace of William IV, who was the former king of England and the uncle of the present queen. The palace was constructed sixty years ago, and the architecture is visibly different from that of contemporary times. It appears to me to be similar to that of China; the wall murals in the palace are filled with drawings of Chinese figures. This proves that the mighty influence of China had already arrived during that period and had obviously aroused the admiration of the people in England.

This afternoon I strolled along the boardwalk of the old pier and watched women and children swimming in the sea.

4TH OF THE EIGHTH MONTH

I went down to the new pier and watched men and women swimming in the sea. Later, I watched a performance of a flea circus and marveled at a flea pulling a cart around.

10TH OF THE EIGHTH MONTH

A letter from China reported uncontrollable floods brought on by incessant rain from the Yangzi Valley to the Yellow River basin. The countryside in China has been devastated by this natural disaster.

12TH OF THE EIGHTH MONTH

The total construction cost of both the old pier and the new pier in Brighton was £30,000.

13TH OF THE EIGHTH MONTH

This afternoon, I returned to London with my family.

The British Foreign Office brought a new map to the embassy. In comparison to the map they gave me in the Third month, some distinct changes have been made concerning the Yunnan-Burma border and the location of the Yeren Mountains.

16TH OF EIGHTH MONTH

I contacted the British Foreign Office and made the following suggestions about the new map of the Yeren Mountains region:

> We agree that the borderline should begin at the latitude of twenty-five degrees north and ninety-eight degrees east on the peak of the Gaolun Hills and follow the mountain slope southwest passing through Walun Peak and Hunchang Village. The village should be included in the territory of Burma. From there the border should run west, tilting slightly southward to pass Saboping and then southward over the shoulder of the mountains to the Dasaier

River. From the mouth of this river, the line should be clearly drawn between Xi on the east and Leiben on the west. From the South Taibo River, the line goes southward until the river runs into the Leigela River and then flows to the mouth of the river at the vicinity of Engelun. From there, with Engelun in the west and the Milei River in the east, the line goes by the Laise River until the river meets the Nanmeili River. From that river, the line goes to the vicinity near Benlang and from there southwest by following the Laise River into the Milei River. From the Milei River, the line goes southwest until the river flows into the Chindwin River. And then from the tributary stream of the river, the line goes from the Manipur River to the Taiping River.

19TH OF THE EIGHTH MONTH

Qing Aitang wrote me with the following message:

I recently had two meetings with the under secretary of the Russian Foreign Office and then two more meetings with the Russian foreign minister. The czar of Russia had briefed the Foreign Office by letter from Denmark to the effect that he totally agreed with my assessment of Sino-Russian relations and decreed that the Foreign Office, in conjunction with the Defense Ministry, must prepare a new agreement after the czar's return in order to negotiate a peaceful settlement of the boundary issue. However, the old agreement, which is still in the possession of the Russian Foreign Office, was written in Manchurian and Russian only, without a Chinese language version. The agreement in Manchurian didn't indicate that the Chinese boundary should go straight southward but has it reach only to Ulughchat. The International Office is probably fully aware of this implication, and we therefore may have to accept a concession. This problem can be easily resolved; however, it's up to the International Office to make such a decision. In my own capacity, I can only propose further negotiations.

At first the Russian Foreign Office tried to stall and then completely ignored our protests. It's because of this total failure in diplomacy that Grand Secretary Sun proposed a change in envoy. Fortunately, the czar maintains a degree of integrity and gave his consent to our proposal for further negotiations. After this briefing, the Russian foreign minister hastened to the capital from his country home and went directly to confer with the minister of defense. Together they prepared a new agreement for further negotiations. I assume I shall learn within seven or eight days the basic details of their new proposal, which, I understand, will be presented to the czar after His Majesty's return in December. The Russian Foreign Office contended that the boundary dispute is hard to resolve and that they must wait for the czar's return. It's a decision for the czar to make and they are unable to dictate the final settlement. Their statement may not be as deceitful as we previously anticipated.

Several days later I received another letter from Qing stating as follows:

I heard that Ambassador Xu's latest advice to the International Office is to accept the Russian demands. In my humble opinion, the date for negotiations has not even been set, but we have already expressed our willingness to retreat. Russia will invariably push further into our territory, and this problem may never be resolved.

I understand that the Russian Foreign Office has completely ignored Ambassador Xu's presence as the Chinese envoy since this spring, which places him in a rather awkward position. In the last two years, Ambassador Xu has talked to only one Russian official and has made no attempt to confer with the Russian foreign minister. It is obvious why he has never made any progress.

6TH OF THE NINTH MONTH

Ancient Chinese scholars claimed that matter is generated from energy. The energy from Heaven is either the purest of the pure or the purest of the impure, whereas the energy from Earth is either the impurest of the pure or the impurest of the impure.[48] The varieties of energy that Western men have discovered are hydrogen, nitrogen, oxygen and carbon monoxide. Hydrogen is the purest of the pure, nitrogen the purest of the impure, oxygen the impurest of the pure and carbon monoxide the impurest of the impure.

Fire and water are the major forces on earth. Water consists of three elements from heaven and four elements from earth. Now the Western men claim that water is two parts hydrogen and one part oxygen. This theory is certainly compatible with ours. Between heaven and earth, the major forces continue to be fire and water, as both these forces are essential to life on earth.

23RD OF THE NINTH MONTH

The office of the viceroy of India is located in Madras, where all the railways meet. However, whenever there is an emergency, all the departments under the viceroy still depend on telegrams for communication.

1ST OF THE TENTH MONTH

The five thousand words of the *Tao Te Ching*, by a Zhou historian [Taishi Dan, third century B.C.], is the earliest record of the philosophy of Taoism. The basic principles are to empty one's mind and not to interfere with the actions of others, to hold firm to one's own ideals and be self-reliant and to meditate relentlessly. With the assistance of the power of patience and the

---

48. The Chinese understood all matter in the universe to be composed of *qi*—"energy," "ether" or "material force." As Hsieh explains, heavenly *qi* was purer than earthly *qi*, and it was the mix of these degrees of *qi* that determined the nature of a thing. Here, though, Hsieh is attempting to correlate the Chinese theory of *qi* to Western chemical theory on the study of gases. Chinese translated chemical "gas" as *qi*.

belief that the meek will dominate the forceful and that retreat will defeat aggression, the doctrine is not too far from that of Confucianism. Philosophers of the latter Zhou, such as Zhuangzi, Lizi, Wenzi, and Guanyinzi branched out from this philosophy and established their own theories. Sunzi and Hanzi made a few changes in the idea and formed the School of Names and School of Logicians, respectively. *The Scripture of the Secret Symbol*, which deals with military strategy, is another form of the same philosophy. In later centuries, with the hope of achieving immortality, the Taoists began their earnest search for an elixir to prolong life and prescriptions to reverse the aging process.

To reach a state of immortality, the Taoists followed two different paths: bodily manipulation and alchemy, which are known as the Nei Tan [Inner Elixir] and Wai Tan [Outer Elixir]. Those who practice Nei Tan claim that there are but water, fire, ying and yang in the human body. If we learn how to control these elements through breathing, we will extend our life expectancy. This theory was initiated by Wei Boyan, Zhang Botan and Wang Tao, who wrote several books, including the *Dragon and Tiger Scripture*. It's a rational interpretation. However, some of their concepts, such as the newborn infant and the pure virgin, the golden castle and the vermilion palace, the blue dragon and the white tiger, and the precious metal goblet and the red-hot kiln, are definitely not the words of Lao Tzu but their own ideas. Wai Tan is the technology that supposedly can turn stone into gold, which is simply absurd. Therefore, the philosophy of Taoism has deteriorated into a fraudulent cult several thousand years after its inception.

4TH OF THE TENTH MONTH

On the 1st of the Seventh month I received a telegram from the International Office stating:

> According to the map provided by the governor of Yunnan, the Cheli chief controls the region of the Thirteen Meng. Unless you can identify all the names of the places in this border region, it will be difficult for us to bring them into negotiation.
>
> This office will inform the French ambassador that the border in their map doesn't coincide with that in our Chinese map. We must check with the governor of Yunnan Province before we can give him an answer. Furthermore, China has the right to maintain her interests in the territory of the Cheli chief but shall not interfere with the government policies of either Vietnam or Siam. We would like to suggest to the French ambassador that he appeal for a decisive policy from the French Foreign Office by telegram, and we will patiently wait for a reply. This action we consider to be as binding as a treaty, but it doesn't display any aggressiveness on our part.

On the 9th of the same month, I received another telegram from the International Office that stated:

> The border between Vietnam and China should cease at Mengbin, as the territory in the west may be included within the region of the Cheli chief's Thirteen Meng. The boundary from Mengbin along the border of Siam to the Mekong River should be drawn from the south toward the west and then circle Cheli. It should not be placed straight toward the west. Your map is incorrect. We must check with the governor of Yunnan Province before we can give you a definite statement. If France insists that the boundary should be drawn from Mengbin through the Mekong River, we may accept their proposal as long as they recognize China's rights within the Cheli region. We will also observe the rights of France in Vietnam and Siam. Please tell the French Foreign Office that we are urgently awaiting their reply, and keep reminding them until you receive an answer from them.

On the 24th of the Ninth month, another telegram arrived, stating as follows:

> Yesterday we visited the French embassy and asked Lemy why French forces still remain in Siam after Siam had conceded her territory and paid her indemnity. Lemy pretended he was not aware of these facts and promised he would telegram the French Foreign Office for confirmation. Later, British ambassador O'Connor came to our office and claimed that the British ambassador to France is urgently negotiating with the French Foreign Office on the issue of Siam's autonomy rights and is in dire need of China's support. Please brief Qing Aitang by cable to relay the message to the French Foreign Office that China would like to take the role of mediator during their negotiations and report back what kind of response they give. Watch for your opportunity to induce France to fulfill her promises. This action will invariably help Britain during the negotiations.

Today I received another telegram from the International Office stating as follows:

> Ambassador O'Connor suggested that Britain and China should sign an agreement and give full support to Siam in case France fails to fulfill her promise. He claimed that if France heard of such an agreement, she will not break her own agreement. However, we are afraid that if we sign such an agreement with Britain, we may offend France. If our cooperation with Britain fails to intimidate France into submission, she may extend her power further into Siam. This problem will then get out of hand.
>
> Please discuss this issue with the British Foreign Office and find an alternative way to protect Siam. If they mention Ambassador O'Connor's suggestion, tell them China has never signed a secret pact with any other nation but is merely interested in acting as mediator. This move may be the best policy. What is your opinion? We would like to hear from you.

6TH OF THE TENTH MONTH

A cable from Rangoon reported that a Chinese official came to Bhamo with a native chief, and in a few days time he left with Mr. Wally. Further news stated that Captain Davis led an armed force 500 strong to the three passes of Huju, Tianma and Hanlong. His intention was to camp his army by the Huju Pass because it is located at the end of the Chinese territory. The gate is about seventeen miles east of Bhamo, and China contended that the border should be placed there, according to the old official map of China.

7TH OF THE TENTH MONTH

A French newspaper reported that a former British military officer claimed that France's recent close relationship with Russia may pose a problem for Britain, and the Siam case is a good example.

13TH OF THE TWELFTH MONTH

A cable from the International Office stated that according to the British ambassador, after their negotiation on the Pamir affair, both Britain and Russia reached an agreement that Russia should have the territory from the Aksu-daria River to Andizhan at the north of the Lesser Pamir Hills.

Another cable from Ambassador Xu stated that the Russian Foreign Office claimed that they will take over the Lesser Pamir Hills as agreed upon during the negotiations. He contended that we should dispatch more troops to the garrisons in both the southern and eastern regions next spring when Russia enters these territories. He asked further whether or not our placement of more garrisons at Andizhan may be negotiated during the finalization of the pact.

I immediately lodged a protest at the British Foreign Office and accused them of deliberately surrendering Chinese territory to Russia without China's consent. They flatly deny any such action.

Later, I received a letter from Ambassador Xu that stated:

> Last winter, the Russian Foreign Office was willing to draw the boundary along Mt. Sarakoran and later even willing to include the territory west of the mountain in compliance with China's proposal. Subsequently, the International Office gave them a list of the names of these places according to the Kashgar agreement, but the Russia Foreign Office refused to accept it; therefore negotiations were again postponed.
>
> When Qing Aitang came to Russia, he suggested that we allow Russia to take over half of Baroghil west of the mountain, which is too far from the original plan of the International Office; therefore, I cannot accept his proposal.

A month ago he urged me to pursue his idea, as he heard that Britain will soon terminate negotiations with Russia. He also claimed that the International Office would like to feel out Russia's intention regarding the territory west of the mountain. Russia's proposal to take over the territory south of the Baroghil Pass is definitely out of the question. As far as the territory in the Andizhan region is concerned, it is still in the negotiating stage.

22ND OF THE TWELFTH MONTH

Ambassador Xu sent a letter to me with the following message:

Xinjiang has dispatched troops to Taghdumbash and set up a garrison there. Russia so far has made no protest. According to the Russian map, this area is not included within her boundaries, and apparently she has no desire to occupy the land there. As far as the Andizhan region is concerned, it should extend from the north to the south and cannot be included within the boundaries of either Britain or Russia.

Ambassador Xu also enclosed the cable he sent to the International Office, which read:

I continued negotiations with the Russian Foreign Office as instructed. The Russian foreign minister claimed that the issue over the southern region of Andizhan has since been resolved between Britain and Russia. Further negotiations between our two countries should be focused on the eastern region only, and the foreign minister wishes China would follow the original Russian map.

After repeated protests from Qing Aitang, the Russian foreign minister agreed that he will wait until our International Office hands out the list of the names of the places in the western region; then we can begin further negotiations.

Part V

Twentieth Year of the Guangxu Emperor (1894)

1ST OF THE FIRST MONTH

There were six articles in the original Paris agreement between France and Siam. Ten more articles were added in the final treaty at Bangkok. Siam lost nearly half her country to France. Within the lost territory, there is the city, Luang, a prosperous city that many British merchants have called home for several decades and where they do a large volume of business. The northern territory, which stretches almost to the Chinese border, is rich in minerals. It is for these reasons that the British merchants banded together and sent a petition to their government for the protection of their mining rights. However, the new treaty didn't specify that the northern territory should be ceded to France but merely stated that Siam shall not have exclusive territorial rights on the left bank of the Mekong River. Apparently, France is afraid of rousing protests from other powerful nations and therefore left some elbow room for Siam.

7TH OF THE FIRST MONTH

On the 22nd of the Twelfth month of last year, the International Office sent a telegram to Ambassador Xu with the following message:

> Yesterday the Russian ambassador came to this office and inquired about our terms regarding the boundaries both east and west of Pamir. We replied that since his honorable country prefers a peace settlement, China is willing to meet it halfway. We contend that Karakul and Andizhan are originally Chinese territory, and we absolutely will not yield these two places.
>
> However, we are willing to negotiate the territory west of Andizhan. The Russian ambassador made no protest over these two places we claim as our territory but urged us to set a date for negotiations within this year.
>
> Our intention is to allow Russia to have the western side of the Lesser Pamir Hills, and we will keep the eastern side. Please discuss this with Qing Aitang and persuade Russia to accept these terms.

Since then, Qing Aitang has had the opportunity of seeing Gortchakov twice, who gave his word that Russia will respond within a few days.

14TH OF THE FIRST MONTH

Ambassador Yang Zitong in Chile informed me by letter that he recently received the news from a Chilean consul in British Columbia that the number of Chinese immigrants there has reached a record high of 10,000. The consul suggested that China should establish a consulate there.

19TH OF THE FIRST MONTH

The letter for my official release has not yet arrived. The queen of England will soon leave for vacation in Italy. I expressed to the British Foreign Office my urgency in going home. They suggested that I should bid my farewell to the queen today while Her Majesty is receiving the ambassadors of both Japan and the Netherlands at Windsor Palace. I can then submit my letter of release to their office at a later date.

I accepted their suggestion and went to the train depot at noon. Both Sandison and another official were already waiting at the station. Later, the ambassadors from Japan and the Netherlands joined us for the journey to Windsor Palace.

Dinner was served to us at the palace, and subsequently I was the first one to be ushered into the throne room. I read aloud my tribute to the queen. Her Majesty expressed regret over my forthcoming departure and praised the good work I have accomplished during my assignment. The queen concluded with a wish for enduring friendship between our two nations. I then retreated by bowing deeply.

The ambassador of the Netherlands was then ushered into the throne room and was followed by the ambassador of Japan. After the official business was concluded, Sandison led us on a tour of the palace. Later, we boarded the train and returned to London.

20TH OF THE FIRST MONTH

A letter from Qing Aitang brought the following message:

> I encountered problems after several days of negotiations with Gortchakov. First of all, when crisis broke out on Pamir two years ago, we withdrew all our garrisons from there. Consequently, Russian forces took over the region and claimed Pamir as their territory. Second, we never lodged a strong protest over that affair. Third, the passive nature of our soldiers invariably generates considerable contempt among their Russian counterparts, especially after our second retreat of several hundred miles near the border. These are three major reasons for our diplomatic failure regarding Pamir. The Russians have been playing for time and have refused to negotiate with us for almost a year. Not until recent months did they finally agree to negotiate and expressed their willingness to yield the Karakul area to us. This is due to our repeated protests, which have undoubtedly brought forth this comparably good result. However, Gortchakov suddenly became seriously ill, and according to his doctor, the minister may not have too long to live. Consequently, the Russian Foreign Office suggested that further negotiations ought to proceed in Beijing and will let us know the date within this month.

According to the telegram Ambassador Xu sent to the International Office on the 2nd of this month:

> Yesterday Gortchakov informed Qing Aitang that the czar claimed our new proposal to be similar to the old one; therefore, Russia cannot accept these terms. He further contended that both sides should make an effort to reach a compromise before we can proceed with further negotiations.

In a telegram of the 12th of this month, Xu stated:

> After several attempts on my part to persuade Gortchakov to resume the negotiations as instructed, he finally informed Qing that he had sent a telegram to the Russian ambassador in China and conveyed the czar's wishes. He contended that we must wait for an answer; however, if China would accept Russia's terms, we could go ahead with the negotiations. Now, due to Gortchakov's sudden illness, we have ceased negotiations.

21ST OF THE FIRST MONTH

The International Office's cable to Ambassador Xu on the 14th of this month stated:

> Russia's new map has been delivered to our office, and we received your telegram last winter. Russia is too demanding. We have retreated as far as we can, yet they are still not satisfied. The Russian foreign minister mentioned that Russia would negotiate if we made certain concessions according to Russian terms. Now, the minister is seriously ill and the negotiations are unable to proceed. It's time for us to prepare for the event of further negotiations and to set down a definite plan with the correct name of each place. Please send a cable dispatch with the names of these places in explicit detail according to the Russian map and include your own assessment.

On the 16th of the same month, Ambassador Xu sent his reply:

> According to my map, the boundary ought to follow the west slope of the Karakul Mountains toward the Aksu-daria. Following the river, it then trails south toward the north of the Lesser Pamir Hills. However, Gortchakov previously informed Qing that Russia absolutely will not yield the territory east of the Aksu-daria. This is obviously the problem area of the whole boundary dispute. Gortchakov's condition remains critical.

22ND OF THE FIRST MONTH

We attended Ladies' Night in the evening.

24TH OF THE FIRST MONTH

The Burma-Yunnan boundary dispute reached a settlement in the Third month of last year and the trade agreement was resolved on the 5th of this month. Consequently, I sent a cable dispatch to the International Office and received the decree of approval on the 12th. Since there were a few adjustments to be ironed out, it again took a few more days to resolve the differences. At three o'clock today I went with Margary to the British Foreign Office. Lord Rosebery was ready and waiting for our arrival. Two copies of the agreement in each language were prepared for our signature, and we both signed the four documents. The British Foreign Office kept two copies, one in each language, and I brought the two other copies back to the embassy. A special courier will thus be sent to deliver these two copies to the International Office. And I intend to prepare two more copies in both languages so that I may have them both framed and then present them to His Majesty the Emperor through the International Office.

6TH OF THE SECOND MONTH

Since the signing of the Yunnan-Burma boundary treaty, I have concentrated all my efforts on finishing up the official business at the Chinese embassy in England, as I have to go to Paris for my voyage home.

This afternoon I took my family and my own staff and boarded the train for Dover. It was a stormy day and the ship rocked violently throughout the crossing to the port of Calais in France. Fortunately, I didn't vomit, but on the way to the pier I caught a cold and was sick for several days.

12TH OF THE SECOND MONTH

I received the decree for my official release from His Majesty the Emperor to present to the Queen of England. And I found out that Gong Zhaoyuan, minister of the third rank, will replace me as the next Chinese ambassador to England.

27TH OF THE SECOND MONTH

My successor, Ambassador Gong, returned to his hometown, Luzhou, after a month's stay in Shanghai during the Twelfth month of last year. He asked for a month's vacation at Luzhou so that he may visit the gravesites of all his ancestors. It seems he may not reach Europe for some time to come. I have been living abroad for more than four years now and am extremely anxious to return home. I am also worried that if Gong arrives late, in the first part of summer, then our return voyage through the Red Sea may be extremely unbearable. I may have to take a different route through Canada, which would be most inconvenient for my family.

Consequently, I decided to send my wife and second daughter home first. In addition to their personal maids, I dispatched several of my staff and my military attaché to accompany them on their voyage. In the evening of the 24th of this month we rode the train to Marseilles and arrived the following morning. We stayed at a hotel, and at two o'clock on the 26th I saw them off on a French ocean liner. Afterward, I returned to the hotel and left on the eight o'clock train for Paris.

28TH OF THE SECOND MONTH

On the 13th of this month, Ambassador Xu sent a dispatch by cable to the International Office stating that Gortchakov has informed Qing that the czar is willing to yield the places that Qing demands. He then asked for a list of the names of those places so that both sides can speed up the process of negotiation. As far as Gortchakov's illness is concerned, Xu believes that he has not yet fully recovered.

A reply from the International Office arrived on the 14th of this month instructing Xu to urge Qing to be more conciliatory during the negotiations, because British ambassador O'Connor has recently informed the International Office that Russia is preparing for an invasion in the Fourth month if negotiations collapse this time.

On the 16th, another cable from the International Office arrived. It reported that Ambassador O'Connor had come to the office again and reaffirmed Russia's desire for a peace settlement. It further urged Xu to resolve the differences within a certain time limit.

On the same day, another cable was dispatched by Xu to the International Office informing them that Qing had gone to the Russian Foreign Office the day before as instructed and had given them a list according to the instructions of the previous cable from the International Office.

On the 20th, the International Office sent a decree by cable to Ambassador Xu:

> By order of this decree through the recommendation of the International Office in the case of Pamir, Xu Jingcheng is entrusted with the responsibility of negotiating the border dispute in Pamir with the Russian Foreign Office, according to the terms formulated by the International Office. The strategic points along the frontier from Karakul to Andizhan should be negotiated with extreme care. You should not yield an inch but try to induce Russia to fulfill her promises. As soon as you complete these negotiations, you must immediately contact the International Office and seek a decree for the final approval.

4TH OF THE THIRD MONTH

After several years of negotiations with America's Foreign Office, the unfair laws that discriminate against Chinese immigrants were finally abolished. The previous agreement of the year Wu-zi [1888] was amended, and a clause providing protection with registration was again implemented. Workers from both America and China must register when they are residing in the other country. Since there are only a handful of American workers in China, the American missionaries are also included under this ruling.

For some four years, we have strived to resolve this dispute with the American government but were treated with utter contempt. Last winter, we finally were contacted by America for negotiation on this issue. And it took three more months to resolve this problem.

13TH OF THE THIRD MONTH

This afternoon I went underground to observe the waterworks of Paris. The watchman led us with a candle through a narrow path. There is another level underneath, but I didn't go under on account of the diminishing candle. I understand the total cost of construction was 900 million francs, which amounts to 200 million ounces of gold in China. After completion there is only the expense of hiring a watchman for the place.

17TH OF THE THIRD MONTH

Ambassador Xu's telegram to the International Office on the 13th of last month indicated:

> I repeatedly sent Qing to ask for a negotiation date, and finally Gortchakov replied that the czar cannot accept our terms because their Ministry of War is strongly opposed to capitulation on those strategic points. He further contended that his office has to formulate a plan to meet the mutual demands of both sides and cautioned us to keep the soldiers inside our garrisons so as not to trigger any unnecessary incident. Then he concluded that he would cable the Russian ambassador to furnish us with more details for future negotiations. Russia's excessive demands leave us no room to retreat and give us no alternative but to hold firm to our original terms. Please give me further instructions.

The answer from the International Office arrived on the 11th of this month, indicating:

> Gortchakov sounded reasonable this time; we must not add more pressure on him. He used their Ministry of War as an excuse; we should report the indignation of the Chinese public. We absolutely cannot agree to the Russian terms, as

we have retreated to our ultimate limit. Since both sides will not make an advance, we will wait for a reply from Russia. When the negotiations begin, you must firmly hold your ground in case Russia forfeits her promise later on.

This office will cable the Xinjiang governor and instruct him to keep troops alert and not to let them stray over the border.

12TH OF THE FOURTH MONTH

A month ago I went on a tour to the Pathological Museum and saw human cadavers lining the place. The most gruesome sight was the dissected body parts exhibited in various containers of liquid. I said to the tour guide that in China physicians are knowledgeable about human anatomy without this cruel act of mutilating dead human bodies. The guide gave me a blank look and was speechless.

25TH OF THE FOURTH MONTH

When I received the news of my successor's, Ambassador Gong's, date of arrival, the 16th of this month, I sent Qing Aitang to welcome him in Marseilles. I moved out from the embassy to a hotel on the 15th and returned the next day to await his arrival. He reached Paris shortly before noon with his entourage. We both paid homage to our emperor before a temporary altar set up in the courtyard and then discussed various official business and personal matters until five o'clock in the afternoon. I handed over all the official documents, which I had put in order, and the remaining embassy expenses from both embassies in England and France. The sum total came to the amount of £5,000. In addition, there were £2,000 that Hunan Province had entrusted to me for the purchase of textile machinery.

I left Paris on the 21st and arrived in Marseilles the following day. Today I went aboard an ocean liner, which will set sail in the evening. As soon as we left the harbor, we were hit by a storm. Many people became seasick and refused to eat. It was not until late night that the wind finally died down.

5TH OF THE FIFTH MONTH

Since the ship entered the Red Sea on the 3rd of this month, the weather has remained nice for two days. However, tonight we were hit by a storm again. I was unable to eat for three days and four nights.

16TH OF THE FIFTH MONTH

The ship arrived at Singapore. Consul Huang entertained me with a banquet at the consulate; it was eleven o'clock in the evening before I was able to return to the ship.

19TH OF THE FIFTH MONTH

The ship arrived at Saigon, and the president of the local Chinese Chamber of Commerce, Zhang Peilin, entertained me with a banquet at his home. I came back to the ship by midnight in the rain.

20TH OF THE FIFTH MONTH

A Chinese merchant, Liu, invited me for dinner and wine at noon, and later I went to a banquet given by five merchants' groups.

24TH OF THE FIFTH MONTH

The ship arrived at Hong Kong but didn't enter the harbor because there was an epidemic raging in the city.

26TH OF THE FIFTH MONTH

As the ship passed Taiwan, we received a cable warning of an approaching hurricane. Since there was no land at which the ship could anchor, the captain reduced the speed of the ship and allowed the vessel to float for fear of direct contact with the hurricane. Outside the porthole, huge waves rose as high as a towering mountain, followed by drenching rain. The wind finally died down during the night, and the ship was able to pick up speed to continue the voyage.

27TH OF THE FIFTH MONTH

The storm resumed as fiercely as yesterday. After the ship entered the China Sea, the velocity of the wind decreased somewhat. While the ship was sailing along the Chinese coast, a rainstorm prevented the ship from going any farther. It rained throughout the night.

28TH OF THE FIFTH MONTH

The rain stopped momentarily in the early morning, and the ship began to sail again. Another rainstorm developed a few hours later, and the ship had to make another stop. The rain finally ceased around noon, and the ship entered the harbor of Wusong. There was a steamboat provided by my family waiting there; I went aboard and reached Shanghai in the evening.

Postscript

Hsieh Fucheng died in Shanghai twenty days after this last entry and thus never had the opportunity to return to his beloved hometown, Wuxi. After his untimely death, the Yunnan-Burma agreement he signed with Britain was never fulfilled. An incompetent Manchu minister compromised the agreement under pressure from France, and Britain subsequently withdrew the agreement.